EXPLAINING
THE EAST ASIAN PEACE

D1219233

NIAS – Nordic Institute of Asian Studies

ASIA INSIGHTS

A series aimed at increasing an understanding of contemporary Asia among policy-makers, NGOs, businesses, journalists and other members of the general public as well as scholars and students.

NIAS Press is the autonomous publishing arm of NIAS – Nordic Institute of Asian Studies, a research institute located at the University of Copenhagen. NIAS is partially funded by the governments of Denmark, Finland, Iceland, Norway and Sweden via the Nordic Council of Ministers, and works to encourage and support Asian studies in the Nordic countries. In so doing, NIAS has been publishing books since 1969, with more than two hundred titles produced in the past few years.

UNIVERSITY OF COPENHAGEN

Nordic Council of Ministers

EXPLAINING THE EAST ASIAN PEACE

A Research Story

Stein Tønnesson

Explaining the East Asian Peace
A Research Story
by Stein Tønnesson
Nordic Institute of Asian Studies
Asia Insights, no. 9

First published in 2017 by NIAS Press
NIAS – Nordic Institute of Asian Studies
Øster Farimagsgade 5, 1353 Copenhagen K, Denmark
Tel: +45 3532 9501 • Fax: +45 3532 9549
E-mail: books@nias.ku.dk • Online: www.niaspress.dk

© Stein Tønnesson 2017

A CIP catalogue record for this book is available from the British Library

ISBN: 978-87-7694-222-9 (hbk)
ISBN: 978-87-7694-223-6 (pbk)

Typeset in Arno Pro 12/14.4
Typesetting by BookWork

Printed and bound in Great Britain
by Marston Book Services Limited, Oxfordshire

The cartoon on the cover page, showing weapons and arms factories being re-forged into office buildings, trains, ships, fire engines and electricity masts, is a copy made by the Cambodian artist Chan Wai of a Japanese drawing from 1947. It is remembered by post-war Japanese generations, who saw it in their textbooks at school. The cartoon was drawn in order to explain Japan's new role as a 'peace nation'. The original version (displayed on p. 38) carries a text using Chinese characters that are no longer used in Japan: 戦争放棄 (sensō hōki) – 'The renunciation of war'.

The month in question was April, the cruellest month. (…) It was a month that was both an end of a war and the beginning of … well, 'peace' is not the right word, is it, my dear Commandant?

– Viet Thanh Nguyen, *The Sympathizer* (New York: Grove Press, 2015), p. 1.

Contents

Figures

Tables

Preface

The purpose of this book is threefold. First and foremost, it seeks to explain how a region with thirty per cent of mankind made a transition from frequent, intense and widespread warfare to relative peace. Second, it aims to stimulate debates about the quality or viability of the East Asian Peace. Is it authoritarian, on its way to becoming liberal, or perhaps something that transcends these categories? Is it a peace by unpeaceful means? How fragile or threatened is it? How might it be made more robust? Third, the book aims to tell the story of a six-year research programme at Uppsala University in Sweden, involving more than thirty researchers in over ten countries. I shall present my recollections of how the programme came to be, and reflect on the debates we have engaged in while researching the many aspects of peace and conflict. We decided early on to bring together advocates of diverging theories, methods and viewpoints, and were aware that this might lead to contradictory answers to our two central research questions: How deep is the East Asian Peace? How can it be explained?

This personal account is published alongside *Debating the East Asian Peace*, a book edited by Elin Bjarnegård and Joakim Kreutz, which does fuller justice to the many findings of the programme researchers. Below I shall reveal my doubts and prejudices, and not seek to hide the moments where my own views diverge from those of my colleagues. I shall do my best, though, to present their findings and conclusions loyally, even when they challenge my own. Readers may wish to consult our journal articles, op eds, blogs and YouTube videos at www.pcr.uu.se/research/eap/. Together, they display a range of approaches.

What has united us is a desire to explain peace instead of war.

Acknowledgements

L et me thank the Department of Peace and Conflict Research at Uppsala University, which hosted our programme for six years and organized our opening and closing conferences, in September 2011 and June 2016. I am grateful to Yonsei University in Seoul, Peking University, the Diplomatic Academy of Vietnam and the Asia Research Institute in Singapore for hosting our annual conferences 2012–15. The United States Institute of Peace in Washington, DC contributed to kick-starting the programme by hosting me as a Randolph Jennings Senior Fellow during 2010–11. My main employer, the Peace Research Institute Oslo (PRIO), provided generous support and an inspiring environment throughout. Finally, I would like to express my appreciation of the Swedish Riksbankens Jubileumsfond (RJ), which funded the 2009–10 pilot study and then the full 2011–16 programme. RJ is my favourite funder. Its small but competent staff consistently back up our scholarly enterprise. Instead of requiring excessive reporting, they ask for scholarly results. No wonder true scholars love RJ.

I thank our Core Group, our 24 Research Associates, the participants at our conferences, our Advisory Board, Eric Skoog and Martin Tegnander, who helped out with the figures, the artist Chan Wai, who redrew a Japanese illustration for the cover, Anthony Horton, who created the index, and the excellent copy editor at NIAS Press, David Stuligross.

With the exception of Part Two, 'Predicting China', which builds on a project undertaken with the aim of examining the most important recent works on the subject in Western languages, this book does not include a literature review. It does not even provide references to the most compelling works on peace and security in East Asia. I refer only to publications from the East Asian Peace programme itself and to a few works that have been particularly important for our debates. A full list of the publications from the programme, as well as a record of programme events may be found at www.pcr.uu.se/research/eap/.

Introduction

If whole nations can have peace with themselves, and if peace can prevail in vast regions like Europe, the Americas or East Asia, then it should also be possible to achieve world peace. To study regional transitions to peace is a way to approach the question of what it will take to achieve global peace. As a peace researcher, I find it inspiring that the huge East Asian region, where the world's worst wars took place in my youth, could become as peaceful as it has been in the last thirty-eight years. I remember the horror I felt as a boy: while watching TV as the bombs were falling over Vietnam, Laos and Cambodia, I could sense the suffering of the people seeking shelter below. Great was my joy in April 1975, when the war ended and Vietnam could be unified in peace. Just as great was my despair to learn of the Cambodian genocide, the exodus of Vietnamese 'boat people', and China's invasion of Vietnam in 1979. Ten years later, at the age of thirty-six, I walked along the Sino–Vietnamese border for the first time, where the railway had no rails and traders were obliged to carry their merchandise on their backs. I stood before endless rows of graves, of soldiers killed during China's five-week invasion, and saw that virtually all the dead had been younger than myself. Even then, in 1989, I did not realize that China's withdrawal of its troops from Vietnamese territory in March 1979 had marked the beginning of the East Asian Peace. Not one single new war has broken out since then between any East Asian countries,[1] only incidents and minor clashes. And civil wars have become fewer and less murderous than before.

The emerging peace was difficult to grasp in the 1980s, when there were repeated artillery exchanges at the Sino–Vietnamese border, a drawn-out insurgency against the Vietnam-supported government in

---

1. Brunei, Cambodia, China and Taiwan, Indonesia, Japan, the two Koreas, Laos, Malaysia, Mongolia, Myanmar, the Philippines, Singapore, Thailand, Timor-Leste and Vietnam.

Cambodia, and a number of internal armed conflicts in Laos, Myanmar, Malaysia, Thailand, the Philippines and Indonesia – which then included Timor-Leste. The two Korean states remained dictatorships for most of the decade, and the Chinese repression of Tibetan unrest during 1987–89, and of student protests in Beijing 1989, did not convey an image of peace. Yet Uppsala University statistics tell a different story. They show that the East Asian share of global battle deaths went down from 80 per cent in the 1946–79 period to just 6.2 per cent in the 1980s. This had two main reasons: there was no major war in East Asia, even as new and murderous wars broke out elsewhere, notably between Iraq and Iran, and in Afghanistan. I am not sure when I came to realize that East Asia had entered an era of peace, but I think it dawned on me when in 1991 an agreement was made to establish a transitional UN administration and a coalition government in Cambodia. This allowed Vietnam and China to normalize relations without too much loss of face for Vietnam. Four years later, the peaceful trend continued as Vietnam normalized relations with the United States. The cycle of Indochina wars had ended.

Sino–US relations were quickly restored after the Beijing massacre in 1989. China ceased supporting communist rebels abroad, so the Burmese Communist Party collapsed and the leader of the Malayan communist insurgency signed a surrender agreement. I noted these developments while spending most of my time in historical archives, studying the events that had unleashed the Indochina wars: the Vietnamese August Revolution in 1945, the outbreak of war between Vietnam and France in December 1946 and the national liberation struggles and construction of new states in Indochina, Malaya and Indonesia 1945–49. I read about East Asia's bloody history from the Opium Wars onward. There were wars between states, large-scale rebellions and, notably, colonial wars that first established empires and then dismantled them. I found that, since the 1840s, war had marred the history of at least one East Asian neighbourhood in every single decade. The 19th century's worst was the 1854–68 Taiping Rebellion in China, when whole cities were razed to the ground and their inhabitants slaughtered. While the First World War happened mainly in Europe, hundreds of thousands of Asians were shipped to Europe to serve as factory workers or as cannon fodder in the trenches. The East Asian countries were also affected by the European war, with Japan taking over the German possessions in China.

The Second World War began earlier and ended later in Asia than in Europe, with China suffering the second highest number of casualties after the Soviet Union. I was reading Harold Isaacs' prophetic 1947 book, *No Peace for Asia*, based on travels in the aftermath of Japan's 1945 surrender. He predicted all the wars that followed: the Chinese Civil War, the war of Indonesian independence, the Muslim–Hindu wars in India, the Malayan Emergency, the Korean War, the wars in Vietnam, and insurgencies in other countries. There would be no peace for Asia. Isaacs was right – until 1979. He died in 1986.

When did I understand that the East Asian Peace had come to stay? Quite late. At the end of the Cold War, some of my colleagues held hopes of a peaceful world. They believed that the end of the Cold War would bring a 'peace dividend' and foster global cooperation. Although I am a born optimist, my knowledge of history led me to take a darker view at that time. I thought the end of the Cold War would just remove the ideological clothing that various violent regimes and movements had been wearing for some time; ethnic, national-nativist and religious creeds would take their place as emotional drivers of conflict. Developments in the former Yugoslavia and in the Middle East seemed to confirm my gloom. Yet to my surprise, East Asia proved me wrong. In spite of all the tension that kept simmering in the divided Korea, Tibet, Xinjiang and the Taiwan Strait, between China and Japan, between Korea and Japan, in Aceh, Timor-Leste, Mindanao, south Thailand, and several parts of Myanmar, and the complex rivalries concerning sovereignty over islands and maritime zones in the East China Sea and South China Sea, the region was now astoundingly peaceful.

In 1997, after the first Mischief Reef incident – when the Philippines discovered that China had built installations on a submerged reef just outside of Palawan – I initiated a research programme on the South China Sea and have since been following its maritime disputes. Yet the mid-1990s was also the time I began to embrace the concept of an 'East Asian Peace'. This had to do with Vietnam's amazing entry into the Association of Southeast Asian Nations (ASEAN) in 1995, which paved the way for Laos and Myanmar to join in 1997, and Cambodia in 1998. I am old enough to understand how sensational this was. ASEAN had been formed in 1967 as an organization of five non-communist states; by 1976, when Vietnam had been unified under its communist party, ASEAN countries were afraid that it would take control of Cambodia and Laos, as well as destabilize Thailand. At the time it was still assumed that Vietnam enjoyed Chinese backing. Instead, a deadly conflict developed between Asia's two leading communist states. China sustained the Khmer Rouge in Cambodia, whose paranoia led them to initiate a border war and kill anyone suspected of being pro-Vietnamese. In 1978, Vietnam struck back and took most of Cambodia, installing a pro-Vietnamese regime in Phnom Penh. This allowed for the formation of an unholy alliance of China, ASEAN and the USA against Soviet-supported Vietnam. Against this backdrop, events of 1995 can be seen as nothing less than spectacular. Six years after the end of the Cold War and four years after the Paris agreement on Cambodia and the dissolution of the Soviet Union, ASEAN accepted Vietnam, its main historical adversary, as a member. This must be counted among the largest of the 'peace dividends' from the end of the Cold War. And, to my positive surprise, China did nothing to prevent ASEAN's expansion. In the 1990s, notably after the Asian financial crisis in 1997, China pursued a 'good neighbour policy' that earned it many friends in the region. I noticed with pleasure how my Southeast Asian friends' apprehensions about an increasingly powerful and prosperous China began to dissipate.

Another personal experience helped me understand that East Asia is in fact *one region*, defined as a geographically contiguous area consisting of states that are closely connected with each other and have some joint institutions. In February 1996, together with Director Thommy Svensson of the Nordic Institute of Asian Studies I attended a preparatory conference in Venice for the first Asia Europe Meeting (ASEM). At one of the sessions, we were shown maps drawn by Michel Foucher, a French geographer and later ambassador to Latvia. His charts of regional trade flows, air traffic and telecommunications demonstrated that each ASEAN member country was more closely integrated with China, Hong Kong, Taiwan, South Korea and Japan than it was with other ASEAN members, and, despite geographic proximity, each had only modest interaction with the South Asian countries.[2] The same pattern was confirmed in the field of security by a study undertaken a few years afterwards by political scientists Barry Buzan and Ole Waever (2003), who found that the Southeast Asian and Northeast Asian 'secu-

---

2. India, Pakistan, Bangladesh , Nepal, Bhutan, the Maldives and Sri Lanka.

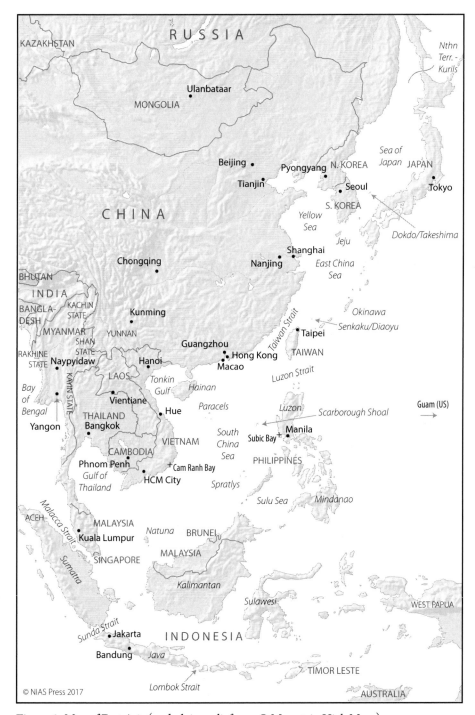

Figure 1: Map of East Asia (underlying relief map © Mountain High Maps)

rity complexes' had merged into a single East Asian complex. Hence I decided to replace my 'Southeast Asianist' hat with one that covers the whole of East Asia, a region characterised by the centrality of China and of Sino–Japanese relations, dense communication networks, business networks centred on Japanese and Korean investments and an influential ethnic Chinese diaspora, a complex set of security arrangements based on Sino–US cooperation and rivalry (including US bases and US bilateral alliances along the region's maritime rim), and frameworks for dialogue built around ASEAN, including East Asian Summits.

What further prompted my attention to the East Asian Peace was a manuscript I reviewed for the *Journal of Peace Research* in 1999, at a time when many peace researchers were consumed by the idea of a democratic peace. The article was written by Finnish political scientist Timo Kivimäki, and published in 2001 under the title 'The Long Peace of ASEAN'. His argument goes like this: the ASEAN countries have long been at peace with each other. This is not a democratic peace. It is based on a perception of shared interests among the national leaders in the Southeast Asian countries.

Kivimäki's article kept resonating in my head on each New Year's Eve, when I could toast to the fact that East Asia had remained peaceful for yet another year. This peace never struck me as self-evident, because there was so much tension, but I grew more and more convinced that the regional transition from war to peace warranted careful study. In 2005, in connection with a visit by the Norwegian Crown Prince and Princess to Thailand, I presented my ideas about a Southeast Asian Peace at Thammasat University in Bangkok. This was not long after the massacres at Kru Se and Tak Bai in Thailand's Deep South, and I was met by a storm of criticism from peace- and freedom-loving Southeast Asian students with diverse ethnic and national backgrounds. They insisted that their societies were far from peaceful. My talk, they asserted, would not merely flatter their authoritarian leaders, but also encourage their regimes to uphold their repression of opposition movements. I sympathized with their longing for a deeper, more genuine peace. Yet I did not agree. The absence of war and direct violence is essential for human well-being – even in non-democratic societies. I began to send research proposals to various funders, who invariably turned me down. Only when Kivimäki and I submitted a joint application in 2008 did we meet with success, due to the good judgment of the Swedish Riksbankens Jubileumsfond and its reviewers.

In the years 2009–12, Kivimäki and I worked closely together. He explored all the databases he could find in order to test if there was such a thing as an 'East Asian Peace' and – in case there was – how it could be explained. His fascinating and eye-opening tables, graphs and analyses convinced me that East Asia had not just avoided war but had also seen a reduction in violent crime. We agreed that democratic peace theory had little to contribute to an explanation, since so many of the East Asian countries were not democracies and peace among the few democracies (Japan, South Korea, and Taiwan) could be explained by their adherence to the same camp in the Cold War. Yet, both of us were also sceptical that another liberal theory, the idea of economic interdependence, could adequately explain the peace. The key factor, we thought, was in the heads of the national decision makers. We disagreed, however, on our theoretical approach. Inspired by constructivism, Kivimäki found it impossible to distinguish between cause and effect in explaining peace. If elite discourses are peaceful in content, then they cannot be separated from their peaceful effects; they are both cause and effect at the same time, indistinguishable parts of a discursive totality.[3] I thought this was gibberish and insisted that classic causal reasoning can yield valuable insights. If we were to explain peace as an outcome of ideas held by national leaders, then we would have to show that those ideas preceded the peace and motivated the actions that created or upheld it. We discussed this back and forth, and he came up with an intriguing idea that fit well with my approach: identify those leaders whose main priority was economic development and those who had other main priorities,

---

3. A key statement in Kivimäki (2014) that I cannot agree with is: 'It is the developmentalist identity that has causal powers relevant for peace, but since that cannot be directly measured, I will have to use proxy indicators: if the state identity is developmentalist, it is likely that state documents use the word development a lot. Yet the use of the word does not create peace in East Asia, but instead the immeasurable developmentalist identity does' (p. 23). In my view, a state does not have any 'identity', except in the imaginings of its representatives, so it is not immeasurable identities that 'have causal powers' but identifiable ideas (goals, priorities, perceptions). Uses of the word 'peace' in state documents are not 'proxies' for collective identities but expressions of ideas held by decision makers. Case studies must determine if these are genuinely held, and serve as motives for actions, or if they are used to legitimise actions undertaken for other reasons.

and see if more peace followed when the former were in power. It would be particularly helpful if we could find leaders who set out to achieve economic development, but failed. If peace followed from an unsuccessful attempt to focus on national development, then this would confirm that it is not development per se that pacifies but the known intention of a government to strive for it. Kivimäki found that the most peaceful period in the contemporary history of the Philippines was under President Ramon Magsaysay (1953–57), who tried his best to generate economic growth, but failed. Kivimäki speculated that Magsaysay – by contrast to the later president Ferdinand Marcos (1965–86) – managed to dissuade would-be rebels from resorting to violence by instilling hope for social improvement.

When setting up our programme, together with Isak Svensson at Uppsala University, we had to make some fundamental choices. First, we decided to make full use of the Uppsala Conflict Data Programme (UCDP), as well as of the Correlates of War (COW) database and PRIO's battle death data. Next, we decided to expand a core group based in Uppsala to include research associates in various countries. These associates would form a programme network, take part in our conferences and carry out specific research projects financed by grants from within the programme. Then we decided to organize four of our six main conferences in East Asia. This happy choice helped establish collaborative relationships with Korean, Vietnamese, Chinese and Singaporean scholars. As Professor Evelyn Goh of Australian National University would say later, 'I have not come across such a diverse group of scholars in any other conference setting. So bringing together these scholars in and of itself, repeatedly, is an important enterprise' (Heldmark & Wrangnert 2015). Only the first and the last conference were held in Sweden. Our eight-member Advisory Board, led by Peter Wallensteen, Dag Hammarsköld Professor at Uppsala University from 1985–2012, has taken part in all the conferences and served as moderators and discussants for the papers presented. Altogether, 140 conference papers were discussed at the six conferences.

Finally, Kivimäki and I decided that our main publications would be of article length and submitted to peer-reviewed journals. In addition, we would produce a few monographs. Much later, I decided that we should also produce a special issue of the journal *Global Asia*, two short video films, and an edited volume: *Debating the East Asian Peace*. In addition to understanding the East Asian Peace, we sought, and continue to seek, to draw public attention to the phenomenon and inspire debates about what can be done to make it last.

Part I

Explaining Regional Peace

When seeking to explain something, we must first decide what that something is. What is peace in a region? Although there is no agreement among peace researchers on how to define 'peace', I was drawn to a narrow definition when trying to explain the regional transition from widespread warfare to relative peace. The definition I chose is simply 'absence of armed conflict'. To the extent that a region avoids 'armed conflict', both between and within states, it has peace. I employ the definition of 'armed conflict' provided by the Uppsala Conflict Data Programme (UCDP) and which serves as the baseline for the UCDP database:

> An armed conflict is a contested incompatibility that concerns government and/or territory where the use of armed force between two parties, of which at least one is the government of a state, results in at least 25 battle-related deaths in one calendar year.

Peace researchers often count armed conflicts and cite their number to point out changes over time and differences between types of states or between regions. Yet armed conflicts vary hugely in severity. One big war can kill more people than a hundred small armed conflicts. In our programme we have thus chosen the individual battle deaths in armed conflict rather than the armed conflict as a whole as our main 'dependent variable', the key indicator of the (lack of) peace. This means that if there is one big war with thousands of battle deaths in a region, then it is not peaceful. However, a region may be regarded as peaceful even if it has several small-scale armed conflicts. The 'East Asian Peace' has never been total, if by total we mean absolutely no armed conflict. As yet, there has not been a single year without a registered armed conflict somewhere in East Asia, and – as can be calculated from Table 1 (p. 12) – the average annual number of East Asian battle deaths in the period 1991–2015 was 967. So the East Asian Peace is just *relative*, with dramatically fewer battle deaths than before.

The UCDP's definition of armed conflict differs from that used in the American Correlates of War (COW) project, which counts 'wars' having reached the level of 1,000 battle deaths since the year when conflict began.[1] Using the much lower 25-death threshold, the UCDP has compiled a robust dataset that is comparable across countries and regions. It is sufficiently broad to include most of what we normally consider to be conflict between organized parties, while it omits most of what we see as terrorism or crime.

In our research proposal from 2009, Kivimäki, Svensson and I asked: how deep is the East Asian Peace? And how can it be explained? We put the questions in that order, meaning we intended to first gauge its depth and then explain it. Kivimäki loyally followed this recipe. He first set out to map the peace, reporting his results in 'East Asian Relative Peace – Does It Exist? What Is It?' (Kivimäki 2010) and then sought to explain the peace in a monograph four years later. I instead moved directly to explaining, and only later began to gauge the quality or sustainability of what I had tried to explain. This is also the way I have organized the book in your hands. In Part I, I discuss how to explain the peace, and it is only in Part III that I turn to the question of its viability. I must acknowledge that Kivimäki's approach is more logical. One should define exactly what is to be explained before starting to explain it.

My problem was that I knew it would be difficult to agree with my colleagues how to measure the depth or quality of peace, and any consensus-based definition would likely be complex, leaving us with a whole cluster of dependent variables. A clear causal explanation requires a precisely defined dependent variable and measurable independent variables. Our main dependent variable should therefore be battle deaths in armed conflicts. For me, this meant that we should define a condition with fewer conflict-related deaths as 'more peaceful' than a condition with more such deaths. I wanted a narrow definition of peace in order to have a tangible change to explain: a dramatic reduction in battle deaths. If I had approached the research questions in the more logical order,

---

1. In the COW dataset, the last interstate war in East Asia ended in 1987, the last year of fighting at the Sino–Vietnamese border. There were intrastate (civil) wars in Cambodia 1979–91 and 1993–97, Aceh (Indonesia) 1989–91 and 1999–2004, Myanmar 1983–1988, and the Philippines 2000–2001, 2003 and 2005–2006: CowWar list at: www.correlatesofwar.org/data-sets/COW-war (accessed 4 November 2016).

I could have ended up with multiple dependent variables, such as in the Global Peace Index (GPI), which consists of 22 indicators, each of which needs to be explained with its own set of independent variables. It is impossible to give a scientific explanation of a country's GPI rank or value without first explaining each of the indicators. To confine our explanatory endeavour to one dependent variable, battle deaths (over a threshold as low as 25), made sense to me, both because it simplified the explanatory endeavour, and because the absence of armed violence is a precondition for human well-being: when few people are killed, there is normally also less fear of being killed.

My insistence on using an absence-of-armed-conflict definition of peace is also due to my general dissatisfaction with the common but misleading distinction between so-called 'negative' and 'positive peace'. This is in my view a false dichotomy, mixing up the descriptive and normative meanings of the words 'negative' and 'positive'. If absence-of-armed-conflict is 'negative peace', then the presence of armed conflict must be 'positive peace', which is absurd. An analogy with medicine can make this clear. If someone tests negative for a certain illness (or for symptoms of an illness), no one would call this 'negative health'. A negative test for an illness is of course something positive. The same goes for peace. Armed conflict is negative, so if there are no armed conflicts in a nation or a region, then this creates a double negative, which is positive: $(\div (\div \text{peace}) = (+ \text{peace}))$. So the absence of armed conflict must already be 'positive peace'.

What people actually mean when they say negative peace, is a shallow, insufficient, fragile or unsustainable peace. Most of us will agree that a genuine peace must include something more than just absence of armed conflict. There should be this – plus something more. But what is this something more? One possibility is to demand absence of more than just armed conflict. Peace could be absence of all direct and indirect violence, physical as well as psychological. It could be absence of incidents, threats, weapons, human rights violations or some people's exploitation of others (so-called 'structural violence'). Another possibility is to broaden the concept of peace by including values such as justice, freedom, equality, legitimate governance or trust. This makes sense, but it is hard to agree on exactly which values to include. When it is broadly defined, 'peace' tends to simply mean a 'good society'. Attempts to explain transitions to peace may then degenerate into a discussion of what is required for creating a good or harmonious society.

Some peace researchers have made an effort to make sense of the term 'quality peace'. Peace is then understood as a continuum, with total war on one end and any of a number of ideal conceptions of a just or harmonious peace on the other. People often say that it is better to die than to endure suppression or humiliation, or that 'peace on these terms would be worse than war'. As a starting point, I disagree. Many more people die and are wounded as a result of state action during wartime than in times of peace. Further, even those qualities theorists of 'quality peace' emphasise – health, justice, human rights, equality – are typically more circumscribed during wartime than during periods when troops are in their barracks. Peace, as I define it, is far from an ideal condition. But it is better than war, and almost always provides a better basis for building a just or more harmonious society.

Peter Wallensteen (2015a, 2015b) defines quality peace as 'the creation of post-war conditions that make the inhabitants of a society (be it an area, a country, a region, a continent, or a planet) secure in life and dignity now and for the foreseeable future'. He thus identifies peace with being 'secure in life and dignity', and he links peace to a process ('the creation') instead of to a static condition. His definition presupposes the absence of war ('post-war conditions'), and has an inbuilt concern for viability ('now and for the foreseeable future'). Wallensteen's proposal may be the best that we have, yet it is probably too broad and imprecise to be operational in scholarly research. He discusses a number of possible indicators, which will need to be explored independently if a statistical study of 'quality peace' shall be meaningful.

Erik Melander (2017) has coined an alternative definition: 'the conduct of politics with respect for the physical person of one's adversary, using consensual decision making, on the basis of strong equality values'. His definition is also about a process ('conduct of politics') but it does not include Wallensteen's concern for dignity (which is hard to operationalize). It instead includes respect: a fully respectful environment is one in which no violence (including torture, arbitrary arrest, etc.) can be used to violate one's adversary's physical integrity. Melander then adds two values that are crucial to his idea of peace: consensual decision-making and equality. The approaches taken by Wallensteen and Melander make sense, but both are fraught with methodological challenges. In order for Melander's definition of peace to be employed in rigorous research, his subcategories must be clearly defined and indicators for each must be identified. Melander engages in this theory-building process, but his result is no less complex than Wallensteen's. While there is nothing wrong with complexity per se, this approach risks the appearance of distracting our attention from the essential task of finding out how nations and regions escape, with lasting effect, from the scourge of war.

I prefer a research strategy that sticks to a narrow definition of peace as 'absence of armed conflict' while seeking to identify the independent variables that are required to make such absence viable. These variables tend to be the same as those that are proposed as constitutive elements of 'quality peace'. My research strategy allows peace researchers to explore the whole spectrum of possible contributing factors, while maintaining a precise and operational definition of peace. Instead of incorporating justice, freedom, good governance, equality or trust in the definition itself, one may look at how these factors affect the duration of peace: its viability or sustainability. My emphasis is on duration, on what enables a peace to last.

In addition to my preference for a precise dependent variable, I have two other reasons for using an absence-of-armed conflict definition. First, the East Asian Peace seems less sustainable than peace in some other regions. From an heuristic point of view, this is an advantage. The East Asian Peace is not over-determined by the presence of the peace triangle made famous by Russett and Oneal (2001): democracy–international institutions–economic integration. East Asia is strongly integrated economically but has a mix of regime forms ranging from well-established democracies (Japan, South Korea, Mongolia, Taiwan) to the world's only really totalitarian regime (North Korea).[2] Although most East Asian states are members of the UN and other global organisations, they have not built much institutional cooperation on the regional level. The first trilateral summit of the region's most economically powerful nations (Japan, China and South Korea) was organized less than a decade ago, and although the Association of Southeast Asian

---

2. A totalitarian regime may be defined as a government that subordinates its citizens to the state by strictly controlling all aspects of life by coercive measures.

Nations (ASEAN) has a longer history, it can in no way be compared to the European Union with regard to regional political integration.

Despite the absence of a robust East Asian peace triangle, the region has enjoyed astoundingly little armed conflict for almost four decades. If we had started our investigation on the basis of a definition of 'quality peace', I'm not sure we would at all have discovered the region's momentous transformation from widespread warfare to relative peace. Instead we would have seen a region full of tension, risk, repression and human rights abuse. Admittedly, it is also desirable to explore the East Asian Peace from the perspective of a continuum from low- to high-quality peace, focussing on how a region enters the continuum at the low end. Yet scholars framing their research on the basis of this kind of continuum are likely to be tempted to overlook successful entry at the low end and look instead for failure to reach the high end.

Our programme has included three complementary approaches to empirical research: 1) explain East Asia's historical transition to peace as absence-of-armed conflict; 2) gauge the quality of the East Asian Peace on a low-high continuum; 3) identify the independent variables that are needed to make the East Asian Peace viable in the long term. As stated in my introduction, we also have a more lofty ambition, 4) to evaluate the extent to which the East Asian Peace may contribute to the goal of world peace. We have touched on this in the programme, by discussing if East Asia's turn toward peace has been a uniquely regional trend (as in the 1980s) or part of a global trend (as in the period 1990–2010), analyzing risks in the Sino–American relationship that are essential for world peace (see Part II of this book), and discussing whether or not the causes of the East Asian Peace may yield peace in other regions as well.

What is a region? In the Introduction, I defined it as 'a geographically contiguous area consisting of states that are closely connected with each other and have some joint institutions'. Buzan and Waever (2003; 43) say that the region 'refers to the level where states or other units link together sufficiently closely that their securities cannot be considered separate from each other'. One could perhaps add that there should be some kind of regional identity among the population. They should have an idea that 'we' are a group of nations that belong together and have certain cultural, social or historical characteristics that make us different from other neighbour nations as well as from nations further away. Yet such identities are hard to ascertain. I've therefore decided to stick to the definition above, with its emphasis on contiguity, communication and cooperation. In our programme, we quickly agreed that East Asia is a single region and not two or several regions. There are undeniable differences between Northeast and Southeast Asia. The former has 72 per cent of East Asia's population and 87 per cent of its economic output (see Table 6, p. 152 and Table 2, p. 50). Northeast Asia (China, Japan, Korea and Mongolia) also has fewer, larger and stronger states, with longer recorded histories. By contrast, the Southeast Asian kingdoms in the pre-modern period – except Vietnam – were weaker, more fluid and territorially overlapping. In the 19th century, all of Southeast Asia except Thailand was colonized by European powers and divided into states with fixed boundaries. They gained independence only after the Second World War, while China and Japan were incorporated as sovereign states in Europe's global system already in the 19th century and simply forced to trade with Europeans on unequal terms. These differences may help explain why the Southeast Asian nations found it more difficult to end their civil wars than China, Japan and Korea. On the other hand, the Southeast Asian nations have been better at reconciling their differences, while interstate tensions have continued to plague Northeast Asia, which does not have a regional organization of its own.

In spite of these differences, there is good reason to consider East Asia as one region. As Michel Foucher demonstrated in 1996, each Southeast Asian country communicates more with Japan, South Korea, China and Taiwan than with one another. In the Second World War, Japan conquered much of China and Southeast Asia, and sought to create an East Asian Co-Prosperity Sphere. The Allies divided the region militarily into a US Southwest Pacific Theatre and a British South-East Asia Command (SEAC) but later, as the Europeans pulled out, the USA became the dominant maritime power in all of East Asia. China is both a Northeast and Southeast Asian power, and the ethnic Chinese diaspora plays a key economic role in all of the Southeast Asian countries. The South China Sea links Northeast and Southeast Asia through some of the world's busiest sea lanes. China, South Korea and Japan are all keenly interested in the security of the sea lanes, where tankers pass continuously with oil from the Middle East. Institutionally, ASEAN has served as a vehicle for regional consultations encompassing the

Northeast Asian states through the ASEAN+3 (China, South Korea and Japan), the ASEAN Regional Forum (ARF) and the East Asia Summits (EAS). There is more communication between Northeast and Southeast Asia than between any of the East Asian countries and Russia or India.[3]

If today's East Asia is more than just itself, then it belongs to the Asia-Pacific. I hold, however, that economic integration across the Pacific, and the US and Australian security roles in East Asia, are best accounted for within a global framework of analysis, with global modes of trade and divisions of labour, alliance patterns, institutions like the UN, the World Trade Organization, G7 and G20. The Asia Pacific Economic Cooperation (APEC) has played only a modest role. Yet, when studying peace and security in East Asia, it is impossible to neglect the fundamental role of the United States. In security terms, the region is dominated by a power triangle of China, Japan and the USA, where the United States remains the most powerful and, moreover, has Japan as an ally with US bases on its territory.

Peace Statistics

My main figurative presentation of the East Asian Peace is a graph showing the annual estimated number of battle deaths in East Asia, as compared with the rest of the world, from 1946 until 2015. It is based on my choice to see regional peace as the (relative) absence of armed conflict, measured in battle deaths. And I have defined my primary task as explaining the decline of East Asian battle deaths from the 1970s to the 1980s, their further decline in the 1990s, and their low number since. As mentioned above, East Asia's share of global battle deaths dropped from 80 per cent in the 1946–79 period to 6.2 per cent in 1980–89. Since 1990 the East Asian share has been 1.7 per cent, and in 2015 it was a mere 1.3 per cent.

In the programme we needed a good strategy for trying out various explanations. Explaining the absence of something is tricky. In the

---

3. South Asia is a region apart. In the pre-modern period, Hindu, Buddhist and Islamic customs penetrated eastwards from India and the Arab world, and in the 19th and 20th centuries, the Indian influence continued under British protection. However, the main external influence now came from Europe and America, and the process of decolonisation, with its focus on creating coherent nation-states based on indigenous ethnic groups, reduced the interaction with India.

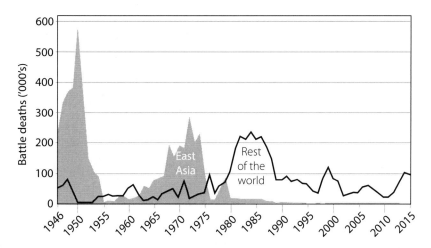

Figure 2: Battle deaths in East Asia (filled shape) and the rest of the world (dark line), 1946–2015

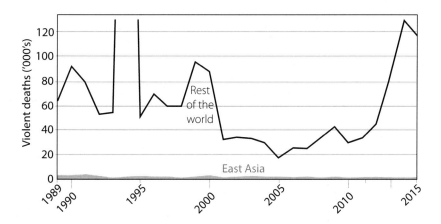

Figure 3: Violent deaths in armed conflicts, non-state conflicts and one-sided violence, East Asia (filled shape) and the rest of the world (dark line), 1989–2015

Note: The reason why the dark line breaks through the roof in 1994 is the Rwandan genocide.

words of Robert S. Ross, a research associate of the East Asian Peace programme and a member of our Advisory Board (2009: 75), 'Proving a negative is difficult; establishing why there has not been greater conflict in East Asia, why East Asia has experienced less conflict than in the past,

Table 1: Battle deaths in East Asia and the rest of the world

Period	East Asia	East Asia %	Rest of World
1946–50	1,890,455	88.90	236,147
1951–55	732,383	92.80	56,472
1956–60	81,548	33.80	160,070
1961–65	225,106	61.60	140,353
1966–70	705,435	81.60	158,852
1971–75	990,809	84.10	186,629
1976–80	168,428	31.30	369,198
1981–85	72,633	6.40	1,065,157
1986–90	35,275	4.70	711,838
1991–95	6,865	1.80	368,793
1996–00	2,065	0.60	372,606
2001–05	5,286	2.50	205,089
2006–10	4,556	2.10	215,914
2011–15	5,393	1.60	327,620

Sources: PRIO Battle Death data 1946–2008, UCDP armed conflict data 2009–15. Best estimates have been used when they exist, low estimates when there are no best.

is a dubious task'. It is much easier to analyse an outbreak of war – or a peace agreement – than conflict avoidance. Most people and most governments live in peace most of the time. So, a peaceful period in a region may be understood as an expansion of the normal. Peace in a region is the cumulative effect of a vast number of more or less conscious decisions not to resort to arms. Many of these decisions were taken long before the peaceful period began, others at the time when the last war ended, and yet others during the peace itself. Peace is only sometimes created. Mostly, it is upheld through a repetition of more or less self-evident decisions to eschew violence. In principle, each instance of peaceful behaviour can be explained through a set of preceding factors. Admittedly, it is difficult to single out the most important reasons why a region with 16–17 states representing thirty per cent of mankind could make a transition from frequent warfare to relative peace. We have to retrace the transition by examining two classes of independent variables: how disputes did not turn violent (i.e., become armed conflicts). and how armed conflicts came to an end. This, I have felt, is only feasible if we stick to one measurable dependent variable: the conflict-related death.

The causes of a decline, or of a constantly low number of battle deaths, may differ from one phase of a conflict to the next: onset, escalation, de-escalation, and termination. As Joakim Kreutz, member of our core group in Uppsala, has pointed out (2015, 2017), the fact that fewer new wars have begun or escalated, and the fact that ongoing conflicts have ended or become less violent, are two separate aspects of declining warfare that are not necessarily causally interlinked.

When a dispute arises – that is, at its onset – the parties may avoid escalation if one party backs off or both agree to turn to institutional mechanisms of conflict resolution, such as negotiations or settlement by a court. The dispute may then be resolved without anyone considering the option to use violence. If the parties cannot resolve their dispute, they may nonetheless disregard or shelve it while sticking to their mutually incompatible claims. Alternatively, the parties may resort to non-violent means of struggle. A rebel group can demonstrate in the streets or occupy public buildings. A government may issue protests against another government's actions, mobilize its people in the streets, or organize a display of force designed to prevent its active use. In any of these cases, there is no onset of armed conflict. Among the factors that avert the onset of new wars, we must distinguish between those preventing an outbreak in a situation where the use of force is actively considered from those ensuring that disputes are managed in ways that make violence unnecessary or even inconceivable.

If a dispute escalates into armed conflict, the parties may seek to limit it and prevent its further escalation by conducting only defensive operations. Firearms may be used in predictable ways or against a target with no human presence so there are no casualties. During much of the Cold War, the Taiwanese-held islands on the Chinese coast were strafed with artillery fire by the People's Liberation Army (PLA) on particular weekdays so people could know when to move around and when to stay in their bunkers. In the 1980s, at the Sino–Vietnamese border, artillery fire often targeted areas where no one would be hurt. In the border dispute between Cambodia and Thailand during 2008–11 around the temple Preah Vihear, artillery was mainly used to demonstrate a will to fight if need be. And in August 2015, artillery shells were fired across the Korean DMZ, carefully calibrated to not target humans. In recent years, cyber warfare has emerged as an option that damages communication systems without inflicting loss of life. It is also possible to limit the number of casualties in active warfare through precision bombing from aircraft or drones.

An armed conflict in progress might de-escalate through unilateral or negotiated ceasefires, or by a show of restraint by one or all parties. A third party may be used as a go-between, facilitator or mediator.

Finally, a conflict may be *terminated*. Sometimes, one side backs out or is defeated. Sometimes the fighting simply peters out.[4] War termination may also take the form of a negotiated peace, with or without third party involvement.

Various explanatory factors may play out differently at each of the stages just enumerated. My sense is that soft factors such as attitudes, discourses, laws, norms, forms of governance and mechanisms of conflict management play their main role in securing a peace once it has been established. Soft factors can reduce fear and threat perceptions, thus making peace viable, but they are not decisive in preventing a crisis or militarized dispute from erupting into war.

I surmise that *political priorities* and *perceptions of economic and security risk* are key factors when governments or rebel leaders choose to shelve a dispute, avoid armed clashes, manage ongoing conflicts so they do not escalate, or de-escalate and terminate them. While some nations have established stable systems of governance and a culture of peaceful conflict resolution, others have not. While some bilateral relationships are characterized by trust and stable economic, diplomatic and cultural exchange, others are imbued with suspicion and recurring incidents that reinforce mutual distrust. Hence shared norms, ideas, culture, discourse or institutions are of limited consequence in regional transitions from widespread warfare to relative peace. Yet these soft factors may have an important role to play as the peace perpetuates itself, allowing regional integration not just economically but also culturally and politically.

---

4. For example, the communist insurgency in Malaya is normally considered to have ended by the mid-1960s if not earlier, but its leaders did not surrender until 1989.

Turning points

When did the East Asian Peace begin? In order to explain its onset, it is of course important to ascertain when it happened. We will not be misled by the graph above and suggest 1979 as a general starting point, tempting though this would be. This was the statistical turning point, the year of the last big war. 1978–79 was also the time when China launched market economic reforms, and the USA and China established full diplomatic relations. A new leader in Beijing, Deng Xiaoping, examined the international situation. After the Soviet Union had failed to intervene on behalf of its ally Vietnam when China invaded in February–March 1979, Deng concluded that China could enjoy a period of peace with the great powers. While retaining heavy military pressure at the Vietnam border and engaging the Vietnamese army repeatedly over the following years, he accepted the risk of channelling resources into market-driven economic growth and reducing China's overall military spending.

Yet, the transition cannot be pinned down to just 1979. Armed conflicts continued beyond that year in the Philippines and Myanmar, and the Third Indochina War, which began in 1978–79 with Vietnam's invasion of Cambodia, China's invasion of Vietnam, and the provision of Chinese, Thai and US aid to a rebel coalition in Cambodia, continued until 1989 in the form of an insurgency in Cambodia. Rebels with external support also fought against the communist regime in Laos, a close ally of Vietnam. And the war at the Sino–Vietnamese border did not end with China's withdrawal from Vietnamese territory in March 1979. For the whole period 1979–87, there was heavy intermittent fighting at the border, with artillery exchanges and raids into each other's territory and thousands of soldiers killed. In March 1988, Chinese and Vietnamese forces also clashed at a submerged reef in the Spratly area of the South China Sea. So the end of the Third Indochina War in 1989, when Vietnam withdrew its troops from Cambodia and China lifted its military pressure on the Sino–Vietnamese border, could be considered an even more important turning point than 1979. Indeed Robert S. Ross (2003; 2017) sees the regional turn to peace as having happened in 1989, at the end of the global Cold War. UCDP statistics report that the estimated number of battle deaths in East Asia dropped from around 16,000 in 1988 to just 3,000 in 1989. They have never since risen above this number and typically are much lower (see Figure 2 and Table 1, pp. 11–12).

On the other hand, the origin of the East Asian Peace may be found in events occurring long before 1979. My story of the regional peace begins in 1945. Japan, I argue, deserves far more credit than it has received for creating a pioneering model of peaceful development. All countries in the region had been drawn into the Second World War, but, although much of East Asia was consumed by war also afterwards, there were two exceptions: Mongolia and Japan, which emerged as independent states after a period of Soviet or US domination. I therefore place the origin of regional peace in Japan's 1945–46 reaction to its military defeat. By contrast, Kivimäki finds the origin of the East Asian Peace in changes happening in Southeast Asia during 1965–67, when ASEAN was established. According to Kivimäki, the five original members of ASEAN instituted a developmental peace under the slogan *The ASEAN Way*. Its consensus culture, built on mutual respect, conflict avoidance and non-interference, spread later to the rest of East Asia. I concur with Kivimäki that the regional peace is developmental: the leaders of the peaceful transition were not pacifists; they sought stability for the sake of economic development, but my developmental peace story begins in Japan. So we actually have four consecutive turning points, with different geographical foci: 1945–46 (Japan and Mongolia), 1965–67 (non-communist Southeast Asia), 1978–79 (China; Sino–US relations), and 1989–91 (Cambodia, Sino–Vietnamese relations). In addition, there was a particularly interesting peaceful interregnum during 1954–57, with little armed fighting (see Figure 2, p. 11). Its geographical focus was on Korea and Indochina, and it marked the entry of the People's Republic of China on the international, diplomatic scene.

The Short Peace (1954–57)

In his monograph *The Long Peace of East Asia*, Kivimäki aptly calls this interregnum *The Short Peace*. It needs both to be understood on its own terms and compared with the later Long Peace. In brief, the Short Piece was a product of Cold War dynamics and, specifically, institutions and relationships that emerged from negotiations to end the Korean and the First Indochina War. The Short Peace was not just East Asian, but represented an attempt to overcome the global Cold War and make détente between East and West. The details are worth pursuing.

The story of the Short Peace begins with Soviet dictator Josef Stalin's death in March 1953, which provoked a search for new Cold War security strategies, including greater emphasis on diplomacy, both in Moscow and Beijing. The Chinese People's Volunteer Army had suffered disastrous losses in Korea. It needed a respite, and was allowed by China's leader Mao Zedong to sign an armistice with the US-led UN forces. The Americans were also ready to talk. In April 1952, the brisk General Douglas MacArthur had been replaced as commander of the UN forces in Korea; the war had become a stalemate with a front line just north of the 38th parallel, which had also divided Korea during 1945–50. Ceasefire negotiations began before Stalin died but took two years. In July 1953, an armistice that built on an Indian proposal was finally signed. It paved the way for a great power conference, held in Geneva, where a Korean peace treaty was expected to be hammered out and the powers would also explore ways to end the war in Indochina. While the first never happened, the second did.

The French now depended on US support for their war against the Democratic Republic of Vietnam, led by the communist leader Ho Chi Minh. While it proved impossible to make any further progress concerning Korea, the leaders of China, the USSR, the United Kingdom and France talked seriously about Indochina and put pressure on the rival Vietnamese governments of Ho Chi Minh and former emperor Bao Dai to accept a truce. The Geneva conference was a diplomatic breakthrough for the People's Republic of China (PRC), which was not yet a UN member and had not been recognized diplomatically by either France or the USA. The United States refused to talk with Chinese representatives, but the French were eager to get out of their Indochinese quagmire and were thus ready for a compromise. While the conference was going on in Geneva, the French army suffered an ignominious defeat at Dien Bien Phu in the Vietnamese highlands, where a fortress was besieged and overrun by the People's Army of Vietnam, with massive Chinese support. With the fall of Dien Bien Phu and the decision in Geneva to recognize Vietnam, Cambodia and Laos as three sovereign states, while dividing Vietnam temporarily at the 17th parallel, the number of battle deaths in East Asia dropped to well under 30,000 in each of the years 1955–57, which in comparison with the previous and subsequent years was a small number.

The Short Peace also included a rapprochement between China and India. Prime Ministers Jawaharlal Nehru and Zhou Enlai signed a joint declaration in December 1953, enumerating Five Principles of Peaceful Coexistence: mutual respect for each other's territorial integrity and sovereignty, mutual non-aggression, mutual non-interference in each other's internal affairs, equality and cooperation for mutual benefit, and peaceful coexistence. So, in the years 1953–55, China, India and the USSR all supported the principle of peaceful coexistence. In December 1954, the Indonesian academic and politician Prijono (1907–69) and the father of modern Burmese nationalism, the poet Thakin Kotaw Hmine (1876–1964), were among the second to last recipients of the Stalin Peace Prize. (Instituted in 1949, this was renamed the Lenin Peace Prize in 1956 following the denunciation of Stalin by the new Soviet leader Nikita Khrushchev.) Priyono and Kotaw Hmine were staunch supporters of their countries' non-aligned foreign policies.

In spite of these many peaceful initiatives, there was nonetheless a short war in the early phase of the Short Peace: the First Taiwan Strait Crisis, which began in April 1953. Both its onset and its termination, in September 1955, are of interest when discussing the failure of the Short Peace. When the Korean War broke out, President Truman sought to avoid its expansion into a Third World War. In 1950, he thus deployed the US 7th fleet to the Taiwan Strait in order to prevent Mao Zedong and Chiang Kai-shek from resuming their civil war, which had ended with Mao in control of the mainland, while Chiang held onto Taiwan and some small islands near the mainland coast. Chiang's hopes for invading the mainland were dashed by the US deployment. In February 1953, at a time when the Korean War had long been at a standstill, Truman lifted the naval blockade of the Taiwan Strait. This enabled Chiang to deploy more troops to the Taiwan-held islands on the Chinese coast and fortify them. Beijing responded with bombardments, and by taking over the least de-fended ones. Shelling with artillery went on for several months; the USA threatened China with a nuclear attack if it did not stop. By April 1955, China was willing to talk, and, on 1 May, the shelling of the Mazu and Jinmen islands ceased – although just temporarily. It resumed in 1958.

This is interesting for our discussion because it created a short-lived 'crisis stability' in the Taiwan Strait. Both sides temporarily put aside their aim of national unification and, after 1958, this state of affairs would become permanent. However, each side demonstrated from time to time that the stalemate was unacceptable. Just as in Korea, there would thus be cycles of incidents and crises, interspersed with periods of rapprochement. Both Beijing and Taipei resented the nature of US involvement. As Mao considered his options, he had to guess whether or not the USA would make good on threats of a full-scale response in the event of an attempt to retake the island by force. Across the Strait, Chiang Kai-shek needed US support to realize his dream of a Nationalist return to the mainland, but he could not understand why this support was not forthcoming. He watched in wonderment as Presidents John F. Kennedy and Lyndon B. Johnson chose to immerse themselves in a hopeless counterinsurgency war in Vietnam, rather than taking the war to what he viewed as the source of communism in Asia: China.

The outcome of the Short Peace was a continuing stalemate in Northeast Asia and an increasing volatility in Southeast Asia, where new independent political initiatives went hand in hand with new armed conflicts.

This returns us to the question of when the East Asian Peace began. In Northeast Asia, a peace of sorts began already in 1953, with the Korean armistice agreement. That peace has lasted until now. It allowed for normal diplomatic relations to be established between Japan and South Korea in 1965, between Japan and China in 1972 and between South Korea and China in 1992. Sino–Japanese relations remain difficult today, however, with China preventing Japan from gaining permanent membership in the UN Security Council. And the absence of armed conflict on the Korean peninsula is a frosty, militarized stalemate 'peace'. Northeast Asia has avoided war since 1953 without any political integration.

Developments in Southeast Asia have been different. During the Short Peace, Southeast Asia and indeed much of the developing world was awash in new political initiatives. In April 1955, an Afro-Asian conference was held in the Indonesian city of Bandung to reject the East-West divide, confirm the Five Principles of Peaceful Coexistence and develop a 'third force' composed of developing countries. Burma's neutralist president U Nu was among the conveners. Chinese Prime Minister Zhou Enlai was there, as was his North Vietnamese counterpart, Pham Van Dong. The Bandung Conference, which marked the height of Indonesian president Sukarno's international influence, is seen as the origin of the non-aligned movement, in which even North Korea – although it was not present in Bandung – became an eager participant. Ten years later, when Kim Il Sung and his son Kim Jong Il visited Indonesia to celebrate the anniversary of Bandung in the company of President Sukarno, the spirit of the Short Peace was long gone. In 1958, there was heavy fighting in the Taiwan Strait when China again laid siege to and shelled Taiwanese-held islands close to the mainland coast. In 1959, China brutally repressed an uprising in Tibet, and in the same year, the Vietnamese communists reopened their armed struggle for national unification. By 1965, the Vietnam War was entering its most intense phase, with the US bombing North Vietnam and dispatching combat troops to South Vietnam.

The Short Peace resulted from a bargain made in a situation of military stalemate and fatigue, both in Korea and Indochina, and also from a strategic realignment within the socialist camp. The armistice that ended the war in Korea was signed by a US general on behalf of the UN Command, a representative of the Korean People's Army and a representative of the Chinese People's Volunteer Army – but not by South Korea. The main reason why the armistice has remained in force till this day is most likely that the USA, USSR and China have always considered a resumption of the war as too risky: Korea is close to the Chinese heartland. Since 1991, when China and South Korea established diplomatic relations and both Koreas became members of the UN, it has been evident that all external powers are opposed to the use of force in Korea.

In the 1960s–70s, however, this was far from evident. The United States remained convinced that communism would continue to expand and had to be contained militarily. This seemed to have been confirmed when the Vietnamese communists reopened their armed struggle in 1957–59. Under inspiration from its apparent success, the North Korean leader Kim Il Sung also wanted to resume his armed struggle for national unification, but was unable to get a green light in Beijing or Moscow and could not do it alone. The communist movement in South Korea had been crushed, and it was impossible for North Korea to dispatch any substantial number of troops to the south clandestinely. Hence the long stalemate, interrupted by unsuccessful attempts at national reconciliation during 1972 and 2000–08, has led to the situation we have today: a prosperous South Korea that is allied with the USA, and an impoverished and lonely North Korea, economically dependent on China but enjoying only the kind of security that military deterrence can provide. Kim Il Sung, his son and grandson were losers standing in contrast to Ho Chi Minh who got the Chinese and Soviet aid he needed to defeat the US-supported South Vietnamese regime and achieve national unification on communist terms, although this victory only came six years after his death in 1969.

Why was the Short Peace not viable? Why did it endure as 'crisis stability' in Korea but not in Indochina? I identify three components of an explanation, the third of which crucially distinguishes the Short Peace from the Long Peace.

The Short Peace could not last in Indochina because, first, the USA never committed itself to the 1954 Geneva agreement, which stipulated that national elections be held in both parts of Vietnam by July 1956. By that time, South Vietnam's new leader, Ngo Dinh Diem, now opting for US support, had thrown out France – which was bound by the agreement. This led to the Vietnamese communists' decision to resume the armed struggle. At first they were not allowed to do so by China, the Soviet Union or even by Ho Chi Minh's government in Hanoi. But in 1959, the Vietnamese Workers Party made a formal decision to fight an all-out armed struggle in South Vietnam in order to undermine Diem's regime. This provoked the US intervention, thus spelling the end of the Short Peace.

Second, Mao's personal convictions had a deleterious impact on the Short Peace. He was sure there would be a Third World War. After the bloodletting in Korea, he sought a respite, but not more than a respite, before he would launch his next assault on the Western imperialist forces, revolutionize the Chinese society and engage in a cataclysmic global war. In 1958, shortly after the People's Republic had consolidated itself under the pragmatic daily leadership of Zhou Enlai and Deng Xiaoping, Mao launched his Great Leap Forward, an attempt at hyper-rapid industrialisation that neglected the needs of agriculture and thus caused a famine that took the lives of 30–50 million people. In the same year, he ordered his army to make a new attempt to conquer a Taiwan-held island. It failed. In 1959, Mao sent his army to quell unrest in Tibet, with the death toll certainly in the tens of thousands. Meanwhile, China launched support programmes for communist parties abroad, not just in Indochina and Burma but also in other parts of Southeast Asia and the world. China entered into a special relationship with the big but unarmed Indonesian Communist Party, which was tolerated and to some extent relied upon by the charismatic president Sukarno. Mao's attempts to export the Chinese revolution led the USA to engage with non-communist governments in the region and enhance their capability to counter communist insurgents. The new US strategy was one of 'flexible response' to communist expansion, the main results of which were Sukarno's fall from power, an orchestrated massacre conducted against Indonesian communists, thirty-three years of General Suharto's authoritarian New Order – and the Vietnam War.

There is one more reason why the Short Peace failed: it was not underpinned by a shared quest for economic development. Japan was already developing, but other countries in the region remained preoccupied with their struggle for independent statehood and control of their home territories. Economic growth was not yet an overriding regional priority. As soon as economic development becomes the primary goal of a government, it sees a pressing need for external and internal stability.

Intrastate and Interstate War

Diplomatic developments during the Short Peace had a strong impact on the formation of the East Asian state system, which today consists of 16 independent states with UN membership and one de facto state (ROC Taiwan), which is diplomatically recognized by just a small and dwindling number of mainly Latin American states. Like elsewhere in the world, the international state system forms the basis for deciding if an armed conflict is intrastate (civil) or interstate (international). When Timo Kivimäki, Isak Svensson and I designed the East Asian Peace programme, we all felt that we would have to study both interstate and intrastate peace, and not distinguish too strictly between them. It is now time to expand on our reasons for that choice. The most important one is that most of the armed conflicts of the past were linked to the formation of the states whose borders are used as basis for deciding if an armed conflict is intra- or interstate. It is therefore difficult to decide if these conflicts were one or the other.

Until the middle of the Short Peace, conflicts in Indochina were neither, or rather both, intra- and interstate. The Geneva conference resolved the international status of French Indochina. Until then it remained possible to imagine that the whole of Indochina, which France had formed as a 'Union' in 1897, would become a federal state. The Geneva conference resolved, however, that Indochina would give way to three independent nation states: Cambodia, Laos and Vietnam. Vietnam would be one nation, although two rival Vietnamese states were present in Geneva: general elections (which never happened) would be held in the whole country before July 1956.

When the Short Peace began (1953), only five East Asian states were fully recognized members of the international system: Japan, the Philippines, Thailand, Myanmar (the Union of Burma), and Indonesia. Japan had just been readmitted as an independent member of the US-dominated international system via the 1952 San Francisco Peace Treaty, which formally ended the US occupation. Thailand had been a member all along; until the Second World War it had been the only independent state in Southeast Asia. The Philippines had gained independence in 1946 but continued to depend on the USA, its former colonial overlord. Myanmar had gained independence from the UK in 1948, and Indonesia from the Netherlands in 1949, but Indonesia did not include West Papua until 1962. Timor-Leste remained a Portuguese colony until 1975, when it was invaded and annexed by Indonesia, and gained independence only in 2002. Until 1957 and 1984 respectively, Malaya and Brunei remained under British rule. Malaya gained its independence during the Short Peace and, in 1963, joined up with Singapore and two of Britain's colonies in Borneo (Sabah and Sarawak) to form the Federation of Malaysia. Singapore was forced to leave the Federation two years later, and became an independent state. The Sultan of Brunei declined membership in Malaysia, and formed the independent state Brunei Darussalam in 1984.

The picture is further complicated by the existence of rival regimes in Korea, China and Indochina. Their rivalries were strongly affected by the diplomacy of the Short Peace. The Korean armistice of July 1953, and the failure of the great powers to follow up with a peace agreement, cemented the division of the Korean nation, and it was not until 1991 that the two Koreas became UN members. Until 1971, China was represented in the UN by the ROC although it only controlled Taiwan, but the Short Peace provided the PRC with other chances to develop a high-level diplomatic standing, first by negotiating the Korean armistice, then by taking part in the Geneva Conference on Indochina alongside the USSR, the UK and France, next by establishing a working relationship with India, and finally by taking part in the Bandung conference. So, to sum up, the Short Peace provided the PRC with an international profile, confirmed the division of Korea, declared Laos and Cambodia as independent, held out the unification of Vietnam as a goal, and saw Malaya gain independence, but the process of decolonisation had not been completed. West Papua remained Dutch until 1962, Timor-Leste Portuguese until 1975 and Brunei British until 1984.

For the period of decolonization and state formation just described, it is not easy to distinguish civil from international wars. They overlapped with and fed on each other. Civil wars were internationalized by spilling over borders, as when Chinese Kuomintang troops took refuge in Myanmar from 1950 onward, or by drawing external support for one or the other side, as when North Vietnam's decision to sustain an insurgency in South Vietnam triggered US intervention. The opposite could also happen: a war that was international at the outset could provoke civil war between resisters and collaborators in occupied territories. During 1942–45, the Burma National Army led by Aung San (Aung San Suu Kyi's father) fought alongside Japan against pro-British ethnic Kayin, Chin and Kachin fighters. This forms a background for the failure of the independent Union of Burma (Myanmar) to make peace internally after its establishment in 1948.[5]

Indeed, most East Asian wars defy the intra/interstate divide. The Chinese Civil War was civil until 1949, but the clashes in the Taiwan Strait in 1953–55 and 1958 are perhaps best seen as interstate, although the same old parties did the fighting. Was the Korean War a civil or international war? At that time, no one recognized two Korean states and both claimed sovereignty over the nation as a whole; until 1972, Seoul was North Korea's formal capital – although it was in South Korea. What we call *the* Vietnam War or *the* Second Indochina War included many wars, some intra- and some interstate: civil war in Laos, civil war

---

5. This book uses Myanmar as the name for the country throughout, although it became the official name only in 1987. The earlier name, Burma, is used only when referring to proper names, such as the Burmese National Army or the Union of Burma.

in South Vietnam, civil war in Cambodia, war between Laos and North Vietnam, war between North and South Vietnam, US counter-insurgency in South Vietnam, US bombing of North Vietnam as well as Laos and Cambodia. The picture is further complicated by China's and the Soviet Union's massive support to North Vietnam, including Chinese troops. Today, it is similarly difficult to categorize the war(s) in Syria/Iraq.

The many armed conflicts in Myanmar are clearly intrastate. Yet for many decades, the Chinese Civil War continued on Myanmar's territory, where substantial Kuomintang forces had found a sanctuary, and Chinese communist voluntary fighters played an active part in the communist insurgency in Myanmar during the 1960s. Myanmar's government has never controlled the Wa territory at the border between Shan State and China, and, if Kachin or Rakhine State should gain independence from Myanmar in the future, we will consider the wars we now call 'civil' as national liberation struggles against Myanmar's occupation. The war in Timor-Leste presents a similar problem. Was it an interstate war during the twenty-two years of Indonesian occupation? During the 1975–99 period, it was common to interpret it as an internal armed conflict in Indonesia, even though the UN never recognized Indonesia's annexation of the former Portuguese colony.

On the background of all these overlaps and linkages between international and domestic warfare, we decided to analyse both types of war in one go. The distinction between intrastate and interstate war often does not make sense when we deal with periods of colonisation, de-colonisation and nation building. For the contemporary period, however, after the current East Asian state system had been established, including sixteen internationally recognized sovereign states (and one de facto state in Taiwan, considered diplomatically as a part of China), the distinction makes better sense. A key factor in developing the state system has been the drawing of international, mapped borders in the fashion introduced to the region by the European colonial powers.

Border Agreements

Border treaties are not normally seen as peace agreements, but they are conducive to long term peace. Disputes leading to international war are often about territory. For peace to be established on a durable basis it is therefore vital to agree upon clearly demarcated borders. While fully agreed borders are mostly open to passage, disputed borders are often closed. Paradoxically, a 'borderless world' may be defined as a world with fully agreed borders. A recent book by the three American scholars Gary Goertz, Paul F. Diehl and Alexandru Balas (2016), building on the work of Douglas M. Gibler (2012), shows how strongly the resolution of border disputes has contributed to making the world more peaceful. This has happened through normative change. Three norms are particularly important: the norm against conquest (as embodied in the 1945 UN Charter), the norm against secession (except for overseas colonies), and the norm of *uti possidetis*, meaning that when land borders are delineated, one should use pre-existing borders instead of drawing new ones. The resolution of border disputes has also been enhanced by an expanding practice of third-party arbitration, undertaken by international courts. And, say the three authors, the signing of the United Nations Convention on the Law of the Sea (UNCLOS) in 1982, and its entry into force in 1996, created a basis for peaceful resolution of maritime boundary disputes as well.[6] I could not agree more. Among the quiet heroes of world peace are the patient diplomats and surveyors who spend weeks, months and years of their precious lives on settling and demarcating disputed borders.

Although much remains on the agendas of East Asian diplomats and surveyors, many disputes have been resolved. This has been achieved by the East Asian states themselves, with just a little help from their friends. China has signed border agreements with all of its neighbours on land, except India and Bhutan. Mao must take much of the responsibility for the fact that India has been unwilling to enter into a border agreement with China. He dealt such a humiliating blow to India in the 1962 Sino–Indian war that it has been impossible for any Indian leader since to compromise. The 1999 land border agreement between China and Vietnam, and its full demarcation over the following decade, are landmarks in the history of regional peace. In 2000, China also signed its first ever maritime boundary agreement: a bilateral treaty delimiting the Gulf of Tonkin into Chinese and Vietnamese maritime zones. Maritime boundaries between Indonesia and Vietnam, Indonesia and Malaysia, Thailand and Malaysia, and Malaysia and Vietnam have also

---

6. These ideas were further developed by the Chair of our Advisory Board, Peter Wallensteen (2015).

been defined. Yet no bilateral or multilateral negotiations have yet been conducted over maritime boundaries in the contested central part of the South China Sea, where the disputed and widely dispersed Spratly Islands are located, and Cambodia has not agreed on its maritime boundaries with Thailand and Vietnam.

In some cases, East Asian governments have invited the International Court of Justice (ICJ) to settle their territorial disputes. It has decided twice (1962 and 2013) on the question of sovereignty to the area around the temple Preah Vihear on the Thai–Cambodian border. In 2002, the ICJ settled a dispute between Malaysia and Indonesia over two small islands east of Borneo/Kalimantan, and it did the same in 2008, with a dispute between Singapore and Malaysia over the little island of Pedra Branca. In each case, the losing side has accepted the verdict. Former Malaysian Prime Minister Mahathir Mohamad, whose government won Malaysia's case against Indonesia but lost against Singapore, has boasted about how Asians resolve their disputes peacefully. He spreads the word that war is an 'uncivilized' and mainly Western practice, and claims that the more civilized Asian nations use negotiations and international arbitration to resolve their disputes.[7]

China, however, has insisted that it will not accept any third party arbitration (except in trade disputes under the WTO) and will only negotiate bilaterally about its maritime boundaries, not multilaterally. In 2013, after failing to engage China in negotiations, the Philippines requested that an arbitral tribunal be established under UNCLOS to resolve certain issues of interpretation that are important for its disputes with China in the South China Sea. China refused to take part in the arbitration, which went ahead all the same and issued rulings in October 2015 (accepting jurisdiction) and on 12 June 2016 (settling most of the issues raised by the Philippines). Since China had boycotted the tribunal and refused to nominate any judge, the ruling became unanimous and crystal clear, going against China (as well as Taiwan) on every account. It affirmed that China has no specific historic rights within its so-called U-shaped (or nine-dashed) line, which dates from

---

7. I heard Mahathir speak to this subject at an international conference on political science, public administration and peace studies in ASEAN countries held at the Prince of Songkla University in Hat Yai, south Thailand, on 6 September 2012, and at the Jeju Forum for Peace and Prosperity in Korea on 29 May 2013: https://www.youtube.com/watch?v=MBclmDtqKDw.

1947, and encompasses most of the South China Sea. The Tribunal decided that the tiny Spratly islands do not qualify legally as 'islands' but are just 'rocks' or 'reefs'. They cannot therefore have any Exclusive Economic Zone (EEZ) or continental shelf but only a 12-nautical-mile territorial sea. This means that China can claim an EEZ only out to a distance of 200 nautical miles from its main coasts. The court also stated that China's dredging, and construction of seven artificial islands on submerged reefs in the Spratly area has aggravated and extended the dispute between the parties, notably concerning the protection and preservation of the natural environment. The ruling makes sense from a legal perspective, and also from a perspective of peace, since it drastically reduces the areas under possible dispute and thus should make conflict resolution easier. What is so marvellous with the law of the sea is that boundaries are calculated on the basis of geography, not on any history of military or administrative control. In international law, land dominates the sea. A state has sovereign rights only within zones that are measured by distance from its coasts. As long as this principle is accepted, there is not so much to quarrel about. This precludes warfare. A problem arises, however, when tiny islands are disputed and claimants to those islands also claim a 200 nautical mile EEZ and continental shelf around them. This is what could have been the case in the Spratlys if the Arbitral Tribunal had not determined that none of the Spratlys satisfy the conditions for generating an EEZ or continental shelf. This is the part of the ruling that is toughest for China and Taiwan to swallow.

The problem now is that China and Taiwan do not recognize the jurisdiction of the arbitral tribunal and consider its ruling null and void. China upholds its claim to sovereign rights within its U-shaped line, and Taiwan sticks to its opinion that Itu Aba (Taiping Island), the largest of the Spratly Islands, which is occupied by Taiwan (on behalf, one might say, of the One China), does fulfil the criteria defined in UNCLOS for having an EEZ of its own. By refusing to take part in the arbitration, China painted itself into a corner. That is a dangerous place for a great power to be. A key challenge for China in the period ahead is to dissociate its boundary disputes with its neighbours from its contest with the United States for naval supremacy in the seas along its coast, which include some of the world's busiest shipping lanes. China's neighbours have been looking to the USA for protection of their sovereign rights at sea and under the seabed. If China could reassure them by entering into boundary agreements on the basis of the law of the sea, it would drastically reduce their need for US protection.

Psychologically, however, this is extremely difficult for China since it will end up with a much smaller Exclusive Economic Zone (EEZ) and continental shelf than it has been claiming as its inalienable right. All Chinese – and Taiwanese – are used to seeing the map with the U-shaped line. As the arbitral tribunal made clear, this line has no legal status in international law as a claim to any 'maritime territory', and can only be understood in the eyes of the law as a notice that China claims all of the islands inside it and their 12 nautical mile territorial seas. Beijing will find it difficult to accept such a narrow interpretation of the U-shaped line and retreat from its excessive historical rights claim since it has become a focus point for Chinese nationalism that is portrayed as self-evident and undisputable in the Chinese media, school curriculums and public statements. There is also some competition between mainland China and Taiwan in promoting China's claims, which have their historical origin in the actions and official statements of the Republic of China before it retreated to Taiwan, and basepoints on the Taiwanese coast must be used to measure the extension of the Chinese – or separate Taiwanese – maritime zone claims. A modification of China's stance would therefore need to include cooperation and mutual understanding between the PRC and the ROC (Taiwan), which will be hard to realize as long as there is no agreement on Taiwan's own legal status.

However difficult it is emotionally and politically, from a strategic perspective the only sensible thing for China to do is to withdraw from its maximalist position, which others see as threatening, and ground its claims in a justifiable reading of the law of the sea. This would reassure its neighbourhood, reduce the risk of US interference, allow China room to continue its naval expansion, and facilitate agreement with the countries around the South China Sea on how to protect the marine environment, manage fish stocks, and set up joint ventures to explore for oil and gas under the various countries' continental shelf. It is essential both for the Chinese and international media to understand that a state does not 'control' its continental shelf or EEZ. It has a sovereign right to all resources in the sea and under the seabed, but is obliged to respect the freedom of navigation, and also of laying cables on the seabed. For navigation purposes, the EEZ is considered international waters in just the same way as the High Seas (waters more than 200 nautical miles from all coasts).

The disputes in the East China Sea are quite different. China, Taiwan, South Korea and Japan have not resolved their boundary disputes but they have reached fishery agreements. And in a short period during the mid-2000s there was a deal in place between China and Japan jointly to explore for oil on a part of the continental shelf straddling the median line between the Chinese and Japanese coastlines. The agreement fell apart, however, and in 2009, both South Korea and China submitted data to the UN meant to demonstrate that their continental shelf (and therefore their sovereign rights to all resources underneath), continues beyond the median line and all the way to the Okinawa Trough, just outside the Japanese Ryukuyu island chain. This claim is unacceptable for Japan, which insists on using the median line both for the EEZ and the continental shelf. In the East China Sea, there is also a contentious high-profile dispute between China, Taiwan and Japan over sovereignty to five rocks that Japan calls the Senkakus, and the Chinese Diaoyu, and which may or may not have a right to an EEZ and continental shelf of their own.

The division of Korea and the question of Taiwan's status are also territorial issues that need to be resolved in order to perpetuate the East Asian Peace. Between North Korea and South Korea there is moreover a highly contested maritime boundary, the so-called Northern Limit Line, which was drawn by the US military right after the Korean War. If North and South Korea were to recognize each other as independent states or as members of a Confederation, their sea boundary would have to be redrawn, yielding more maritime space to North Korea. North Korea does not recognize or respect the Northern Limit Line, and many dangerous incidents have occurred in the disputed zone, including the sinking of the South Korean corvette *Cheonan* in March 2010.

If this is not enough, I must also mention the long-standing dispute between Japan and Russia over sovereignty to Japan's Northern Territories, which the Russians call the Kuril Islands. They were occupied by the Soviet Union in the aftermath of the Second World War, and populated with Russians. Japan demands them back. The dispute hinders a closer relationship between Japan and Russia, and thus strengthens Russia's dependence on its strategic partnership with China.

Much remains to be done before we can say that the East Asian state system has been fully developed with clear and internationally recognized borders. Border agreements are 'proactive peace agreements'. They are results of preventive diplomacy and remove possible causes of war. Another kind of peace agreements are those that end wars, and which normally include a ceasefire or armistice. Such peace agreements have also played a role in the East Asian Peace.

Peace Agreements

Peace is sometimes established through victory for one side and defeat for the other, as in the Second World War and the Vietnam War, and sometimes because one side gradually loses the capacity to fight, as in the communist insurgencies in Malaya 1948–89 and Myanmar 1946–89. Peace is also sometimes established through a peace agreement, as in Cambodia 1991. The jury is out as to whether victories or peace agreements lead to the most viable peace. The problem with victories is not only their cost in human lives but also that they tend to humiliate the defeated party in ways that motivate new generations to resume the struggle. The problem with ceasefire and peace agreements is that they often do not satisfy any of the parties, and leave the key disputes unresolved, with the effect that war breaks out anew.

When examining the history of the East Asian Peace I realized how important ceasefire and peace agreements have been for ending armed fighting temporarily, and sometimes for years or decades. Ceasefire agreements have saved many lives and occasionally laid the foundation for a viable peace agreement. Ceasefire and peace agreements are sometimes signed between states, sometimes between a state and a rebel group. The latter kind is most common since there are many more civil wars than international wars. What roles have ceasefires and peace agreements played in East Asia's transition to peace? When answering that question, I part ways with some of my colleagues in Uppsala. Svensson (2011) and Kivimäki (2014) count peace agreements around the world and find that East Asia has had fewer than other world regions, and that the number has gone *down* since 1979. This leads them to posit that peace agreements have played a modest role in East Asia's transition to peace. I argue, however, that the impact of peace agreements is more telling than the number. Also, their relevance cannot be understood by just looking at whether or not they ended all armed fighting immediately. We must look, case by case, at their impact on the conflicts they were meant to resolve.

The agreements to end the conflicts in Korea 1953, in Indochina (primarily Cambodia) 1991, and in the Indonesian province Aceh 2005 were essential steps to regional peace. Standing head and shoulders above these, however, is the umbrella of institutions and ideas that shaped Japan's pioneering status as a US-protected 'peace nation', starting with its adoption of a 'peace constitution' in 1946, and being consecrated with the San Francisco Peace Treaty of 1952. All of these have had an impact on regional peace. If Myanmar's ongoing national political dialogue should arrive at a workable federal compromise, and if the current negotiations between the Philippines government and the Communist Party of the Philippines, as well as with the Moro Islamic Liberation Front (MILF), the Moro National Liberation Front (MNLF) and other groups, can lead to social and economic reforms and the establishment of a social and federal compromise in the Philippines, then we would have further evidence of how negotiated agreements contribute to peace in East Asia.

After World War II, the first comprehensive peace agreement in the region was the San Francisco Peace Treaty, which was signed on 8 September 1951 and entered into force on 28 April 1952, one year before the Korean armistice. Japan had surrendered unconditionally and signed its instruments of surrender to the Allies on 2 September 1945, so the San Francisco agreement was not a negotiated treaty to end an ongoing war but one imposed on the vanquished by the victors, allowing it to re-enter international society as a 'peace nation'. Japan signed the agreement with forty-eight of its former adversaries, including the Asian states of Indonesia, Pakistan, the Philippines, Ceylon, Cambodia, Laos and South Vietnam (most of the rest were in Europe or the Americas). The treaty restored sovereignty to Japan after seven years of US occupation, and integrated it in the non-communist part of the international system. The treaty did not, however, include either of the two Koreas, which were at war with each other at that time. As mentioned above, South Korea established diplomatic relations with Japan as late as 1965, while North Korea has yet to do so. Nor did the San Francisco treaty include the People's Republic of China (PRC). The Japanese government wanted to re-establish commercial and political relations with Mainland China, but was told by the USA to instead sign a separate peace agreement with the Republic of China (ROC) in Taiwan, which it did in 1952, at the same time as the San Francisco Treaty entered into force. Although the Soviet Union was present in San Francisco, it did not sign the treaty.

Due to the Cold War, the San Francisco system was full of deficiencies. Okinawa did not come under Japanese sovereignty until 1972 and remains a US base area today. The United States also keeps bases in other Japanese islands. A number of Japan's territorial issues were left unresolved, with Russia in the Northern Territories/Kurils, with North and South Korea over the Takeshima/Dokdo islet, and with China and Taiwan over the Senkaku/Diaoyu islets, which remained under US administration until 1972 – along with Okinawa. Japan renounced its claim to sovereignty over the Paracel and Spratly Islands in the South China Sea, but did not say to whom. As we have seen above, all of these territorial issues continue to fester today. Japan's separate peace also delayed what might have been a process of justice and reconciliation after the crimes committed during Japan's rule in Korea and its occupation of huge parts of China. The historical wounds could not be healed. Furthermore, Japan's subordination to the USA in an alliance treaty signed in 1951, and renewed in 1960, has created problems for Japan's national identity. Many Japanese, particularly right wing conservatives, feel that Japan is not treated as a 'normal nation'.

In spite of all these deficiencies, the San Francisco system created a partial foundation for regional peace by re-establishing Japan as a sovereign nation with UN membership and a chance to reinsert itself economically in its region and the world. Japan became sufficiently independent to resist US pressure for rearmament and participation in US wars, and established itself as a democratic, peaceful and increasingly prosperous nation. Tokyo shifted its recognition from the Republic of China to the People's Republic of China in 1972 – seven years before the USA. These are all essential premises for the current East Asian Peace. As will be further discussed below, Article 9 of the 1946 constitution, which renounces Japan's right to wage war, and commits it to abstain from having military forces, played a significant role in paving the way for the East Asian Peace. There has been little reason to fear a resurgence of Japanese imperialism in the form it had during 1894–1945. Japan's integration into the US military structure through an alliance treaty has also been important. It means that neither Russia nor China can have a separate conflict with Japan but must expect to confront the US-Japan alliance if they allow a crisis to escalate.

The Korean armistice was signed two years after the San Francisco treaty, in July 1953. The armistice has helped prevent the resumption of active warfare for more than sixty years in the absence of a peace treaty. A peace treaty with the USA is North Korea's top diplomatic goal. The United States, however, dismisses this option because of North Korea's nuclear programme. So the stalemate in Korea persists.

The history of war and peace in Indochina could be told as an epic of four failed agreements (Hanoi/Paris 1946, Geneva 1954, Geneva 1962, Paris 1973), and finally a successful one (Paris 1991). France recognized Vietnam as a 'free state' in March 1946 and in September 1946 signed a 'modus vivendi' with President Ho Chi Minh. The agreements were not respected, and war broke out in November–December. After eight years of war, and the French defeat at Dien Bien Phu in May 1954, the Geneva agreement on Indochina divided Vietnam temporarily at the 17th parallel. The story of how the Geneva agreement failed and the Vietnam War began has already been told. What has not yet been mentioned is the role of Laos in the run-up to that war. In the late 1950s, in order to set up transportation lines to the southern battlefront (the Ho Chi Minh Trail), North Vietnam took control of the eastern parts of Laos and sustained a pro-communist faction in Lao politics. This provoked an international crisis, leading to a separate Geneva agreement on Laos in 1962 that guaranteed its independence and neutrality. Yet this agreement proved a third failure. It broke down quickly, under pressure from the mounting struggle in South Vietnam. Laos and Cambodia were subsequently pulled further into the war through US bombing.

The fourth failure was the Paris peace agreement of 1973 between the USA, North Vietnam, South Vietnam and the Provisional Revolutionary Government of South Vietnam. It broke down as both the South Vietnamese and North-supported rebel forces violated the agreed cease-fire. This does not mean that the agreement had no impact. It allowed the USA to withdraw from Indochina and paved the way for Hanoi to reunify Vietnam on its terms in 1975–76. It made no strategic sense for the United States to pursue a costly war in Indochina after President Nixon had gone to China in 1972. At a time when both China and the USA had come to see the Soviet Union as their main adversary, there was no longer any need to contain China. Instead, the USA and China saw a shared need to contain Vietnam's USSR-supported communist regime.

The establishment of a united Socialist Republic of Vietnam (SRV) did not bring peace to Indochina. A Sino–Vietnamese rivalry developed over the treatment of the ethnic Chinese in Vietnam, and over the nature of the new regime in Cambodia, where Khmer communist leaders had seized the capital Phnom Penh two weeks before their big brother captured Saigon. The new Khmer Rouge leaders allied themselves with China against their Vietnamese mentors and established the most paranoid and brutal of all 20th century regimes, killing anyone suspected of pro-Vietnamese or pro-Western sentiments in what is generally considered a genocide, even though it targeted not only the Viet, Chinese and Cham ethnic minorities, but also the ethnic kin of the new Khmer rulers. Vietnam invaded Cambodia and removed the Khmer Rouge from power in December 1978. This marked the beginning of the Third Indochina War, which again affected all of Indochina, although most of the fighting took place in Cambodia and at the Sino–Vietnamese border. Vietnam maintained troops in Cambodia to sustain the new pro-Vietnamese regime, which came under the leadership of the young communist Hun Sen (who had defected from the Khmer Rouge), while China and the United States supported an insurgent coalition dominated by the Khmer Rouge, with sanctuaries in Thailand.

The Third Indochina War turned Vietnam into a pariah within the regional state system, and made it dependent on Soviet aid. When the Cold War approached its end, Soviet leader Mikhail Gorbachev cancelled aid transfers to Indochina and engineered a rapprochement with China. Hanoi was obliged to withdraw its troops from Cambodia in 1989 and seek a settlement. It took two years, with a combination of Indonesian and French facilitation and intense diplomatic efforts by many governments, before the October 1991 Paris peace agreement on Cambodia could be signed. This was the fifth agreement, and this time it was implemented under the UN Transitional Authority in Cambodia

(UNTAC) 1992–93, with with a Japanese Chief of Mission and a 600-member Japanese engineering contingent. The fact that the Khmer Rouge took up arms again afterwards, were deprived of foreign support and collapsed in 1998 should be seen as fortunate effects of the Paris agreement, not as signs of failure. The political outcome in Cambodia, after factional struggles, questionable elections, assassinations and what might be called a coup, is certainly not ideal. Hun Sen, the strongman who came to power with Vietnamese support, has retained his hold on power to this day by using heavy-handed methods against his op-ponents, engaging in border clashes with Thailand and aligning himself with China internationally. Yet the most significant outcome of the 1991 Paris agreement was to remove several bones of contention from the region. As a result, Vietnam and China could repair their relationship and stable relations could be built among three sovereign Indochinese states, which were all invited into ASEAN.

Next came the UN-sponsored agreement between Indonesia and Portugal (Timor-Leste's former colonial power), which led to a refer-endum on Timor-Leste's independence in 1999. After the referendum resulted in an unequivocal vote for independence, Indonesia was compelled by a concert of great and small powers to withdraw from the country it had occupied and supressed since 1975. Timor-Leste's independence, formally acquired in 2002 thanks to a rapid international reaction to stop a frenzy of violence perpetrated by the losers in the 1999 referendum, contributed to strengthening the global idea of a Responsibility to Protect (R2P). Indonesia's defeat also had a sobering effect on Indonesian politics, which had turned ugly with much com-munal strife after the downfall of General Suharto's dictatorship in 1998. Three years after Timor-Leste gained independence, a new Indonesian government was ready to sign an agreement with the Free Aceh move-ment, ending a long insurgency and granting large-scale autonomy to this province at the northern tip of Sumatra. By that time, a mutually reinforcing spiral was already at work in other parts of Indonesia with political violence dying down and government-supported militias being dissolved or deactivated. For more than ten years now, the world's larg-est Muslim country has been a stable, decentralised democracy without much military involvement in politics. Yet the little-known conflict in West Papua should not escape our attention, although information as to exactly which parties are fighting, and the exact number of casualties, is hard to come by.

Many studies have been written about the upsurge of violence in Indonesia during 1998-2003, but I am only aware of one study of how the violence subsided in the following period: Barron, Jaffrey and Varshney (2016). It is based on a comprehensive dataset covering all the main conflict areas in Indonesia, and finds that only the large-scale deadly violence has subsided. Less serious forms of violence have continued, and there has been an increase in violent incidents in relation to land disputes and elections. The authors conclude that the local drivers of conflict have not disappeared, and that the main reason why deadly violence has subsided is a change in the attitude of the political elite, who no longer see any advantage in stimulating or condoning the use of violence. The security forces therefore often intervene in a timely fashion to stop local violence from escalating, while in the past they either stood aside or quietly supported militia groups. There may be lessons to learn from the Indonesian experience for the three regional countries that still have large-scale deadly violence: the Philippines, Myanmar and Thailand.

Many dangerous territorial disputes also remain in the region but others have been settled, with each settlement establishing a precedent for how border agreements can be reached. What is most striking, from a historical point of view, is that none of the region's most serious territorial interstate disputes has led to open warfare since the 1980s. This may be related to the fact that governments in the region have put so much emphasis on ensuring the stability needed for achieving economic growth.

Developmental Peace

Here comes my own theory, which is inspired by the work of Jeffrey Legro (2000; 2008) and William Overholt (2008), and partially developed in my own work (2015c and 2017). I see the East Asian Peace as the cumulative effect of a number of national priority shifts and changing risk perceptions among national decision makers in the region, and also to some extent among rebel leaders fighting against governments. The former have sought to overcome or avoid armed conflict both externally and internally, while the latter have shifted from

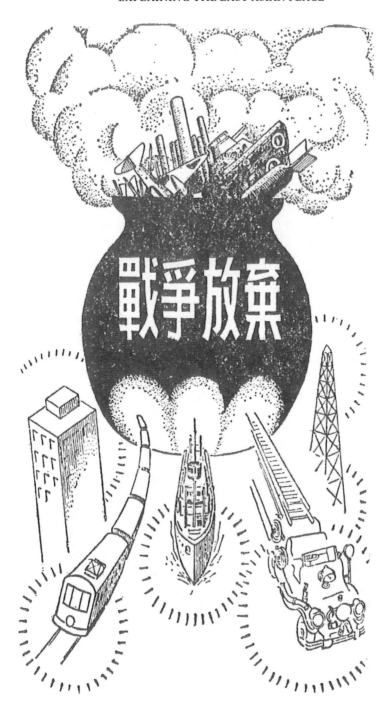

Figure 4: Renunciation of war – a Japanese drawing from 1947

armed to unarmed tactics. My theory includes an element of learning: politicians have learned from each other. In situations of perceived national crisis, new government leaders have made economic development their main priority and seen external and internal stability as a prerequisite. The East Asian Peace is linked to the emergence of the 'developmental state', which may be defined as a state governed by a determined developmental elite with a powerful economic bureaucracy, a weak civil society, and effective management of public as well as private companies. This is not a socialist state. Its aim is to prosper by competing on the global capitalist market. Yet it is also not a liberal state since it actively promotes its business interests abroad, and also intervenes in and 'governs' the national market instead of just providing macroeconomic management.

The history of national priority shifts in East Asia, leading to the creation of highly organized developmental states, began in 1945–46, in the wake of Japan's defeat in the Second World War. A pro-Western diplomat, Yoshida Shigeru, took over as prime minister under US tutelage and remained in power for most of the time until 1954. At the beginning of his tenure, Japan was in a deep national crisis with its cities in ruins and its honour destroyed. Yet its leaders decided, as John Dower (1999) so eloquently put it, to 'embrace defeat'. Not a single US soldier was killed in anger after the war, and Japan adopted a constitution that forbade it from ever again waging war or having an army. Radical reforms were carried out, including redistribution of land and the creation of a Ministry of International Trade and Industry (MITI) to coordinate economic reconstruction. Figure 4, a redrawn version of which is on the cover of this book, is a Japanese drawing from a 1947 school textbook that shows arms factories and weapons being dropped into a huge melting pot, where they are beaten not into ploughshares but into office buildings, trains, ships, fire engines and electricity masts.

This is the Japanese model in a nutshell, the basic elements of which would later be reproduced again and again by other East Asian nations. At the cost of allowing the USA to keep bases on its territory, Japan regained its sovereignty in 1952. It resisted US pressure to rearm rapidly and take part in the Korean War, and instead made money from it. Internally, Yoshida maintained a system of close surveillance and police control to prevent leftist rebellion. His economically oriented foreign policy and his emphasis on economic growth would later become known as 'the Yoshida doctrine'. It was opposed both from right and left, but nonetheless led Japan to prosper. Only after the country had reached first world status in the 1980s, and was viewed by some commentators as a threat to US global hegemony, did its economy begin to stagnate. And despite being a staunch US ally, at least until 2016 Japan was constitutionally prohibited from fighting in the many US wars.

Japan went through a national purpose transition and created a model that would later be used by other East Asian countries. In each country, the political process included the following sequence of choices. A deeply felt national crisis brought to power new leaders:

- who decided to prioritize state-driven economic growth,
- learned from other nations that had done this before,
- undertook policies to achieve external and internal stability,
- accommodated the USA in order to avoid becoming targets of US hostility and to benefit from US aid, investment and market access,
- adopted pragmatic and reassuring policies towards their neighbours,
- effectively repressed or accommodated internal opposition movments, and finally
- achieved rapid economic growth. (Tønnesson, 2015c)

All the choices are logically connected, stemming from the same quest for national development, but the logic is not deterministic. Leaders could take other choices if they had competing priorities, and some East Asian leaders did. Some who really tried anyhow failed. In order to succeed, they depended on the capacity of institutions to implement their policies. What distinguishes East Asia from other world regions is that so many nations shifted at some stage to an economy-first policy, and had sufficient institutional capacity to implement reforms and keep their population under control. This allowed the region to enter its era of peace.

I see the package of choices above as constituting a 'Japanese model'. This does not mean that all countries following that model would apply the same kind of economic policies or the same level of domestic repression. The various developmental states differed in the degree to which they controlled their big companies, in their level of openness to external trade and investment, in their mix of export-oriented and import substitution strategies, in how radical their land reforms were, and in the relative weight of repression, co-optation and legitimation in achieving domestic stability. The key elements in what I call the Japanese model was the pursuit of external and internal peace in order to generate economic growth, and accommodation of the United States as the world's most powerful nation with the largest market and the most advanced productive technologies.

Learning was key. South Korea's dictator Park Chung-hee (1961–79) was deeply inspired by Japan. He normalized relations with Tokyo in 1965 so he could get aid and investment. He avoided war with North Korea, but sent troops to Vietnam in exchange for massive US aid, and set South Korea on a course to prosperity by promoting massive industrialization within a well-governed market. To govern the market means not just to rely on free markets but to allocate resources through a synergetic mix of administrative decisions and utilization of the market mechanism (Wade 1990). When possible, developmental states combined elements of import substitution with efforts to target export markets, thereby generating huge surpluses in their balance of trade.

When Lee Kuan Yew's Singapore was thrown out of the Malaysian Federation in 1965, it applied, with astounding success, a developmental policy that emphasized both internal and external political stability. Indonesia made a similar change under General Suharto after 1965. It abandoned president Sukarno's confrontational policy towards Malaysia, sought rapprochement with Japan and the USA, formed ASEAN in 1967 (with Malaysia, the Philippines, Thailand and Singapore), and applied a successful economy-first policy combined with extremely harsh internal repression. After a national crisis caused by ethnic riots in 1969, Malaysia adopted a New Economic Policy (NEP) in 1971, giving ethnic Malays a preferential stake in commerce and industry in order to enhance ethno-political stability. In 1981, when Mahathir Mohamad took charge as prime minister, he modified the NEP by adopting a growth-promoting 'Look East' policy. Chiang Ching-kuo, Taiwan's prime minister from 1972–78 and president from 1978–88, abandoned any remaining hope to reconquer mainland China and carried out a thriving developmental policy, boosted Taiwan's trade with Japan and the USA, obtained implicit US protection under the

Taiwan Relations Act of 1979, and began a process of enhancing regime legitimacy through democratic reforms.

Most important of all: when Mao died in 1976, his Cultural Revolution ended and a sense of acute crisis spread among the communist elite. Deng Xiaoping took charge in 1978, not long after the Maoist 'Gang of Four' had been arrested. He gave up Mao's idea that a Third World War was inevitable, undertook study tours to Japan and the USA, and set China on its way to peace and development. Since 1979, China has not engaged in any armed conflict, except for a number of clashes with Vietnam in the 1980s. China's huge internal security forces have long prevented any armed rebellion on its territory. Just as China made its transition, Vietnam was bogged down by its costly counter-insurgency in Cambodia, its border conflict with China and the end of its alliance with the Soviet Union. When Mikhail Gorbachev announced his *perestroika* reforms and made it clear that the aid to Vietnam would end, Vietnam's leaders understood that they had to emulate Japan, South Korea and China. When party chief Le Duan died in 1986, the stage was set for *doi moi*, Vietnam's version of reform, which was adopted, paradoxically, at a time when the veteran doctrinary Marxist Truong Chinh (1906–88) took over as party leader. The country encouraged export-oriented industry and withdrew its troops from Cambodia, allowing Hanoi to normalize relations with Beijing and Washington, join ASEAN in 1995 and initiate rapid economic growth. After the 1991 Paris agreement on Cambodia, the demise of the Khmer Rouge movement in 1998, and Cambodia's membership in ASEAN that same year, the government of Hun Sen also implemented some of the basic tenets of the Japanese model, with a fair degree of success.

Once all these countries had opted to avoid external and internal war in favour of developmental policies, East Asia began its long era of peace. Peace was thus the cumulative effect of a series of national priority shifts. Mine is a historical theory, meant to explain the emergence of the East Asian Peace as such. It does not predict that similar priority changes will happen elsewhere but it could provide inspiration for policymakers in other countries and regions.

The exceptions to the rule may help to refine the theory. Laos and Brunei have implemented parts of the model. Myanmar is only really trying now. Former military dictator Than Shwe began to open up the national economy in the 1990s, but his brutal repression of the democratic opposition led to international sanctions. He retired in 2011 and left his chosen President, Thein Sein, with a mandate to get rid of sanctions and catch up economically. Myanmar has long enjoyed international peace, but has been ravaged by internal warfare. A key condition for peace in Myanmar will be a successful national political dialogue between its new government (from 2016 led de facto by State Councillor Aung San Suu Kyi), the powerful military, the elected national, state and regional assemblies, and its many ethnic parties and armed groups. The big question is whether or not they can reach a federal compromise. We cannot yet say if Myanmar's bid for developmental peace will succeed.

Thailand has had substantial growth, but without a sustained developmental policy. Its long-term monarch Rama IX, who served from 1946 until he died in 2016, hewed to a regressive economic self-subsistence philosophy and the Thai military has always eluded civilian control, seizing power on numerous occasions and withdrawing to the barracks only when its economic failures have been too evident. In the 2000s, Thailand became a regional outlier when its government was unable to prevent a drawn-out insurgency in its Malay-Muslim south, the army engaged in a border conflict with Cambodia, and a polarized power struggle took place in Bangkok between two national factions or 'networks'.

The policy-making elite in the Philippines has never reached consensus on a developmental policy, much less implemented one. Some presidents have tried (Ramon Magsaysay 1953–57; Fidel Ramos 1992–98). Their failures were largely due to weak state capacity; rich landowners were powerful enough to ignore or obstruct government policies. In contrast to the main growth countries, the Philippines has not carried out genuine land reform and never managed to subdue its communist or Muslim separatist rebels. Under the presidency of Benigno Aquino III (2011–16), Manila reached a peace agreement with the Moro Islamic Liberation Front (MILF) about setting up a new autonomous region (Bangsamoro) but the Senate failed to adopt the law that was needed to implement it. The new president, Rodrigo Duterte, who took office in August 2016, made the agreement with the MILF contingent upon the inclusion of the smaller MNLF. He saw the establishment of Bangsamoro as a possible building block for a larger, more comprehensive, and more time consuming federal reform. The result was dissatisfaction among the Moro youth and worries that everything would be left in the air once again (see also p. 172). Meanwhile, Duterte kick-started negotiations with the country's communist rebels, which had been neglected by his predecessor, let the Communist Party of the Philippines nominate several key members of his government, released a number of leading communists from jail, and agreed to an indeterminate ceasefire. Duterte has identified economic development as a key priority, notably for the island of Mindanao, which he hopes can catch up with Luzon.

If Duterte should succeed in his endeavours, persuade the world to tolerate his use of extrajudicial killings against drug dealers, move his own people to accept the rehabilitation of the late Ferdinand Marcos, get women to tolerate his sexism, prevent journalists from criticizing his administration, link up successfully with China, obtain large-scale Chinese investments, co-opt the Communist Party of the Philippines, accommodate the Moro demands for autonomy – and generate rapid economic growth – then he might be seen in the future as one of East Asia's successful, elected dictators. As has been argued above, peace is not always pretty. Yet this chain of events seems unlikely. While some are impressed by Duterte's heavy-handedness, others are abhorred and provoked. He could well be repeating the mistakes made by Thaksin Shinawatra in Thailand, who unleashed a wave of extra-judicial killings in the early 2000s and launched a violent clampdown on the Malay Muslims in Patani, thus greatly stimulating an insurgency that might plausibly have been managed to greater effect through more delicate means. The Philippines is more likely to be heading for new waves of political violence than a successful developmentalist Dutertism.

The greatest aberration remains North Korea. The Kim dynasty has never felt sufficiently secure to demilitarize its system and open up to international trade and investment. Instead, it has sought security through a military-first policy, emphasizing nuclear weapons and thus provoking sanctions and resentment from abroad, and further boosting Pyongyang's sense of insecurity while condemning most of its people to poverty. North Korea's downward spiral since the 1960s is like an inverse mirror of the peaceful growth spiral entered into by other countries in the region.

These exceptions show that a successful developmental peace depends on the priorities of national leaders, but not on that alone. It also depends on state capacity and control of the armed forces. It depends on the ability to overcome internal armed conflict through repression or agreement. And it depends in the first place on a sense within the national leadership that its national security is sufficiently safe for it to bet on export-driven economic growth. This points toward the two key calculations that must be processed in the minds of decision makers before they undertake a shift in national purpose. One is security risk for both nation and regime. The other is economic risk. I shall soon recount the discussions we have had in the Uppsala-based programme on whether or not a combination of nuclear deterrence and economic interdependence is sufficient to guarantee the continuation of regional peace, but first I will delve into the special role played by Japan and its 'peace constitution' in paving the way for the East Asian Peace. This is not sufficiently recognized by its neighbours, who tend to identify Japan instead with its wartime militarism and to focus on demands for an official apology from the Japanese Emperor.

Japan as Pioneer

Article 9 of the Japanese 1946 Constitution says:

> (1) Aspiring sincerely to an international peace based on justice and order, the Japanese people forever renounce war as a sovereign right of the nation and the threat or use of force as means of settling international disputes.

> (2) To accomplish the aim of the preceding paragraph, land, sea, and air forces, as well as other war potential, will never be maintained. The right of belligerency of the state will not be recognized.

The article is 'pacifist' in content, and pacifists have always been in the forefront of defending it. It could not, however, have survived in Japanese politics without support from the left wing as well as from pragmatic conservatives. And it has always been helped by the constitutional provision that amendments require a decision by a two-thirds majority in both houses of the Japanese parliament, followed by a referendum.

The argument I have explored when presenting my historical theory above is that Article 9 was instrumental in allowing Japan, under the Yoshida doctrine, to stay out of the wars in Korea, Vietnam, and other US wars so it could concentrate on its economic reconstruction and growth (Tønnesson, forthcoming). This did not just benefit Japan but all of East Asia, since it reduced fears of a Japanese militarist revival and provided a model for peaceful economic development. One nation after another could shift to a Peaceful Development strategy, inspired by the successful Japanese example, without having to fear that Japanese aid and investment would lead to military aggression. Absent this threat, other governments could also limit their military spending and give priority to developing good relations with not just Japan but the United States as well.

Article 9 has helped Japan stay out of war for almost seventy years. It has consistently aligned its foreign policies with Washington. In return it has reaped benefits from not having to waste resources on maintaining a strong military of its own. The US alliance and the US nuclear umbrella gave room for Japan to concentrate on its economy, and set the region on its road to Peaceful Development.

Article 9 has been controversial in Japan continuously since its inception. Some prominent conservative politicians have seen it as a straitjacket that prevents them from constituting a 'normal nation' and signifies that neither they nor their offspring can be proud of their national history, but instead must submit to American domination and constantly apologize to their neighbours for incidents belonging to a now distant past. Yet Article 9 has stood its test. It has not yet been revised, only reinterpreted. For a long time it was defended by a coalition of convinced pacifists, left wing socialists and conservative pragmatists. The support for and use of Article 9 by conservative politicians, who aim to ensure Japan's re-entry into the world community as a sovereign nation, was the main force that kept Article 9 alive. Yoshida Shigeru and his successors embodied this policy.

At the outset, Article 9 was included in the new Japanese constitution at the suggestion and insistence of the US occupation authorities. This was before the Cold War had begun. The stated purpose was to prevent any future resurgence of Japanese militarism but General Douglas MacArthur's more immediate concern was to forestall criticism from US wartime allies regarding the US decision to let the Emperor remain on his throne. The 'Peace Constitution' was a way for MacArthur to reassure other countries that the USA would not tolerate any Japanese militarist revival. As the Cold War took hold, and before the outbreak of the Korean War in June 1950, the USA regretted having imposed Article 9 on Japan and began asking the government to rearm. During the Korean War, the United States wanted Japan to take part. Yet the Anglophile aristocrat Yoshida saw no need to sacrifice Japanese blood in a war under US command. Neither did he want to underwrite an unwelcome return to Japan's former colony. And he did not want a resurgence of militarism in Japan itself.

Yoshida was by no means a pacifist. He had, after all, called for the use of Japanese force in China in the 1920s, but now warned against antagonising the UK and the USA as the world's leading powers. In the 1930s he struggled as a diplomat to prevent the developments that led to Pearl Harbor and ultimately to Hiroshima, Nagasaki and the Emperor's decision to surrender. He blamed Japan's fateful mistakes on its militarism and concluded that military officers must not again be allowed to interfere in politics. He saw the intervention by 'military cliques' in Japanese politics in the 1930s as resulting from the budgetary cuts undertaken by the civilian government during the world economic crisis of 1929–30. For a government intending to reduce its military budgets it is essential to keep its officer corps under firm civilian control. One of Yoshida's reasons for resisting requests for a rapid rearmament in the 1950s was his fear of creating conditions where the military could again intervene in politics. His worry extended from the officer corps to the common soldiers. He was afraid of providing guns to young men recruited from the lower classes, who might on occasion be inspired by communist or socialist leaders to use them against the government.

Until 1950, Yoshida was the most prominent exponent in Japanese politics of a strict interpretation of Article 9: Japanese rearmament in any form was prohibited. When defending the Peace Constitution in 1946, he declared: 'Now that we have been beaten, and we haven't got a single soldier left on our hands, it is a fine opportunity to renounce war for all time'. And on 26 June that year, he told the House of Representatives that not just the right of belligerence but also of self-defence was renounced. Yet he could not avoid being swayed by US pressure and the Cold War mentality. In January 1950, after the communist victory in the Chinese civil war and following General Douglas MacArthur's New Year's address, which called explicitly for Japanese rearmament, Yoshida stated that the Constitution 'of course' did not preclude self-defence. The recreation of Japanese armed forces began in July 1950, just a few weeks after the outbreak of the Korean War. In February 1951 Yoshida stated publicly that Japan had 'a right and obligation to defend its own security'. Yet he resisted pressure to allocate substantial resources to its new 'Police Reserve', and set Japan on a path of a gradual and modest remilitarisation. The 'Police Reserve' was after some time re-baptised 'Safety Force' and then 'Self-Defence Force', which it is still called today. In order not to violate Article 9, it was at first said to be without 'war potential'.

An amendment of the Japanese constitution requires a 2/3 majority in both houses of the Diet, as well as a simple majority in a subsequent national referendum. This had never been possible before 2016, when the Liberal Democratic Party and its coalition partner, the Komeito party, which already had a 2/3 majority in the lower house won a 2/3 majority in the upper house as well. For the first time, therefore, it was now possible for both houses of the Diet to approve a constitutional revision, which then would need to be approved by simple majority in a popular referendum. Abe Shinzo's government (2012–) might still choose to avoid the acrimony of a heated public debate, since there is a groundswell of support for Article 9 in the Japanese population, in particular among those who keep the memory of Hiroshima and Nagasaki alive. Abe Shinzo may therefore resign himself to the same procedure that he and his predecessors have used repeatedly: reinterpret the constitution through legislation and government decree.

The Yoshida government established this pattern as a substitute for revising the constitution when it allowed the Self-Defence Force to be created. Yoshida did not see any direct military threat to the Japanese home islands, except from a Soviet Union that was deterred by US power. He did not want to stir up further anti-Japanese sentiments in other Asian countries, so he did not need a strong Self-Defence Force. If the SDF had been allowed to grow much further at the time, Japan might have found it difficult to resist pressures to dispatch troops to US wars. The pro-British Yoshida resisted 'war-loving America' throughout his premiership. Only towards the end of his life, perhaps under the impression of the Chinese Cultural Revolution and at a time when he had lost all of his influence, did he change his position on rearmament, claiming that his past policy had been based on political expediency and that he had never envisioned 'eternal' disarmament. Once Japan was restored to great-power status, he said, not to have a national army would be a 'deformity'. So, if this was what Yoshida had been thinking all along, then his doctrine was just meant to be a temporary expedient. Yet, even as such, it played a significant role in the gradual pacification of East Asia. It stabilized relations among the non-communist Asian countries and paved the way for stabilizing the East Asian region as soon as China and the USA had reconciled in the 1970s. It seems unlikely that Japan's economic miracle could have been embraced and emulated by other countries in the region if it had not been for Article 9.

The greatest imitator was China. When Deng Xiaoping went to Japan in December 1978, his explicit aim was to learn from its government as well as its big companies, and attract Japanese investments and technology transfer. He did not of course copy every aspect of the Japanese example. Instead of forbidding China from having an army, he used it to invade Vietnam, but afterwards he cut the number of troops and military costs in order to channel resources into the civilian economy. Thus began China's astounding economic rise. It could not have happened without the Japanese model and Japan's active participation. The model inspired Chinese policy making, and Japanese technology provided through official development aid (ODA) and commercial investments were essential for China's economic rise. So was access for Japanese and Chinese products on the US and European export markets. A division of labour emerged over time between Japan and China in the global trading system. Japan exported machinery to China, and China used it for producing end products for the Western markets. While Japan enjoyed a surplus in its trade with China, China gained an even greater surplus in its trade with the West.

It is a travesty that Japan's contribution to China's peaceful rise is not more actively recognized in China today, and that memories of past wars are allowed to poison relations among the Northeast Asian nations, creating an environment where apprehension for national security is allowed to overshadow the need for promoting human and environmental security. It is similarly tragic that Article 9 is being emptied of its remaining content because Japan has become so fearful of China's military build-up. Please accept my apology for making this emotional statement in a text that is meant to be scholarly. I shall now try to resume my analytical detachment.

Table 2: China's economic preponderance: 2015 GDP and GDP/PPP in all East Asian countries – and in the USA, India and Russia for comparison (World Bank figures)

	GDP 2015 (bill. USD)	% of E. Asia	% of World	GDP/PPP (bill. USD)	% of E. Asia	% of World
China	10,866.4	55.1	14.8	19,524.3	56.6	17.2
Japan	4,123.3	21.0	5.6	4,738.3	13.7	4.2
ROK (S. Korea)	1,377.9	7.0	1.9	1,748.8	5.0	1.5
Indonesia	861.9	4.4	1.2	2,842.2	8.2	2.5
ROC Taiwan[a]	523.6	2.7	0.7	1,099.0	3.2	1.0
Thailand	395.3	2.0	0.5	1,108.1	3.2	1.0
Hong Kong SAR	309.9	1.6	0.4	414.4	1.2	0.4
Malaysia	296.2	1.5	0.4	815.6	2.4	0.7
Singapore	292.7	1.5	0.4	471.6	1.4	0.4
Philippines	292.0	1.5	0.4	741.0	2.1	0.7
Vietnam	193.6	1.0	0.3	552.3	1.6	0.5
Myanmar[b]	64.9	0.3	0.1	194.6	0.6	0.2
Macao SAR	46.2	0.2	0.1	65.4	0.2	0.1
Cambodia	18.1	0.1	0.0	54.3	0.2	0.0
Brunei Darussalam	15.5	0.1	0.0	30.0	0.1	0.0
Lao PDR	12.3	0.1	0.0	38.6	0.1	0.0
Mongolia	11.8	0.1	0.0	36.1	0.1	0.0
DPRK (N. Korea)[c]	3.1	0.0	0.0	9.3	0.0	0.0
Timor-Leste	1.4	0.0	0.0	2.8	0.0	0.0
East Asia	19,706.0	100.0	26.8	34,486.7	100.0	30.4
Northeast Asia	17,262.1	87.6	23.5	27,635.5	80.1	24.3
Southeast Asia	2,443.9	12.4	3.3	6,851.2	19.9	6.0
Greater China[d]	11,746.1	59.6	16.0	21,103.1	61.2	18.6
USA	17,947.0	–	24.4	17,947.0	–	15.8
India	2,073.5	–	2.8	7,982.5	–	7.0
Russia	1,326.0	–	1.8	3,579.8	–	3.2
World	73,433.6	–	100.0	113,612.5	–	100.0

Source: World Bank: http://databank.worldbank.org/data/download/GDP.pdf and http://databank.worldbank.org/data/download/GDP_PPP.pdf.

Notes: (a) The World Bank does not publish data for Taiwan, so the figures here have been taken from the International Monetary Fund's estimate for 'Taiwan, province of China'.

Risk and Interdependence

Since the 1980s, China has seen phenomenal economic growth and, in 2014, surpassed the USA as the world's largest economy when measured in purchasing power parity (ppp) terms. If measured in nominal terms, following currency exchange rates, it is set to surpass the USA around 2023. Opinions differ as to which method best reflects a nation's power. If the ability to pay soldiers and produce ordinary weapons is the most important, then it makes sense to use the ppp figures. If what is most important is to buy oil or sophisticated weapons, or to be a powerful economic actor on the world market, then we should stick to calculating wealth and value on the basis of the exchange rate between the local currency and the relevant international currency. Regardless of method, the Chinese economy is now much bigger than all the other East Asian economies combined, as can be seen from Table 2.

State control of a high share of GDP adds further to China's economic power. State banks and state-owned enterprises control a high share of the national revenue. Private household spending represents a low share of the national income, both because of low salaries and because households save much of their income in state banks. The same is the case in Japan, although the average household income there is much higher. The Japanese and Chinese states are now among the most heavily indebted in the world, but they owe most of the money to their own population.

Like South Korea, Taiwan, Hong Kong and Singapore, China followed Japan's lead in the regional quest for prosperity. Yet China's growth since the 1980s has been even more rapid than Japan's was in the 1950s–80s, and China's growth has been more export driven than Japan's. In this sense, China has differed from Japan. While Japan has a huge internal

(b) The World Bank has no GDP/PPP figure for Myanmar. The figure here has been calculated by multiplying the nominal GDP by three, assuming that Myanmar has roughly the same difference between nominal GDP and GDP/PPP as Cambodia.
(c) The World Bank does not publish data for the DPRK, and estimates vary greatly. The nominal GDP here is based on the Bank of (South) Korea's estimate of North Korea's GDP per capita (USD 1,224); the GDP/PPP figure has been calculated by multiplying the nominal GDP by three, assuming that the DPRK has roughly the same difference between nominal GDP and GDP/PPP as Cambodia.
(d) Comprising China, Hong Kong, Macao and Taiwan.

market, China has relied on the global market, and now urgently needs to stimulate private consumption if it shall have any hope of maintaining its growth momentum at a time when the global market is no longer able to absorb its products. China is now on its way to becoming less dependent on exports and may be moving in the direction of a more balanced foreign trade. This is likely to reduce the government's share of the revenues while households become more prosperous. While a more balanced Chinese economy will reduce its macroeconomic dependence on exports, it will not mean that China pulls back from its integration in the global economy. Just as Japan, which has long had a strong domestic market, China will also depend just as much as in the past on international peace and stability.

The rigorously analytical and realist scholar Robert S. Ross (2014) has examined the effect of China's economic growth for East Asia's regional security. He assumes that the governments of small states in the region make security and economic risk assessments before deciding whether or not to align their foreign and security policies with either China or the USA. China is now second only to the USA as a world economic power and is East Asia's most important market. A regional economic order is developing, with China's domestic market as its anchor. China's economic rise has already challenged the ability of the United States to shape the world trade and financial orders. But the ways in which the rise of the Chinese economy has influenced East Asian security is less clear. The key analytical issue is whether economic power can independently determine the security alignments of states. If China could use its growing market power to realize new security objectives, it could destabilize the existing order.

Political economists often claim that trade dependence on another country's market can lead small states to realign their security policies, with scant regard for military power. Recent developments in China's bilateral relations with some Southeast Asian states, which look to China for financial and other support while having difficulties with the United States, seem to confirm the political economy thesis. However, through multiple bilateral case studies, Ross (2014) examines the merits of this argument. He isolates those trade dyads in which China possesses superior economic power vis-a-vis the USA, reflected in greater economic dependence on China than on the United States, but inferior military power. This allows him to assess the independent ability of trade to affect strategic alignments. Contrary to the expectations of the political economists, Ross finds that those states in East Asia that depend significantly on exports to the Chinese market but continue to experience and perceive US military dominance have not adjusted their strategic alignment to develop closer military cooperation with China. Thus, more generally, his research suggests that the economic dependence of a small state on a great economic power is an insufficient force to influence its strategic alignment and that China's rising economic power has not generated and will not generate strategic accommodation by East Asia's smaller states.

Interestingly, Ross's realist Chinese colleague, Yan Xuetong of Peking University, reacted to the coming to power of Donald Trump in January 2017 by suggesting that time had come for China to abandon its principled opposition to formal alliances, and forge military alliances with Cambodia, Thailand, Malaysia and the Philippines (Yan 2017). If this should happen, either Ross would be proven wrong or the security realignment of these smaller states would result only from uncertainties with regard to the US military commitment and not to China's growing economic strength.

Ross's findings have implications for our understanding of how economic power affects international politics. They indicate that security alignments do not directly reflect challenges to the international economic order but also require changes in the balance of military power. If security alignments change in ways that destabilize the regional order and threaten international peace, then this is likely to follow from changes in the US–China military balance, not merely from greater economic strength. In this respect, given continued US ability to deploy military power to sustain its regional security partnerships, the East Asian power transition does not, according to Ross, challenge the East Asian Peace in the short to medium term.

Ross' findings (see e.g. Ross 2017) seem reassuring: the East Asian Peace finds its main explanation in the military superiority of the US–Japan alliance, which is likely to continue. Not one single country has yet opted out of an alliance or shifted to another as an effect of China's rise. This means China could be free to continue its economic growth without destabilizing the region. Let me add, though, that Yan (2017) does not take his radical alliance proposal out of just thin air. There has been some political and diplomatic movement, with Cambodia, Thailand, Malaysia and the Philippines, flirting with China, while Myanmar and Vietnam have moved closer to the USA. South Korea, a strong US ally, also moved closer to China after Park Geun-hye became president in 2012, but Sino–Korean relations worsened when South Korea in 2016 decided to let the United States deploy a Terminal High Altitude Air Defence system (THAAD) on its territory. In consonance with Ross' theory, security related concerns trumped the quest for economic gain. Under President Benigno Aquino III, the Philippines reaffirmed its US military alliance, which had been weakened by the departure of the USA from its naval Subic Bay and Clark air base in 1992, but President Rodrigo Duterte changed the Philippines foreign policy soon after taking office in August 2016, attacking the USA and seeking Chinese investment in Mindanao. On the other hand, North Korea has openly defied its Chinese protector with frequent nuclear tests and missile launches; its young leader has not yet made a visit to Beijing and would no doubt prefer to go to Washington, and surely dreams of having nuclear arms and a US peace treaty, too.

These diplomatic adjustments are interesting for the way they reflect a combination of geography, patterns of economic integration, and domestic political situation. If a country shares a border with China and/or is involved in a boundary dispute with it (Vietnam and the Philippines), its perception of security risk tends to make it resent its dependence on China and want a US counterbalance. Yet China's proximity also calls for caution; Vietnamese communist leaders who appear too critical of China have on several occasions been removed from power in Hanoi, and the Philippines has had an ambiguous relationship with the USA as ally and former colonial power. Small developing countries feeling weary of domination by other regional states than China, such as Timor-Leste, Laos and Cambodia, have tended to welcome Chinese aid and reciprocate by aligning themselves with Chinese foreign policies, and more developed countries such as Brunei, Malaysia, Singapore and Thailand may also seek to accommodate China in order to safeguard their concern for access to the Chinese market. Furthermore, if a country's domestic politics faces US criticism (Thailand's military rule, Malaysian corruption, Myanmar's discrimination against the Rohingya, the Philippines because of extra-judicial killings), then they are likely to orient themselves towards China, which does not interfere with other countries' internal affairs as long as they are not of direct concern to China. By contrast, the rich and internally stable but internationally vulnerable city state of Singapore looks constantly for ways to preserve the global balance of power. It strives actively to maintain the US security role in the region, while doing its best to prevent this from damaging its relations with China.

Ross is right that the recent political or diplomatic adjustments do not amount to a security realignment. After a failed Japanese attempt to move closer to China under the short-lived Democratic Party governments of Hatoyama Yukio (2009–10), Kan Naoto (2010–11) and Noda Yoshihiko (2011–12), Japan returned to a policy of reinforcing its US alliance. Although South Korea shares China's historical animosity towards Japan, has a similar boundary dispute with Japan as China in the East China Sea, has China as its main trading partner and also for some years has enjoyed a more confident relationship with Beijing than North Korea, the government in Seoul has stuck firmly to its US alliance.

It seems pertinent to ask what each government sees as its main priority, and to what extent it allows its policy to be influenced by assessment of economic risk. Ross examines the trading pattern of each bilateral relationship. One important consideration is what kind of dependence we talk about. A sense of economic dependence is no mere reflection of the total volume of trade or its share of GDP. The kind of goods a country exports or imports matters, as does the kind of foreign direct investments it receives or makes abroad. A key question is how easy it is to replace a trading partner. The East Asian countries have different kinds of economic relations with China, depending on their level of development. Some invest directly in China and export machinery and technology to it (Japan, Taiwan, South Korea, Singapore). Some import Chinese manufactured goods in exchange for agricultural products (Myanmar, Laos, Vietnam, the Philippines). Some compete with China in the US, Japanese and European markets (Thailand, Vietnam, Indonesia). Regardless of all these differences, Ross is right to observe that there has not so far been any security realignment. So far, the US Cold War system remains intact, and was indeed reinforced under President Obama's pivot to Asia. This should mean that there is no acute need for the states in the region radically to change their threat perceptions. If national leaders keep their heads cool and Trump does not break radically with the traditional foreign policy of the USA, the East Asian governments may continue to prioritise Peaceful Development and concentrate on fulfilling the needs of their domestic constituencies. Yet, if just one of the US allies, such as Duterte's Philippines, should prove ready to send the Americans packing and instead form a close and lasting partnership with China, then this would tend to refute Ross' point and confirm the political economy thesis.

Some structural theories seek to explain how economic interdependence affects conflict behaviour. The theory of the 'capitalist peace' comes in several versions. Some think economic interaction creates cultural affinities that prevent conflict. Others hold that big transnational companies are empowered and lobby governments to yield terrain to their adversaries in order to keep the peace. Business thrives on predictability. Yet others think that interdependence makes war too costly. A conflict would disrupt access to the international market and unleash an economic crisis, with shares and currencies plummeting, and people losing their jobs. The anticipation of such events is thought to have a constraining effect on government behaviour.

In the most recent years, according to Kreutz (2015), even minor signs of Sino–Japanese hostility have led to drops in regional stock markets and created a joint interest among powerful economic elites to de-escalate interstate disputes. He claims that economic risk plays a much greater role in East Asian decision-making today than before. Yet peace research explorations of how perceptions of economic risk influence government behaviour in a crisis have not yet made much progress. Is it the top decision makers themselves who worry about the costs? Does the impact of economic concerns depend on the influence of ministers of finance, trade and industry? Does the central bank have a say? Who else lobbies governments? Do transnational companies intervene to prevent or shape the trajectories of international crises?

East Asia's intra-regional as well as extra-regional trade have grown tremendously during the East Asian Peace. It is therefore reasonable to assume that there is a causal connection, which could run in both directions. Peace may be safely assumed to have facilitated trade, and trade may also have prevented armed conflict. Within our programme, the most elaborate attempt to explore the relationship between peace and international trade has been made by Ben Goldsmith, University of Sydney, who has compared the extent to which trade has had a more or less pacifying impact in East Asia than in other parts of the world. He focuses (2013, 2017) on pairs of states (dyads) and two aspects of their bilateral trade: interdependence (which he defines as bilateral trade in proportion to the larger country's GDP) and the volume of trade between them (the total amount of bilateral exports and imports). He wonders if one or the other reduces the chance that the two states get into conflict and, if they do, affect the probability of their conflict escalating. He argues that interdependence creates an economic opportunity cost (a loss of potential gain from choosing other alternatives than conflict) and thus hinders conflict initiation if it is sufficiently high. High trade volumes could play a similar role in preventing conflict escalation, because high trade volumes allow states to interfere with their own trade and use such interference as a signalling device. By accepting the loss to themselves of reducing trade they can signal resolve, or an intention to compromise, in the midst of a crisis.

In his data, Goldsmith finds evidence that supports both hypotheses, but in each case the statistical association between trade and peace is weaker in East Asia than in other parts of the world. He thus suggests that East Asia's developmental states (and also developmental states elsewhere) 'more freely, but less credibly, use trade as a foreign policy tool', but given the exceptionally high intra-regional East Asian trade volumes after 1980, the conflict dampening effect may nevertheless have been very large. As mentioned earlier, a 'developmental state' is governed by a determined elite with a powerful, economic bureaucracy, which effectively steers the behaviour even of private companies. Interestingly, Goldsmith finds evidence to support his second hypothesis: high volumes of trade prevent conflict escalation, when developmental states are involved.[8]

---

8. Ben Goldsmith (2013). I have some doubts, though, about the data used in this study. The Militarized Interstate Dispute (MID) data include many small disputes, such as fishery incidents at sea, which have not drawn much attention from governments and where escalation has not been on the cards. The MIDs that have escalated in East Asia are also so few that any statistical association they may have with other factors can hardly be meaningful.

Goldsmith's argument relies on the economic value of trade, either because opportunity costs prevent conflict initiation, or because high volumes of trade represent a resource used by states to communicate their intentions in ways preventing a conflict from escalating. Goldsmith thus challenges my characterisation of the East Asian Peace as developmental rather than capitalist by suggesting that structural incentives and constraints, rather than the priorities of national leaders, have helped East Asia become and remain so relatively peaceful.[9]

Explaining Internal Peace

In the modern state system, intrastate armed conflicts have been more common than interstate armed clashes, have often lasted longer, have sometimes been more deadly, and have obstructed economic development. This has notably been the case when the two kinds of warfare are mixed through external intervention or support to opposite factions in a civil war. Intrastate warfare also tends to perpetuate itself. In societies where the state fails to establish a monopoly of violence, armed politics becomes a permanent state of affairs, with fighting flaring up from time to time, interspersed with standoffs or ceasefire arrangements (Staniland, forthcoming). All of this makes it at least as important to theorize about intrastate as interstate peace: How do nations establish a durable civil peace?

East Asia offers a variation of national trajectories, which may be used in comparative studies of transitions from civil war to internal peace. All countries in the region were drawn into the Second World War, which included intense civil warfare, primarily in Myanmar and China. Japan and Mongolia became internally peaceful right after the Second World War. China, Korea and all of the Southeast Asian nations succumbed to internal warfare in the Cold War period, and it took a long time for many of them to achieve internal peace: North and South Korea 1953, Malaya, Brunei and Singapore in the 1960s, Vietnam 1975, China

---

9. Kivimäki (2014: 21) points out that while the ASEAN Way ensured peace in Southeast Asia, the interdependence among those countries actually decreased in the 1960s–70s. However, this is likely to have been due to their increasing trade with the USA and Japan. The most interdependent economic relations in East Asia have not been internal to Southeast Asia (except Malaysia–Singapore) but between the Southeast and Northeast Asian economies, between the economies of Northeast Asia, and between East Asia, America and Europe.

1976 (after the Cultural Revolution), Cambodia 1998, Indonesia 2005. While the Philippines, Thailand and Myanmar have not yet been able to end their civil wars, the first two of these have seen extended periods of internal peace, Myanmar is the prime regional example of a country that has never managed to overcome intrastate armed conflict in its ethnic minority areas, although it also has a rich experience with ceasefire arrangements. In our programme, we have been preoccupied with the challenge of explaining why the Philippines, Thailand and Myanmar have not yet made their transition to peace. Is it due to some common trait not shared by the other regional states? Or does each national failure have its own explanation?

I do not claim that our programme has developed a general theory of internal peace, but we have contributed to moving the attention of peace researchers from studying civil war to explaining civil peace. In our attempts to find fruitful explanations we have followed four main approaches focusing, respectively, on the end of proxy warfare, increased state capacity, change of rebel tactics, and fading of revolutionary ideology. These come in addition to my own approach, as presented above, which explains both external and internal peace with priority changes on the national level, setting economic development as the top priority. I argue that the Philippines, Thailand and Myanmar have not yet been able to establish a developmental state. They have never established any consensus among the main policy makers to gear the state towards achieving economic growth, and this has prevented their governments from doing whatever needs to be done to overcome armed opposition.

The *end of proxy war approach* is grounded in our finding that civil and international conflicts have often interacted in ways that have escalated and prolonged the warfare, notably through great power involvement. Two great powers are located inside the region (China and Japan), and a third has a heavy military presence there (the United States). The United States has military bases in Guam, Okinawa, Tokyo, South Korea, Singapore, and the Philippines) and enjoys superior naval power. India and Russia have also been active in the region. Joakim Kreutz (2015; 2017) has made comparative studies of conflict termination and finds that armed conflicts in Southeast Asia have only ended when all external actors have preferred to see it happen. This would apply to the end of the Korean War in 1953, the First Indochina War in 1954, the Second

Indochina War in 1973–75, and the Third Indochina War in 1991, all of which mixed elements of intrastate and interstate warfare, and various degrees of foreign intervention. In each case all external powers wanted the conflict to end, and then it did – although sometimes just for a while.

Kreutz does not claim that conflicts are bound to end when all external powers want it. The local parties may find ways to continue or reopen their conflict. In such cases, the level of fighting depends on the ability of the parties to fund themselves by taxing local communities or controlling trade in drugs, gems or other valuables. Kreutz argues that the decline in internal armed conflict in Southeast Asia, by contrast to Northeast Asia, has been due mainly to a drop in external support and an end to foreign intervention, that is, an end to 'war by proxy'. The transition to peace has been further enhanced by the efforts of external powers to push actively for conflict resolution. The regional turn to peace does not, he claims (2015), have much to do with what the local governments have done. Instead, the pacification of Southeast Asia reflects a cooperative trend in global politics. This challenges the developmental peace theory advocated by Kivimäki and myself, which builds on the assumption that the identity or priorities of local elites have been instrumental in fostering a need for stability both internationally and internally.

I must admit that Kreutz has a point. The pacification of Cambodia in 1989–91 was not the making of Hun Sen's government, but resulted from Vietnam's retreat, which in turn was precipitated by Gorbachev's downscaling of Soviet commitments abroad. And the Khmer Rouge did not give up their struggle voluntarily. They went back to fighting in 1993 but, without external support, were ineffective. The long-standing communist rebellion in Myanmar collapsed when China withdrew its support in 1989. Yet my emphasis on local decisions finds support in the historical trajectories of Indonesia, Malaysia and Singapore. In those countries the communists never got much foreign support. Their developmentalist governments defeated them. And the loss of Soviet support was not the only reason why Vietnam pulled out of Cambodia. Its decision to withdraw was also grounded in its belief that prime minister Hun Sen could manage on his own, and on an urgent need to save costs and concentrate on reforming Vietnam's own badly managed economy. So let me concede to Kreutz that the end of external support to communist and anti-communist insurgents, as well as to governments engaged in war against internal enemies, made it more costly and difficult to uphold internal wars, and provided developmental states with an opportunity to obtain the stability they needed. I disagree, though, with Kreutz's contention that the creation of an opportunity was the main peace factor. I hold that the main factor was the local will to use it. A regional transition from widespread war to relative peace is a combination of conflict termination, de-escalation and conflict prevention. While external powers may have played a significant role in first sustaining and then ending ongoing armed conflicts, their role has been more limited in preventing conflict onsets. The United States has no doubt had a restraining influence on South Korea, Japan, and Taiwan in times of crisis, but the task of avoiding or preventing conflict through diplomacy and restraint has been handled mostly by the regional governments themselves. They have sometimes avoided escalation and sometimes put disputes aside, and – as we have seen – they have prevented future conflict by negotiating border agreements.

The *state capacity approach* is the nearest we get to a realist explanation of internal peace. I am not aware of any explicitly realist attempt to explain both interstate and intrastate peace in a combined and comprehensive analysis. For realists, the distinction between interstate and intrastate is essential: they see the international society as anarchic, with no overall authority, while national societies are subject to the power of a sovereign government. Most self-proclaimed realists deal primarily with international relations, but some relevant theories include components of internal stability, such as evaluating the capacity of states to control their populations. Well-organized, resource-rich states are not only able to avoid conflict with other states but also to prevent uprisings.

It has always been dangerous to start a rebellion. Those who do so are prepared to accept enormous risk. Once a rebellion has spread and the rebels control some territory, it becomes easier to recruit new fighters. Our increased state capacity approach has been inspired by Dan Slater, University of Chicago, who gave a keynote address to our 5th Annual Conference in Singapore in November 2015. In his book *Ordering Power* (2010), he asks why some authoritarian states are more stable than others, and finds the answer in 'protection pacts' between governments and social elites. What decides the terms of such pacts is the degree to which the elites are afraid of social revolution, separatism or external aggression. The greater their fear, the more power they are willing to yield to the state, and the more they allow themselves to be taxed. Elite threat perceptions are the 'causal motor' of ordered power. The key factor in determining which Southeast Asian states gained the greatest capacity was the relative strength of leftist movements in the aftermath of the Second World War. The Singaporean and Malaysian 'authoritarian Leviathans' became strong and durable because the communist threat was real, whereas the states of Thailand and the Philippines, where communists were less effective, remained fragile. Slater explains the resilience of military rule in Myanmar and Indonesia with the continuous threat from separatist movements. He also briefly discusses the viability of state order in places where the leftist revolutions were successful: China, Laos, North Korea and Vietnam. Some of these revolutionary states have now existed for a long time, but duration is not, he says, the same as durability.

Together with Elin Bjarnegård, a member of our core group in Uppsala and specialist on Thai politics, I have examined the question of why this middle income country has defied the general peace trend. We observed (2015) several violent conflicts since the turn of the millennium: one over government in Bangkok, with protracted street demonstrations that provoked military coups both in 2006 and 2014; one at the border to Cambodia ostensibly over access to the temple Preah Vihear, and the worst one in the country's Deep South, where a conflict between the government and clandestine groups of Malay Muslim rebels has cost thousands of lives. Our main explanation for Thailand's failure to uphold peace is a lack of state capacity. No civilian Thai government has ever gained control of the armed forces and, since the early 2000s, a polarised rivalry between red and yellow political factions has incapacitated the state. Except in times of direct military rule, Thailand has had two parallel governments, one military and one civilian, neither of which controls the other.

A similar situation has now been created in Myanmar, where the military commander-in-chief holds the main power over matters related to internal and external security, while State Councillor Aung San Suu Kyi is expected to take care of economic and administrative management, ensure the provision of services, conduct diplomacy – and keep the country's peace process alive. This kind of hybrid regime is not conducive to peace. It was easy to see that its establishment in March–April 2016 was likely to derail the peace process between the government and the ethnic armed groups, and provoke more armed conflict. Yet, if Myanmar is able to generate substantial economic growth, which should be relatively easy for a country on its low level of development, endowed with both cheap labour and abundant natural resources, then it will also have the resources to develop state capacity. When a state, as has happened in much of the region, is able to build infrastructure (roads, railways, telecommunications, etc.), hire many more bureaucrats, provide education and health services to the population, then this gradually boosts its capacity for detecting, co-opting or repressing opposition movements, and also for systematically consulting the population in ways that may lead citizens to accept government decisions. When this is done by a cohesive government, with full civilian control of the armed forces (army as well as police), then life will become difficult for armed rebels, who may have to look for other ways to accomplish their goals.

The *changing rebel tactics approach* has forced me to widen my perspective from mainly looking at the national policy makers on the side of the government to also studying opposition leaders and commanders of non-state armed groups. Changes in their outlook and behaviour must be taken into account when seeking to explain the regional transition to peace. One of our research associates, Paul Staniland, University of Chicago, has looked at situations where armed groups do not actually fight, or do so only intermittently, but manage to insert or sustain themselves in a certain area as armed groups within a system of *armed politics*. This challenges the basic tenets of statistical peace research, with its emphasis on active armed conflict, measured in clashes, casualties or battle deaths. In the UCDP an armed conflict is considered as 'inactive' if it does not reach the 25 battle death threshold in a given year.

Staniland shares Slater's interest in order and disorder, and seeks to unpack the relationships between governments and other armed actors, identifying contexts in which a lack of violence does not mean that a conflict has ended or that the state is in control, but instead results from collusion and cooperation between non-state armed groups and the state. He looks at alliance patterns and alternation between cooperation and hostilities. His approach, drawing on fieldwork and historical sources in Myanmar and South Asia, lets him analyse armed politics in a way that is not possible if one accepts my crude distinction between armed conflict and peace as absence-of-armed-conflict. Focussing on armed politics rather than conflict, and seeing the question of whether people were killed or not as relatively unimportant, he finds that complex war economies, electoral collaboration, and variants of indirect rule all have an impact on struggles for power. In an East Asian context his findings are above all relevant for Myanmar, but may also inform our understanding of the present situation in some parts of Indonesia, the Philippines, Thailand, Laos and Cambodia, and historically in Vietnam and China before their communists established a centralized government with a monopoly on violence.

Staniland's work may help us understand how, in some societies, armed groups are able to sustain themselves beyond the time when they can have any prospect of toppling a government or liberating a national homeland by military means. His findings suggest that there are ways of creating stability that do not require a state monopoly of violence throughout a national territory. Several armed groups may live side by side for long periods of time without much actual fighting. Staniland looks at the reduction of armed conflict in Myanmar after 1989, and also at how the democratisation process since 2011 has destabilized local arrangements in ways leading to renewed fighting. The 'armed peace' in Myanmar has depended on complex sets of economic and security arrangements between the army, some twenty non-state armed groups and a newly elected government. While Myanmar is not typical for the region, it might exemplify something that affects other Southeast Asian countries as well: when rebel groups stop fighting, they might retain their arms and become latent forces with a capacity for resuming their struggle later on. Increased state capacity is only a part of the explanation for the reduction of internal armed conflict in Southeast Asia, and it is not an irreversible process. Ceasefire and peace, according to Staniland, are not the same. In ceasefires, the latent forces of conflict remain.

Paul Staniland is also concerned with the economics of local patterns of conflict and cooperation between states and non-state armed groups. They may have a shared interest in the benefits of exploiting natural resources, and in either promoting or resisting economic modernization. The extension of mobile telephone networks to areas controlled by non-state groups creates a kind of social change that links up both militias and units of the national army with a broader, indeed global community. In that context it must worry the government in Naypyidaw that the de facto independent Wa territory in northern Shan State is more deeply integrated with China than with Myanmar. It uses Chinese currency and Chinese mobile telephone networks. The two companies Oredoo and Telenor, however, have a concession obliging them to build telecommunications networks on the whole of Myanmar's territory, so they must offer their services also to the Wa. This is one special case that illustrates a more general point: the economics of local conflicts have a huge impact on the prospects of peace. Both government and rebel leaders have to take economic risks into consideration when they choose their strategy and tactics.

Mathilda Lindgren and Isak Svensson (2011) have taken a different approach, looking at how rebels have changed from armed tactics to non-violent forms of struggle, such as street demonstrations and occupation of public buildings. Lindgren and Svensson call their article on the subject 'From Bombs to Banners'. The same process may be captured by the phrase 'From People's War to People Power'. The People's War strategy of guerrilla leaders Mao Zedong, Che Guevara and Truong Chinh, and inserted in a different setting by the Indonesian army's theoretician, Abdul Haris Nasution (1965), disappeared from the agenda at the end of the Cold War. The People Power revolution in Manila 1986 formed a new paradigm of non-violent regime change. Many attempts at non-violent revolt have been repressed, as in Yangon 1988 and Beijing 1989, but some of the failed revolts have shamed governments and induced them to reform. This has been the case in Myanmar, where the military government got tired of repressing its population. After it instituted a constitutional government, it launched democratic reforms from 2011 onward and paved the way for the electoral victory of Aung San Suu Kyi and the National League for Democracy (NLD) in November 2015.

Lindgren and Svensson point to comparative statistics tending to show that unarmed rebellions are more likely to reach their goal than armed ones, and indicate that this may have inspired new generations of would-be rebels to take a non-violent approach. While this may still hold true, the sad fate of the non-violent Arab Spring (and also of People Power in the Philippines), has somewhat weakened the changing-rebel-tactics thesis. More recently Svensson (2017) has taken a different approach, asking why East Asia has remained so relatively peaceful while the Middle East, in the aftermath of the Arab Spring, has seen a tremendous upsurge of armed conflict.

As a historian, I choose to call Svensson's new approach the *enfeebled revolutionary ideology approach*, although he himself speaks of it (2017) as an inquiry into the character of religious conflict. In the period since the end of the Cold War, revolutionary religious ideology has taken over much of the role that various forms of communism used to play in motivating rebellious behaviour. Many rebels used to be motivated by socialist ideology and received support from the communist powers. Rebels fighting against communist regimes were similarly motivated by anti-communist ideologies, sometimes driven by ethno-religious convictions. These anti-communist rebels could get support from the Western powers. Rebels thrived at the time, and the number of internal armed conflicts grew exponentially in the world's developing countries. The last successful leftist rebellion happened in Nicaragua in 1979. Since then, not one single leftist group using terrorist or guerrilla tactics has managed to seize power in any country on this earth. The most successful insurgents in the 1980s were those enjoying US or Chinese support, notably in Afghanistan and Cambodia.

While revolutionary religion – mostly Islamist – has taken over the role of secular communism in urging armed rebellion in the Greater Middle East and also in parts of Africa and South and Central Asia, this has only to a limited extent been the case in East Asia. Svensson observes (2015; 2017) that the relative absence of religious armed conflict in East Asia is not due to lack of religious cleavages or tension. He suggests that there remains a huge potential for religious conflict, particularly in Southeast Asia. In Indonesia, religious conflicts proliferated in the wake of Suharto's 1998 fall from power, with sectarian violence in Maluku, West Kalimantan and other places, intense fighting in Aceh, and also terrorist bombings by a group called Jemaah Islamiyah (JI). There was talk of a 'second Islamist front' in addition to the one in the Middle East, but the JI was effectively suppressed. In 2016, a new group with links to the Islamic State in Syria managed to carry out a bombing in Jakarta, but it mainly killed the perpetrators, thus demonstrating the weakness of Islamist terrorism in the world's largest Muslim country.

Svensson highlights two likely reasons for the relative absence of religious conflict. One is that East Asia's existing internal conflicts with a religious dimension have been inconsistent with transnational religious agendas and have thus not drawn external support or intervention. Since 2005, there has been little armed conflict in Indonesia. Elsewhere in the region, in areas where there are Islamic separatist movements (Mindanao and Patani) the majority of the local militants have had a local agenda that had little in common, and sometimes was at cross-purposes, with a global Jihad to resurrect the Caliphate.[10] In Myanmar's Rakhine State, the Muslim Rohingya have mostly been victims of Rakhine nationalism and Buddhist extremism rather than perpetrators, although an attack was carried out against Myanmar's border guards in October 2016, leading the Myanmar Army to react by putting fire to whole villages, killing or causing the inhabitants to flee. Ethno-religious grievances simmer in Xinjiang and Tibet, but the Uighur fighters have been harshly repressed by the Chinese People's Army Police, and the Buddhist activists in Tibet have chosen suicide tactics instead of killing agents of the state. Svensson's second reason is that East Asia has tough and well-provisioned governments, with a capacity to repress religiously motivated opponents. These two factors mentioned by Svensson contribute to explaining East Asia's downward trend in internal armed conflict since the 1980s.

In conclusion, I ascribe East Asia's downward trend in internal armed conflict to a combination of several factors. The governments of developmental states have needed internal stability in order to generate economic growth, and have allocated substantial resources to obtaining basic stability. The great powers have ended their practice of supporting proxies in their rivalries with each other. Governments have gradually acquired a much higher capacity for controlling their populations. This has contributed to peace except in those cases where there is little civilian control with the armed forces (the Philippines, Thailand, and Myanmar). Armed rebels in some countries have found ways to sustain themselves locally, and keep their arms, without actually having to fight. This kind of 'armed politics' has contributed to the peaceful transition

---

10. In an interview with Jill Sabillo (2016), Miriam Coronel-Ferrer, leader of the Philippines government's negotiation panel with the Moro Islamic Liberation Front (MILF) 2012–2016 and a research associate in our programme, described the agreement made between her government and MILF as 'a containment measure against jihadist extremism'.

by reducing the number of battle deaths, but entails a constant risk that the armed struggle may resume (as happened in Myanmar's Kachin State and Northern Shan State after 2011). There has been a change in rebel tactics from armed guerrilla struggles to un-armed People Power revolutions. This no doubt has contributed to the onset of the East Asian Peace. Yet it may not be a lasting trend, since governments have learned to better repress unarmed rebels, and also use unarmed demonstrations as a tactical counter-force.

All of this is compatible with my 'elitist' approach. I see changes as having occurred as a result of new expectations and priorities among national leaders as well as rebel leaders – who are also a kind of elite. It is now high time to address the criticism I have received for my elitism. I often hear that I do not sufficiently emphasize the role of public opinion.

Rulers, Citizens and Democratic Peace

Kivimäki (2014: 26) and I both hold the position that, if the 'rulers and citizens' prioritize development, they try to avoid both internal and interstate wars. In my view, though, the rulers are more important than the citizens, at least in foreign policy decision-making. In some instances the rulers and citizens think alike, and then we cannot know if the former are influenced by the latter or just happen to have the same view. In other cases, the public does not hold any clear opinion, but leaves decisions to the rulers, either because of disinterest or because they trust the authorities, in which case the leaders decide. If the rulers defy public opinion, we will know that it was they who decided. Only when the rulers accommodate public opinion by making choices going against their own preferences, can we clearly say that public opinion was decisive. This would mainly happen when leaders are afraid of losing power in a coup, revolt or election.

Kivimäki speaks of the developmentalist 'identity' of states where I prefer to look at the priorities of those who hold the reins of power. Decisions on war and peace are taken by a few individuals, who base their choices on their conception of national priorities and their perceptions of risk.[11] Yet concern for public opinion informs the foreign and

---

11. 'FPA (Foreign Policy Analysis) has important contributions to make in explaining the relative peace and economic dynamism of post-Cold War Asia. Unit-level variables intrinsic to FPA, such as threat perception, national identity, ideology,

internal policies of both democratic and authoritarian governments. As Kreutz (2014) has pointed out, when leaders see a need to secure continued support from influential groups, they sometimes engage in policies that contradict their values. This can be seen in de facto government support for attacks against Muslims in Myanmar, and in China's support for Myanmar's process of democratisation. These policies have not been pursued because the government of former president Thein Sein was anti-Islamic or because the Chinese government is in favour of liberal democracy, but because the Myanmar government needed support from anti-Islamic Buddhists, and the Chinese government wanted to protect its economic and strategic interests. Kreutz is right, of course. Leaders do not just act on their overall priorities but also on the basis of risk assessments, and when these make it difficult to pursue a priority or uphold a value, the leaders may adapt to public opinion. Sometimes this mitigates one risk while creating another. The classic case is when a government, in order to secure domestic support, engages in provocations abroad. M. Taylor Fravel (2008) has demonstrated that the opposite can also happen: when China has found it difficult to keep its ethnic minorities under control, it has offered territorial concessions to neighbour states in order to secure the border.

With the use of experimental methods, Allan Dafoe and Jessica Weiss (2015; see also Weiss 2014) investigate Chinese mass opinion and its influence on China's policy vis-a-vis the USA and Japan. Their research speaks more to the future of the peace than to its past and will therefore be discussed below. For now, let me just report that in a time of international crisis, they find that public opinion is responsive to what national leaders say and do. A crisis may be framed in ways that either stir up public demands for tough action or acceptance of backing down. Leaders have more power and more choice than they often presume or pretend.

What has been said about the role of public opinion, may apply also in democracies. As mentioned, Kivimäki and I assumed when we set up the programme, that democratic peace theory had little to contribute in terms of explaining the East Asian Peace. Democratic peace theory observes that democracies rarely if ever fight each other and seeks to

---

and leadership, are indispensable to understanding these outcomes'. Yuen Foong Khong (2014: 81).

explain why this is so, but East Asia has only a few clearly democratic polities (Japan, Mongolia, South Korea, Taiwan). Its mix of regime types should make the region vulnerable to armed conflict. Ben Goldsmith (2014a; 2014b), however, has challenged this assumption. He finds evidence of a 'democratic peace effect' on interstate relations both in the rest of the world and in East Asia. Since there have been so few armed conflicts, he looks at crises instead, and since there are not many full-blown democracies, he looks at levels of internal political competition. Goldsmith finds that East Asian countries with a high level of internal political competition have been unlikely to initiate crises with other countries that also have a high level of internal political competition. He does not, however, find any similarly significant effect from other democratic indicators, such as constraints on the executive or political participation. While Goldsmith's findings may suggest a possible causal effect, I do not think statistical association within a region of just 16 states in a period of 58 years (1948–2006) can yield any conclusive insights.[12]

Soft Explanations

A number of researchers within our programme have sought to explain the East Asian Peace with soft factors such as law, norms, culture, discourse, ideas or networks. Their work, which generally addresses both interstate and intrastate conflict, has brought many interesting issues to light but I remain unconvinced that such factors have led governments to refrain from the use of force in a crisis. Such factors are unlikely to have ended the Third Indochina War or the armed conflict in Aceh, led to peace talks in Myanmar or the Philippines, prevented the outbreak of war in the Korean peninsula or Taiwan Strait, caused the various claimant states to show restraint in the East China Sea or the South China Sea, or induced China, Japan and the USA to refrain from using force against each other. In a crisis situation, perceptions of risk and priorities are more likely to decide the outcome. The soft factors may influence priority set-

---

12. Goldsmith divides the relationships into annual dyads, so the total number of statistical observations in East Asia are as high as 12,346, 0.35% of which experienced crisis initiation by one state against another in the period 1948–2006. I think it must be a methodological problem that a bilateral relationship between State A and B in 2005 is treated as if it were distinct from the relationship between the same two states in 2006. To me this seems an artificial way to create a large N.

ting, and in a situation where there is no crisis, norms and institutions are likely to make peace more viable by offering non-violent ways to manage or resolve disputes. In that case the option to use force may not even be on the table. To use the language proposed by Jong Kun Choi (2016) of Yonsei University in Seoul, 'crisis stability' gives way to 'general stability'.

One soft explanation of the East Asian Peace is 'the ASEAN Way'. It occupies a central place in Kivimäki's thinking. The ASEAN Way, he says (2014, esp. pp. 65–82), consists of developmentalism, non-interference and face-saving. It was established as a discourse or a set of norms among the top Southeast Asian policy makers in the mid-1960s, and from then onwards, no armed conflict broke out among member states until Thailand and Cambodia clashed in 2008–11. Kivimäki claims that the ASEAN Way spread to Northeast Asia at the end of the Cold War, through the frameworks of ASEAN+3 and the ASEAN Regional Forum (ARF). This allowed East Asia to establish an informal and peaceful alternative to the more formal and institutionalised European model of peace. I have not found this convincing. While the importance of ASEAN in the wider region should not be denied, we must remember that the principle of non-interference, which forms an essential part of the ASEAN Way, was actually one of China's Five Principles of Peaceful Coexistence from 1953. It was reconfirmed when Deng Xiaoping took power and is independent of ASEAN, rather than imported from it.

There are two ways of looking at the ASEAN Way. One is to argue, as Kivimäki does, that it prevents conflict by seeking consensus, shelving disputes and upholding norms of non-interference. In that case, the ASEAN Way appears to provide an essential, if not causal, explanation for the regional peace. The other approach, presented by Michael Leifer (1999), is to argue that there was no conflict to prevent among the ASEAN member states, no credible casus belli. The confrontation between Indonesia and Malaysia had ended by the time ASEAN was formed. Subsequently, ASEAN did not really need to dissuade the Philippines from pushing its claim to the Malaysian State of Sabah. For geopolitical reasons, this could not happen anyway. A military conflict would have led the US-supported Philippines into a conflict with the UK-supported Malaysia at the time of the Vietnam War. The five original members of ASEAN were united by their fear of communist expansion, and by a shared priority for national security and economic development. ASEAN actually stayed away from preventive diplomacy. Each time there was a need to end or prevent a conflict; ASEAN left the task to outside powers. This was the case even when the Paris peace agreement on Cambodia was negotiated in 1989–91. Indonesia and Singapore played constructive roles, not ASEAN as such. ASEAN was also unable to do anything effective to persuade Thailand and Cambodia to stop fighting at their border in 2008–11.

The impact of norms is likely to be higher when the risk of armed conflict is low. Decisions in times of peace, when there is little security risk or economic cost involved, may be taken on the basis of norms or customs. Norms give way to other concerns when the risk rises. In crisis situations, norms are often used to legitimize actions taken for other reasons. Ren Xiao of Fudan University in Shanghai has examined the change of Chinese world views from Mao to Deng and beyond. He claims (2015) that 'ideational change' has determined China's international behaviour. When China's leaders have been committed to peaceful coexistence, they have tended to act cautiously. By contrast, when they thought the world was in 'war and revolution', they rejected the international order and backed up revolutionaries in other countries. At one point China identified itself as the 'centre of world revolution'. The cognitive shift to peace and development in the 1980s profoundly influenced China's behaviour. The shift from a revolutionary to a developmental state that integrated itself in the existing international order was consolidated through two major debates in the 1990s. In addition to embracing international institutions, China joined up with neighbouring countries in forging new peaceful institutions and norms. This would not have happened, says Ren, without ideational change: 'Perception conditions policy', and ideas guide policy making. Ren posits that China's doctrine of Peaceful Development is of real consequence, but needs to be encouraged by the outside world and internalized by the Chinese themselves in order to keep its benign influence on foreign policy behaviour.

Liselotte Odgaard of the Royal Danish Defence College has discussed China's principle of peaceful coexistence in the context of its role in the BRICS grouping (Brazil, Russia, India, China and South Africa) and its attempt to revise the world order. She finds (2014) that China's maritime policy calls into question its commitment to respect other countries' sovereign rights. Although this may not result in war, it has increased regional tension and diverted resources towards military spending and away from domestic socio-economic challenges in several countries in the region. So the ideas discussed by Ren Xiao do not seem to prevent China from pushing claims in its maritime neighbourhood in ways perceived by its neighbours as aggressive and in breach of international law. I am on record (2016b) concurring with Odgaard that China's maritime disputes, and its dissatisfaction with the United Nations Convention on the Law of the Sea (UNCLOS) provide a test of China's peaceful intentions. Hence I do not quite subscribe to Ren's ideational optimism. In my view, it is not the Peaceful Development doctrine as such that has determined China's foreign policy behaviour, but the priority given to economic development. The doctrine has reflected a priority, not vice versa. Let me add, with reference to the analysis of Swedish ambassador Börje Ljunggren (2015b; 2017), that Xi Jinping's much-promoted 'China Dream' is ambivalent with relation to peace. On the one hand, it emphasizes economic development. On the other it is about regaining the respected status China enjoyed before its 'century of humiliation'. Steps to realise this part of the dream are unlikely to promote peace.

One finding from our programme is that pacifism as a norm in itself has not had much impact in East Asia. Peace here has been a means to achieve an end: economic development. As I have argued above, this has even been the case in Japan, although pacifist ideas have been stronger there than in other countries. Pacifists on the political left and in the Komeito Party have played their part in preventing the Constitution's article 9 from being revised. They have set limits for military costs and thwarted attempts to open up the opportunity for Japanese forces to take part in military operations abroad. Yet the key factor behind Japan's pioneering role as a 'peace nation' was not pacifism but the pragmatism of a succession of leaders concerned with development. Linus Hagström (2015), the Swedish Defence University, has compared foreign policy debates in the Japanese Diet in 1972 and 2009–12 and shown how elastic the term 'peace' can be. It has been used to justify many different policies, including the recent the build-up of a credible military deterrent.

Mikael Weissmann at the Swedish Institute of International Affairs has published a book on the East Asian Peace, based on his doctoral thesis. He looks at networks among regional elites (politicians, diplomats, bureaucrats, military commanders), and finds that these networks have built trust, increased knowledge and predictability, altered definitions of national interests, and fostered shared regional norms. Thus they have been, says Weissmann (2012), essential for building a stable peace. Well, maybe. While it seems likely that people who know each other are less apt to go to war against each other than those who never communicate, there have been many wars in human history between people who knew each other well. Weissmann provides a rich documentation of the role of elite networks in East Asia, but does not convince me that these networks explain the regional peace. Would war have broken out in the South China Sea without the networks created under the Indonesia-led Managing Potential Conflict in the South China Sea process from 1990 onward? Would there have been open conflict in Korea if it had not been for the networks created by the Six Party Talks among China, Russia, Japan, the USA, North and South Korea 2003–07? I'm not so sure.

Rex Li, Liverpool John Moore's University, provides a constructivist explanation for the absence of military clashes in the Taiwan Strait since 1958: China and Taiwan have engaged in a discursive battle around concepts such as the One China principle, the '1992 consensus', 'two-state theory' and 'one country on each side'. This battle of words has replaced military operations as a means to advance the positions of China and Taiwan. Tension has not disappeared but has not needed to be played out militarily. Li's (2016) position is similar to Ren's. From the early 1970s, China built its national identity on reform and modernisation, resulting in a more conciliatory policy towards Taiwan. By the mid-1990s, when the PRC had achieved substantial economic success with growing military capabilities, its leaders and policy elites were determined to construct a new great power identity. Clearly, a war against Taiwan would undermine international support for China as a great power. China acknowledged this global reality when it enunciated the Peaceful Development doctrine. In Li's view, this explains why the PRC was reluctant to use military force, even during Chen Shui-bian's pro-independence presidency 2000–08.

Since 1986, the identity of Taiwan had been constructed on the basis of democracy, freedom and openness, which were conducive to gradually developing cross-strait exchanges. The military power balance, as emphasised by realist thinkers, may explain why China did not invade in 1995–96, when Taiwan held its first free presidential election. China conducted missile tests in the strait, the USA deployed aircraft carriers, and China backed down. This experience seems to support realist claims that balance of power calculations explain war and peace, but Li responds that realists cannot explain why China did not continue to intimidate Taiwan after the US carriers departed. This, in my view, is a key point. In acute crisis situations, balance of power considerations are decisive. When threats die down, softer factors come into play, such as what Li calls the ideational context of foreign policy-making. In his view, the liberal contention that economically interdependent countries are unlikely to initiate armed conflict with each other is flawed, because it fails to explain why political tension was so high in the 2000s, at a time when cross-strait trade and investments expanded dramatically. Why, asks Li, did support in Taiwan for reunification with the mainland diminish in precisely that period? Both Chinese and Taiwanese leaders have realised that a war over Taiwan would undermine their endeavour to construct a peaceful national identity, each on their side of the strait, with greater recognition by the international community. Yet these identities have come to grow further apart, preventing any solution and upholding the status quo. While I value Li's historical account of continuation and change in the Taiwan Strait, I cannot concur that identity construction explains the lack of military conflict since 1958. My impression, rather, is that the diverging national identities have not got sufficiently in harm's way to destroy a peace built on perceptions of risk. The security risk has been sufficiently high on both sides to allow win-win economic integration.

The most tangible kind of norms that have been studied in our programme as a possible driver of peace is international law. Together with Zou Keyuan of the University of Central Lancashire, UK, and Song Yann-huei of Academia Sinica, Taipei, I have looked at the possibility that the East Asian Peace has resulted from the expansion of international law, including treaties being signed, ratified and implemented by countries in the region, and integrated in their national legislation.[13] Law as an

---

13. Song Yann-Huei and Stein Tønnesson (2013); Song Yann-huei and Zou Keyuan, eds. (2014); Zou Keyuan (2012; 2014); Zou Keyuan and Stein Tønnesson (2015); Stein Tønnesson (2014; 2015a; 2016c). The role of international law in generating peace is also discussed by Shirley Scott (2017), and by Gary Goertz, Paul F. Diehl and Alexandru Balas (2016).

independent variable is often ignored in peace and security studies, and one of the most visible characteristics of our programme is that it has studied the impact of law. Some years ago, a group of Taiwanese scholars developed a Cross-Strait Peace Index and approached Zou for his ideas. He suggested that law should be included into the index as an essential variable. However, due to the difficulty of measuring legal impact and some reluctance from political scientists, nothing came out of it.

The laws we have studied in the programme cover various sectors, from regional economic integration, maritime order and environmental protection to anti-terrorism, arms control and non-proliferation. Our research shows that law has played several parallel roles in promoting and sustaining peace. It offers rules or precedents for how to solve disputes, provides institutional mechanisms for conflict resolution (such as third-party arbitration) and creates a problem-solving language that can be used by negotiators. However, new laws can also institutionalize 'winners' and 'losers', giving that status a permanence that the 'losers' seek to avoid. Hence, we were not surpised to find that the law could produce new conflict, as when the principle of a 200 nautical mile Exclusive Economic Zone was adopted at the UN Convention on the Law of the SEA (UNCLOS) 1973–82. Law can generate conflict when it is either too precise to be acceptable or too vague to provide direction. Although UNCLOS is an impressive body of law – a 'constitution for the world's oceans' – it also contains rules that some of its signatories refuse to accept in practice, and quite a few paragraphs whose vagueness allows for contradictory interpretations.

We have gone into the impact of particular treaties, such as the Charter of the United Nations with its prohibition against aggression, and the ASEAN Charter. We have in addition looked into the impact of 'soft law' such as the 2002 Declaration on the Conduct of Parties in the South China Sea. Zou Keyuan, Song Yann-huei and I agree that international law does not provide the main key to understanding why the East Asian states have not resorted to war against each other, and even less for the reduction of internal armed conflict. When states abstain from using force, it is not primarily because force is illegal; examples abound of governments finding a legal excuse for violent actions that the bulk of the international community interprets as illegal. Nonetheless, we think the law plays its main role in resolving disputes that might, if they were not resolved, give ground for new conflicts. Border disputes are a case in point. I have tried to get political scientists to understand, so far with little success, that disputes over the delimitation of the Continental Shelf and Exclusive Economic Zones cannot be resolved by force: a navy can dominate a certain part of the sea but cannot control a maritime zone by setting up border controls. Hence a navy also cannot provide security to its fishermen and immensely expensive oil rigs unless its sovereign right to the resources in the sea and under the seabed is acknowledged by other states. Such confirmation can be achieved through negotiations based on international law, but hardly by using force.

Conclusion

Changes in international alignments of power have at certain junctures created opportunities for regional peace. This was the case when the Short Peace came about in 1953–54. It was again the case in the 1970s, with the US–Chinese rapprochement and their common response to perceived threats posed by the Soviet Union. The rapprochement paved the way for a reduction of armed conflict in the 1980s. Fighting continued in Cambodia, and flared up occasionally at the Sino–Vietnamese border, as well as in the South China Sea in 1988. Then, the end of the global Cold War further stimulated East Asia's transition to peace.

The fact that an opportunity arose, however, can hardly have been the determining factor for the regional transition to peace. The local protagonists would still have enough to fight about if they dared and wanted to, and there were many grievances that rebels might seize upon. So the decisive factor behind the transition to peace in East Asia was the choices made locally by each East Asian government, as well as by rebel leaders.

The governments were motivated by their overall national priorities, and of their perception of security risk and economic risk. While risk perceptions assume a role mainly when there is tension, national priorities can have a more persistent impact. If the overall priority is economic development, then it can motivate governments to resolve conflicts, shelve disputes, show restraint or avoid open conflict in a crisis. Neither security risk nor economic risk is enough though to prevent leaders from taking actions that lead to war. The risks entailed by the use of force must first be assessed, and then deemed unacceptable. A state may feel so much threatened either from the outside or the inside – or both at the same time – that it decides to lash out, even at great risk to itself. Or, none of the parties involved in an escalating dispute may be prepared to back down, even though they understand that war is the worst outcome. The same goes for economic interdependence. Some national leaders may accept severe economic loss if they feel certain of winning a military confrontation or feel that higher values are at stake.

The likelihood that peace will be maintained, however, increases if leaders see a risk of nuclear war and their countries are at the same time integrated with each other economically: priority for economic development + mutual deterrence + economic interdependence = peace. Fortunately, this combination is likely to prevail in the most important trilateral security relationship of our time, that between China, the USA and Japan. The most fragile variable in the above equation may be the priority for development. If a government has other main concerns than the well-being of its citizens, and resents depending economically on its possible adversaries, then it may seek to reduce such dependence through protectionist or other measures. This in turn increases threat perceptions, and the equation takes a more dangerous form: priority for a non-economic goal + mutual deterrence + reduced economic interdependence = higher risk of war. If deterrence were to be the sole or dominant factor in keeping the East Asian states away from armed conflict, then the whole region might look like Korea: a precarious 'crisis stability'.

Part II

Predicting China

T he (still) rising China holds the key to the future of the East Asian Peace. Will Beijing continue to adhere to its strategy for Peaceful Development and avoid using force in its foreign relations? Can it employ economic and soft power to attract or intimidate its neighbours? Can it uphold peace with America while trying to reduce the US presence and power in the region? Most Western observers emphasize the China factor when discussing East Asia's regional security. There are intense debates about where China and Sino–US relations are heading. As leader of the East Asian Peace programme I felt a need to undertake a review of the Western-language literature about contemporary China, with the aim to evaluate the reliability of predictions made by scholars adhering to various theoretical schools. This chapter reports my findings.

The felt need for such a review has been reinforced by a number of recent developments. Since we initiated the programme in 2009–10, the situation in East Asia has become increasingly precarious, with no end to Japan's economic stagnation, a slowdown of China's economic growth, a US 'pivot' or 'rebalancing' toward Asia, a reinterpretation and possible revision of the Japanese constitution, North Korean nuclear and missile tests provoking UN sanctions and friction between Pyongyang and Beijing, a decision to deploy a Terminal High Altitude Air Defence system (THAAD) in South Korea, a number of incidents in the East China Sea and South China Sea, election of a president in Taiwan who does not hail to the One China principle, an Arbitrary Tribunal ruling under the UN Convention on the Law of the Sea (UNCLOS) strongly in favour of the Philippines, then the election of an anti-American and pro-Chinese new president in the Philippines, Chinese decision-making being increasingly centralized in the hands of a man with a 'China Dream', and – finally – the election of a businessman as US president, who promised to 'make America great again', pledged to apply protectionist measures against Chinese imports and, before moving into the White House, talked on the phone with the president of Taiwan and subsequently suggested he might abandon the One China principle if China did not accommodate his wish to change the terms of US–China trade.

The future can be conceived as dream, hope, vision, proposal, plan, expectation, warning or prediction: Xi Jinping *dreams* of a China that has regained its central position in the world; some Chinese *hope* that China will preserve the peace; Xi Jinping's predecessor Hu Jintao expressed a *vision* of a harmonious society in a harmonious world; some scholars have put forward a *proposal* for China and the United States to meet halfway and manage the world together; Xi Jingping's *plan* is for China to be moderately prosperous by 2021 and a fully modern society by 2049; quite a few scholars have expressed their *expectation* that the Chinese Communist Party will break up under the pressure from mounting opposition and internal factional struggles; others *fear* that China will become a new global hegemon, or that unless the US prevents China's further rise, it will go to war against the United States down the road; I myself lean towards *predicting* that, in spite of much tension and widespread dissatisfaction, the Chinese party state will maintain its cohesion and survive, so China can continue to change, although without either war or revolution. All of these predictions or imaginings will be discussed below, with emphasis on scholarly descriptions of likely future developments, based on various forms of data and studies of the past and present.

I first thought that it would be futile for someone who cannot read Chinese to try and analyse predictions of Chinese future. Predictions made in China would, I thought, be inherently more interesting than those produced overseas. Then I realized that Western scholarship on China is not only diverse but also highly sophisticated and based on profound knowledge of Chinese history, culture and politics. And Chinese scholars are at least as influenced by hopes, dreams and fears as the Western ones. Some relevant Chinese works have been translated into Western languages, and some have been written in English by Chinese scholars. We have texts from President Xi Jinping's hand about his China Dream, emphasizing the rejuvenation of the Chinese nation as it overcomes completely its century of humiliation, continues its

Peaceful Development, wins equal status with the USA in a New Type of Great Power Relations, becomes a moderately prosperous country by 2021 and a fully developed modern nation by 2049 (Xi 2014). There is Colonel Liu Mingfu's *The China Dream* (2015), which goes further in setting out a vision of China becoming the world's most powerful state. There are English language books discussing Chinese expectations of the future. One is Mark Leonard's *What Does China Think?* (2008), based on interviews with Chinese intellectuals and revealing a diversity of views. Leonard, who is co-founder and director of the European Council on Foreign Relations (a pan-European think-tank), met an anti-capitalist looking for an alternative modernity, an environmentalist engaged in fighting the destructiveness of China's rampant capitalism, a liberal experimenting with grassroots democracy, a conservative thinker arguing in favour of a centralized, meritocratic state, a realist international relations scholar heaping scorn on the People's Liberation Army for being so bureaucratic that it cannot fight, an influential constructivist scholar advocating Sino–Japanese rapprochement within a vision of East Asian regional cooperation, and a high-ranking military officer who talks about how to develop a strategy of asymmetric warfare against the United States, since China cannot expect to match US firepower.

More recently I read William A. Callahan's wonderful *China Dreams: 20 Visions of the Future* (2013), which synthesizes the works of twenty Chinese thinkers. Callahan shows that the slogan of the 2008 Beijing Olympics, 'One World One Dream', is misleading. There are many parallel or overlapping China dreams, sometimes supplementing, sometimes contradicting each other. China has many possible futures.

In 2014, our Core Group invited Håvard Hegre, Peter Wallensteen's successor as Dag Hammarsköld Professor at Uppsala University, to give a talk about how to predict the future of peace and conflict in the world. Together with some of his colleagues, he had developed a predictive model for changes in global and regional incidences of armed conflict in the period 2010–50. The predictions are based on statistical data from the 1970–2009 period, as well as various forecasts. He predicts peace in and between countries that have a history of peace, have been independent for a long time, have a large population and low infant mortality rate, are demographically homogenous, are relatively prosperous, have effective education programmes, do not depend on oil exports, do not have severe ethnic cleavages, and are situated in a neighbourhood with few internal armed conflicts. Hegre and his group tested the model by predicting conflict in the 2007–09 period, based on data for the 1970–2000 period, and found that the model was highly accurate. Their resultant article predicted that the ongoing decline in the share of the world's countries that experience active armed conflict will continue, going down from 15 per cent in 2009 to just seven per cent in 2050. The decline will be particularly strong in the Middle East, while the remaining conflict countries will be concentrated in Africa and South *and East Asia*.

Such predictions are of course uncertain, and developments since Hegre and his co-authors published their finding in 2013 do not yet reveal any decrease in the number of Middle Eastern countries with armed conflict, or any increase in East Asian ones. The Middle East has instead seen conflicts spread and intensify, while East Asia remains peaceful in spite of much tension. Although conflict incidence reflects decisions made by a few individuals, whose priorities and perceptions are hard to include in a statistical model, I am not the kind of historian who heaps scorn on the predictive ambition of political scientists by citing the aphorism, 'it is difficult to predict, particularly about the future'. My hunch is that predictions of the kind developed by Hegre et al. will become more accurate and useful as their data become more and more nuanced. Conflict predictions may now be at a stage where weather forecasting was a hundred years ago. Yet the weather is mostly a natural phenomenon, unaffected by human decisions, while human agency is at the core of any process leading to war. At the individual level, humans sometimes act in unpredictable ways; when that human is a national decision maker, it can have enormous implications. Prediction models are generally better at predicting continuity or transformative trends than abrupt changes, since the latter just happen occasionally. A big problem is to find ways of predicting the behaviour of individual great powers like the USA and China, which may greatly affect the prospects of world peace. Great power rivalries and wars do not just affect international relations, but lead to massive amounts of internal armed conflict as well. Thus the Second World War triggered or expanded upon hugely destructive armed conflicts within countries such as Ukraine, Yugoslavia, Greece, Myanmar and China; the Cold War was not cold but a direct contributor to hot war and massacres in the Koreas, Indonesia, Vietnam, Laos, Cambodia, Afghanistan, Angola, Mozambique, Eritrea, and elsewhere.

If a predictive model for the next 40–50 years shall be useful, it must include the likelihood and probable effects of an internal collapse of the Chinese party-state and/or a war or rivalry (cold war) between China and the United States. After hearing Håvard Hegre disclose that his computerized model has predicted conflicts in China that have not yet materialized, I decided that it might be useful to consult the voluminous Western-language literature about contemporary China; how do the various theoretical schools gauge the likelihood that China will either collapse or go to war – or both?

My review yields three insights. First, all the four most relevant scenarios have been predicted by someone: continued peaceful rise on Western terms (Pax Americana); peaceful rise on Chinese terms (Pax Sinica); collapse of the Chinese state; and rivalry or war between China and the USA (Figures 5 and 6, overleaf). Second, I found no systematic difference in the predictions of scholars belonging to the realist, political economy, constructivist, foreign policy analysis, or liberal theoretical schools. Internal disagreements are as vigorous as debates with proponents of the other theoretical approaches. While general theory has implications for the choice of premises, it seems to have little effect on the conclusions. Third, I found that scholarly predictions tend to fluctuate with contemporary developments in China and the world. As can be seen from Figures 5 and 6, the tendency in the 2000s was to move away from predicting war or collapse, and hypothesize instead that China would continue its peaceful rise and establish a Pax Sinica. However, in the 2010s, after the financial crisis had hit the West and China had become more assertive externally and more authoritarian internally, more analysts predicted the collapse or atrophy of the communist regime, and a continuation of the Pax Americana.

I shall expound on these findings by examining predictions made in the most respected Western publications, and conclude with a discussion of whether or not it makes sense to let predictions be informed by the most recent developments. The authorship I have found most exciting in this context is that of David Shambaugh, George Washington University, Washington, DC, who has followed China's developments

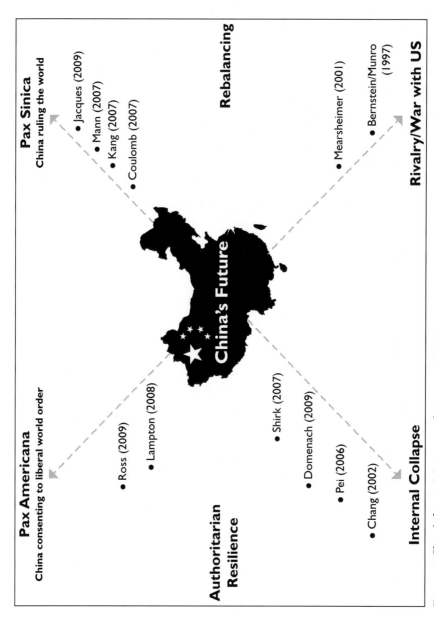

Figure 5: China's future: Western predictions until 2010

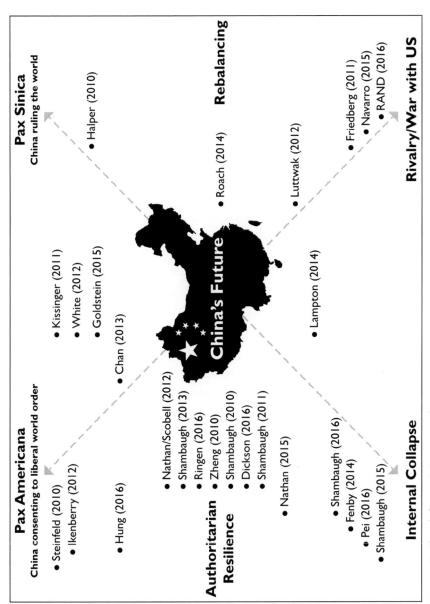

Figure 6: China's future: Western predictions since 2010

closely since he first visited the country in 1979, just after China had withdrawn its troops from Vietnam. There are two reasons why Shambaugh's writings are of particular interest: his predictions are more explicit and less cautious than others, and he has not stuck to one opinion, but rather changed his view like a weathercock. This is not meant as criticism. The fate of the East Asian Peace may well be determined by shifting winds.

Collapse of the Chinese state and war between China and the United States are two of the world's worst nightmares. The former would spell disaster for the global economy, and could provoke armed conflict both in China itself and in its neighbourhood. A Sino–US war could lead to a nuclear Armageddon. In the early 2000s, China sought to dispel such possibilities by assuring itself and the world that it aimed only for a Peaceful Rise or Peaceful Development, and had drawn the appropriate lessons from the failures of earlier rising powers, such as Imperial Germany before the First World War, Imperial Japan before the Second World War, and the Soviet Union in the Cold War. The price China had to pay for its development was to operate on Western terms, at least temporarily. China adapted itself to the global liberal order, produced goods for Western markets, attracted foreign investments, signed and ratified international treaties, joined the World Trade Organization (WTO), used its UN veto power sparingly, and placed savings in US treasury bonds – all the while retaining its own characteristics with its own political system.

Coming War

An early warning against China's aggressive intentions was made in Richard Bernstein and Ross H. Munro's book, *The Coming Conflict With China* (1997), which ends with a war game. It describes a dissatisfied and ambitious China aiming to dominate Asia. Beijing's strategy is to first gain sovereignty and control over Taiwan, then expand its military presence and take control of the South China Sea, and subsequently induce a withdrawal of all US forces from Asia – with the possible exception of a defensive force in Japan, since it may help prevent Japan's re-emergence as an independent military power. The final stage in Beijing's alleged strategy was to keep Japan in a state of permanent strategic subordination. The book is based on purely military thinking and does not take China's economic integration with Japan and the United States into account. In spite of the book's title, the authors do not exactly predict war. Instead they warn against it in order to persuade Americans to strengthen Japan and keep China in its place. Bernstein and Munro's book is an uncomfortable cousin of the realist scholarly tradition, since its focus is on intentions more than capabilities.

Most other contributions within the 'coming war' genre have been even more speculative or prescriptive than Ross and Munro (1997). They have generally aimed to warn US public opinion against the 'China threat' and urge the US government to adopt measures to stop China's economic rise, and build more military strength. This includes three books by the economist Peter Navarro (2008; 2011; 2015). In his latest book, *Crouching Tiger* (2015), Navarro paints a picture of an expansionist China that will continue to expand as long as it is not met with a strong response. Peace can only be achieved through strength. In his prescriptions, Navarro takes up the Chinese concept of 'comprehensive national power,' and calls for implementation of a comprehensive counter-strategy, with a mixture of economic warfare and military preparations, aimed at stopping the growth of China's power. 'No sensible speculator would want to put big money on China's peaceful rise over the next several decades,' he says (2015: e-book loc. 232). He finds war with China 'likely indeed' (loc. 256). The course of history 'at this point appears grimly and inexorably headed for conflict – and perhaps even a nuclear cliff' (loc. 211). Even though Navarro is an economist, he holds that 'while a nation's military strength may be only one element of national power, it will always be *the* most important element when the wolf – or dragon – is at the door' (loc. 3612). Yet the immediate remedy for reducing China's power is to stop its economic growth: 'Reducing the dependence of America and its allies on "Made in China" products would seem to be an obvious policy step to improve both US national security as well as the prospects for peace in Asia' (loc. 3648). This is desirable in spite of the fact that it will have an inflationary effect in the USA, deprive the population of cheap Chinese products, and thus hit 'the poorest segments of American society disproportionately hard' (loc. 3663). American consumers have been 'helping to finance a Chinese military buildup that may well mean to do us and our countries harm' (loc. 3671).

On the basis of a simplistic analysis, where an expansionist China has been playing on divisions in the American society to gain access to markets, investments and technology so it can grow its economy and build military strength and thus challenge the US and its allies, Navarro calls for implementing a counter-strategy where the aim is not primarily to save American jobs but to maintain the position of the US as the dominant global power. His counter-strategy includes heavy military elements, notably the maintenance of overwhelming force projected by US aircraft-carrier strike groups, a small number of forward bases, a space-based system that provides battlefield awareness and control (loc. 3741), the strengthening of US military alliances, and also more classic means of struggle, such as the mining of China's ports and a possible oil embargo. He also evokes the idea of establishing a 'China Policy Czar' within the upper echelons of the American government, 'somebody in charge who looks at both the economic and national security implications of the US–China relationship and recognizes that they are inextricably intertwined' (loc. 3687). Navarro's books, which were mostly ignored by China scholars when they came out, since they did not hold much scholarly quality, suddenly gained much attention in December 2016 when president-elect Donald Trump seemed to take up Navarro's idea of establishing a Sino–US relations czar by appointing Navarro himself to head his new National Trade Council. This suddenly transformed the 67-year-old economy professor from a marginal voice in the wilderness to someone who may impose his views on US policy and thus greatly increase the risk of a Sino–US clash.

In 2016, well before the election of Donald Trump as US president, and his appointment of Navarro, RAND Corporation published a detailed academic scenario study, commissioned by the US Undersecretary of the Army, of a possible war between China and the USA in either 2015 or 2025 (Gombert et al. 2016). This kind of study is rarely made accessible in the public domain (the authors call this a 'gaping omission;' p. 1). The Pentagon does of course have war plans. It also plays war games. Rarely, however, are detailed studies of a future war publicized. Then again, other branches of the US government seem to have been unhappy with the Army's decision to sponsor the study. The authors say one of their aims is to provoke discussions in China, so the Chinese can realize how costly a war with the USA would be for them (p. x). One should think the Chinese already know, and that the publication of this study might rather strengthen their determination to prepare themselves for winning the coming war with America.

The RAND study presents the following arguments:

- The Sino–US war will not be a world war. Although Japan is likely to take part on the US side, the war is unlikely to spread to other parts of the world, despite temptations for Russia and other countries to utilize the temporary inability of the USA to intervene in their region to pressurize such neighbouring states as Ukraine or even the Baltic states.

- The war will not lead to a nuclear exchange (pp. 29–30). Mutual deterrence will continue to work during the war. The United States will be careful not to target China's strategic missile launch sites, and will ensure that war fighting proceeds in a way that does not represent an existential threat to China as a nation or to its communist regime (p. 31).

- The United States will make sure that the war does not become a land war. No American troops will be deployed on Chinese territory. The war will be fought at sea, in the air, in space and cyberspace (p. ix).

- The side that orders the first massive strike will benefit from a significant advantage since it will be able to destroy a huge amount of its adversary's weapons platforms (bases, ships and submarines, missile launch sites, airports, ports, submarines, etc.) before they can be utilized.

- The war is not likely to be short: it may well last more than a year. This is because both sides will concentrate on destroying each other's weapons platforms. The Obama administration pledged to keep 60 per cent of the US naval strength deployed in the Pacific. If that pledge is upheld, then the US weaponry will be superior to China's already in the opening phase of a war, yet not sufficient to force China to its knees (pp. 20–3). In 2025 the US superiority will have been further reduced but by then Japan may be ready to play a more prominent part, and thus compensate for the reduced US superiority (pp. 58, 64–5). After the initial exchange, which regardless of who strikes first will involve the destruction of substantial parts of China's capabilities while leaving many US weapons platforms intact, the USA will need to bring in additional weapons platforms from elsewhere in the world in order to overcome China's will to resist (thus eliminating at least temporarily the US capability to fight wars elsewhere). Only when the USA brings in its overwhelming force will China be ready to sue for peace.

- The military losses to both sides will be enormous, and will include one or more US aircraft carriers (pp. 36, 39).

- The economic losses will also be enormous and much greater for China than for the USA since the latter will lose only its bilateral trade with China while China will lose most of its regional and global trade.

- Because of the huge losses to be expected on both sides, war is 'improbable' (pp. xv, 70). The two sides will understand the need to continue communicating with each other at times of acute crisis in order to prevent a military confrontation.

While I find some comfort in the last of these arguments, I am not in the least convinced by what the study says about the low risk of a world war or nuclear exchange. If the USA avoids targeting China's strategic missile sites, then the Pentagon will need to worry constantly that Beijing might decide, instead of suing for peace, to launch its strategic missiles. And then the US president will keep his hand close to the button. Most war games have shown that if the United States strikes first, it can destroy all of China's nuclear weapons before Beijing has a chance to respond.

I am also not convinced that the United States could attain its goals without taking a war onto the Chinese landmass. The RAND study concedes that this might be difficult if the war starts in the Korean peninsula, with China and the United States entering an inter-Korean war on opposite sides (p. 72). I assume that in any case China would try its best to pull the USA into a confrontation on Chinese territory through asymmetric warfare, such as cyber attacks or terrorist attacks against targets in the US homeland. These would make it difficult for Washington to avoid the temptation to retaliate against the source of the attacks, and it might not then be sufficient to use drones, missiles or air raids, cf. Afghanistan and Iraq. RAND may also underrate China's willingness to continue the fight from a position of great inferiority.[1] The Chinese remember how they remained in the war with Japan for eight years from 1937 to 1945 although they lost virtually every battle. In a coming war, if China were to lose as many people as the whole US population (320 million), it would still have more than a billion citizens left. The extent to which a 21st century Chinese government would be willing to sacrifice its citizens in the face of an existential threat is unclear. I cannot but think of that day in early June 1938 when Generalissimo Chiang Kai-shek decided to blow up the Yellow River dikes in order to inundate areas the Japanese army would have to pass through in order to approach China's wartime capital Chongqing. Chiang could not but know that the floods would cost hundreds of thousands of Chinese lives, yet never seems to have regretted this sacrifice for the purpose of staying in the war.[2] While Americans today know nothing but modernity, the Chinese could survive without it. RAND's reasoning also reminds me of the thinking that came out of the Pentagon computers at the time when Robert McNamara was US Secretary of Defense: they showed consistently that the USA was winning the war in Vietnam. The most likely outcome of a US–China war, as I see it – provided it does not trigger a nuclear exchange – would be that the USA declared victory while the Chinese continued to fight with any means at their disposal.

Realist Predictions

A classic work within the offensive realism school is John Mearsheimer's *The Tragedy of Great Power Politics*, from 2001. It disregards intentions as irrelevant since states can never trust that their strategic rivals will stick to their current attitude. States must plan for the eventuality that a possible adversary will use its capabilities. The problem, in Mearsheimer's realist view, is not Chinese or US intentions, but the relative distribution of power. In an anarchic international society, states seek to defend and maximise their power. War can be avoided either through a balance of power or through hegemony. If a new power rises to the extent that it is

---

1. The RAND study (Gombert et al. 2016: 65) touches on this possibility.
2. Chiang Kai-shek's government later estimated that 800,000 people had died because of the floods, but some historians have suggested that the real number was lower, perhaps as low as 500,000, while others have said it might have reached 900,000 (Taylor 2009: 154–155; Paine 2012: 139–140; Mitter 2013: 159–164).

capable of challenging a hegemon, then conflict will ensue, regardless of intentions. Today's East Asia is characterized by a multipolar power balance among China, Russia and the USA – with Japan as a potential fourth player. The European Union and its member states cannot be included as parts of any East Asian power balance today. The days are gone when France and Great Britain played a security role in the region, and the EU, with its weakly developed common foreign and security policy, is mainly a market and a player in economic diplomacy. As such I think it should be seen as a force for peace; all Asian countries can deal with the EU without facing the slightest security risk.

According to Mearsheimer, the regional balance between the US–Japan alliance and the China–Russia strategic partnership remains as long as neither the USA nor China has a realistic possibility to become a regional hegemon. If the Chinese economy should become bigger than Japan's (this happened in 2010, and in 2015 it was two-and-a half times as big as Japan's), then China would seek regional hegemony and develop a strategy to compromise US power in the region. However, if China should become a regional hegemon, then the USA would have to calculate with the possibility that China would further increase its power, and challenge the USA as the global hegemon. The United States would then be compelled to abandon its accommodating policy vis-à-vis China and put brakes on China's growth.

Unlike Bernstein and Munro, Mearsheimer does not assume that a conflict would be initiated by the rising power. The initiative could just as well come from the incumbent global hegemon, whose power is being challenged. As of 2001, China was still far away from the point where it had enough latent power to make a run at regional hegemony. So it was not too late for the United States, said Mearsheimer, to reverse course and do what it could to slow the rise of China: 'In fact, the structural imperatives of the international system, which are powerful, will probably force the United States to abandon its policy of constructive engagement in the near future' (Mearsheimer 2001:402). As of now, fifteen years later, this has not yet happened, although the Chinese GDP is set to bypass the USA in the next decade. In 2003, however, when Mearsheimer's book appeared in Chinese translation, it became very popular. It confirmed what many Chinese thought about Americans: their talk about ideals and norms is hot air. What counts for the United

States when time comes to shove, is power. And in 2016, when the Americans elected Donald Trump as president, and he – already before entering the White House – created doubts about China's One China principle, many Chinese felt that the 'Mearsheimer moment' was approaching. Trump's selection of General James Mattis to head the Pentagon has not dissipated that feeling, although many say that he will be a voice of caution. Mattis has direct and fresh experience as a commander of combats in Afghanistan and Iraq and enjoys much respect at the Pentagon, so would be a valuable asset for the Trump administration in case of a war with China.

Aaron Friedberg of Princeton University is less of an offensive and more of a defensive realist than John Mearsheimer. Friedberg tried during the Obama administration to get US decision makers to avoid the coming of the Mearsheimer moment by adopting a tougher, more cool-headed approach to China. Friedberg considers not only capabilities but also ideology. Hence, he is less rigorous than Mearsheimer in adhering to realist thinking, but he is similarly concerned by China's increasing military capabilities and worried when writing his book that the USA did not take sufficient account of the threat from China. Although Friedberg travels a somewhat different road, he arrives at a similar conclusion to Mearsheimer's. The ongoing shift of power from the USA to China, in combination with fundamental ideological contradictions between the two countries, may overwhelm the mitigating effects of economic interdependence and nuclear deterrence on Sino–US relations, and increase the risk of war. If China were to democratise, there would be less cause to worry, but as long as this does not happen, the USA should replace its policy of constructive engagement with a policy that combines engagement with containment. Friedberg (2011: 278–9) calls this 'congagement'. The USA cannot rely on either economic interdependence or nuclear deterrence for its security, he claims, but must focus on improving its conventional forces, and maintain command of the world's oceans. This is Friedberg's key to maintaining peace and stability.

Robert S. Ross represents the realist school in our East Asian Peace programme. A number of his analyses were assembled in the anthology *China's Security Policy* (2009a). He has published an article about naval strategy in *International Security* (2009b) and written a chapter for our

2017 edited volume, *Debating the East Asian Peace*. Ross has more confidence in continued peace than Mearsheimer and Friedberg. He claims there has been a power balance in the Western Pacific between China as a continental power and the USA as a maritime power. The balance has been reinforced by a system of US alliances with insular and peninsular states facing the Chinese mainland: Japan, South Korea, Taiwan, the Philippines, and Singapore. The power balance in East Asia has kept peace in the region since the 1980s. What could threaten it, says Ross, would be if China were to challenge US maritime power. What worries Ross is not China's assertiveness in the South China or East China Seas. It is rational for China to build power projection capabilities in the seas along its coast, and deny access for foreign navies. What is worrisome is that China is developing a large and increasingly modern navy. This challenges US naval power in the Pacific and will compel the United States to respond. As China develops a large and high-technology navy, military competition will increase. Yet such competition is also not inherently unmanageable. The impact of US–China maritime conflict can be contained: 'Optimal U.S. management of China's rising power nationalism will require policies that facilitate ongoing cooperation amid growing naval competition' (Ross 2009: 80–1).

Until recently, Ross relied for his basic optimism on the power projection capabilities of the US aircraft carriers, which he doubted China would be able to match. He argued that it would be irrational for China to build aircraft carriers, since this would be bound to produce a US reaction. Two American security experts, Michael Glosny and Philip Saunders (2010: 180) disagreed. A Chinese decision to build aircraft carriers, they said, reflects a reasonable evaluation of new threats to China's security interests. Since the Chinese mainland is not at present under threat, and China is integrated in the global market, the threats against it have moved from land to sea. China has interests to defend far away from its coast. The current aim of the Chinese Navy is not to challenge US sea-based power but to have a limited power projection capability that makes it possible to defend China's regional interests in contingencies that do not involve the United States, protect its expanding overseas interests, perform non-traditional missions, conduct military diplomacy, and increase China's prestige. China's carriers can be used to defend shipping lanes against threats from Japan, India or pirates, and dissuade neighbour states from extracting resources from maritime zones that China disputes. If Glosny and Saunders are right, then China will most likely avoid challenging US power in the High Seas, and use its navy mainly in contests with small and medium size powers. While this may at first sight seem reassuring, there is always a risk that the US Navy chooses to interfere in these contests, and this might lead to a direct China–USA war that neither side wanted. More recently, moreover, Ross (2017) has become more worried that China's naval modernisation programme may unravel the regional power balance, not just by including the construction of aircraft carriers, but through a general build-up of naval strength.

Andrew J. Nathan (Columbia University) and Andrew Scobell (RAND Corporation) are emblematic 'defensive realists'. Their 2012 book, *China's Search for Security*, offers a corrective to Mearsheimer's offensive realism. Where Mearsheimer (2001: 160–2) foresees 'an intense security competition between China and its rivals, with the ever present danger of great power war hanging over them' if China continues its relative economic rise, Nathan and Scobell think China's rise is 'manageable'. Factual interests drive a country's foreign policy, although the causal path from interest to policy may be distorted by misinformation, miscalculation, value commitments, institutional weaknesses or leadership shortcomings. The main driver of China's foreign policy, they say, is its search for security. Beijing wants security, not global power. When Beijing says it wants 'peace' it really means a 'stability' that allows it to 'concentrate on economic development' (p. 28). The most likely future scenario is a 'new equilibrium' that meets the interests of the USA and its allies 'without damaging China's security' (p. 346). China will remain a 'status quo power in a system designed by the West' (p. 357), although future Chinese leaders may challenge US pre-eminence if Washington does not keep up the economic foundation for US power. The main factor that could unravel the global system keeping China in place would be US decline.

The authors see three possible scenarios for China's internal development. The first and most likely is that it becomes 'an enormous Singapore', dominated by a more institutionalised Communist Party. The second is democratisation from above, as happened in Taiwan. China's national interests would then remain the same, but a more influential public would demand more assertive policies. The United States might find it more difficult to 'draw the line' vis-à-vis a democratic than an authoritarian China. Democratisation could moreover lead to a third scenario: internal turmoil and military interference in national politics (as in Thailand). This would weaken China, making it less predictable and possibly more aggressive. However, Nathan and Scobell see US decline as the main risk to East Asia's stability. If 'the West weakens itself to the point of creating a power vacuum', (p. xi) the risk of war would increase. China would acquire bases around the world and replace the dollar with the renminbi in its foreign trade. The United States would then have to decide whether, when and how to resist, which could in turn lead to war. Yet as long as the USA 'holds tight to its values and solves its problems at home, it will be able to manage the rise of China' (p. 359). The preconditions for peace are thus that the USA maintains its strength and pursues a cautious foreign policy. China is in that case likely to act rationally on the basis of its search for security.

Instead of making strong predictions, Nathan and Scobell use scenarios and contingent causal reasoning: Since US power is the main precondition for regional stability, and since China is unlikely to increase its relative power sufficiently to challenge the United States – unless US power declines, peace is likely to continue. Developments in China, whether following one or the other scenario, will in that case not threaten international peace. More recently, however, Nathan (2015) has expressed concern that Xi Jinping may be 'destabilizing China by concentrating so much power in his own hands … As he departs from Deng Xiaoping's path, he risks undermining the regime's adaptability and resilience'. Yet, the election of Donald Trump as US president, and his nomination of 'China hawks' to influential positions in his administration did not completely unravel Nathan's cautious optimism. In a statement to the press, Nathan (2015) said, 'Trump had shown two sides to his personality in dealing with everybody. One is: "Let's make a deal, we are deal-makers." And the other one is: "You hurt my feelings and I'm going to bomb the shit out of you because I never lose – I always win".' Nathan said he could not know whether Trump is 'setting up China for a deal,' but he thought 'Beijing would still be banking on its ability to win over the tycoon … I think predominantly they understand Trump as a businessman – and that, for them is a glimmer of hope.'

In *The China Choice* from 2012, Australian realist Hugh White doubts that China will be satisfied if the USA maintains its current approach. He thinks China has a legitimate claim to a larger security role in its home region and proposes that the USA give up its dominant security role in East Asia. He criticizes Obama's November 2011 'pivot to Asia' declaration in Canberra, and concludes his book with an imagined speech by a future US president, who explains to her fellow citizens the need to share power with China. In stark contrast to Nathan and Scobell, White holds that if the USA tries to hold on to its primacy, a rivalry will ensue that ultimately leads to war. To prevent this, the United States should decide to share power with China, Japan and India in a 'concert of powers' (pp. 25–6).

What makes White's book interesting is not so much his proposal as his argument: the USA has allowed China to grow so vital to the world economy that there is no way to lock it out again at any acceptable cost. For this reason, he predicts, US primacy will end and this will lead East Asia to be 'divided into competing camps in a classic balance-of-power system, punctuated by serious wars'. Strategic containment would cause a huge economic backlash, increasing the already 'significant danger' of war between the USA and China. Washington has three options: resist, pull out, or share power (pp. 98–9). While sharing power means to give up primacy, it does not mean withdrawal. The United States can allow China a greater role while 'maintaining a strong presence of its own' (p. 5). At sea, this means giving up control while retaining a capacity to deny control to others. Since 1945, the US Navy has controlled the seas around China. This cannot continue. China's deployment of land-based missiles and its naval build-up are creating a 'sea-denial era' (p. 72). Naval powers will be able to sink each others' ships but cannot protect their own. Aircraft carriers can no longer project power because they have to focus on threats to themselves. This will reduce the credibility of US power, so White expects Japan to take responsibility for its own defence, build nuclear weapons and adopt an independent foreign policy. India will also have its say, while Russia remains too preoccupied in Europe (pp. 86–8). The United States will maintain a great power role, but will no longer dominate the region.

White's proposal is probably a non-starter in US politics, unless Donald Trump the 'deal-maker' should change a basic US principle. To accept 'spheres of influence' runs against the essence of Washington's global policy. US representatives have completely and consistently dismissed any Chinese suggestion that the Pacific could be divided in a Western and Eastern sphere or that they could share power in the Pacific. As a high-level US delegation made clear when visiting Beijing to defuse the Sino–Japanese Senkaku crisis in 2012, the USA has no intention of pulling back from its role as the dominant military power in the Western Pacific. Yet power sharing could develop organically as a practical consequence of US budgetary constraints, the continued rise of China's economic and military power, improved ties between China and its neighbours, or perhaps a 'grand bargain' between China and the USA. Indeed Obama's 'pivot to Asia', which was more about redistributing and concentrating US forces than expanding them, may have been the first stage in a gradual strategic concentration of US forces in Guam, Diego Garcia, Darwin and Singapore rather than in more exposed places such as Seoul, Okinawa, and the Philippines. Kissinger's (2011: 5) concept of 'co-evolution' is probably more realistic than White's 'power sharing'. The United States will hardly choose to give up its primacy, but may be compelled to let it happen.

This is where Lyle Goldstein's important book from 2015, *Meeting China Halfway*, comes in, although it is not a work within the realist tradition. It does not declare allegiance to any particular foreign policy school, but builds on the assumption that wise leaders can carry out wise policies if they understand what is at stake and have enough political will.

Goldstein declares himself in almost total agreement with White. He warns that the danger of war will be acute unless the USA accommodates China's security interests, and he worries particularly about the situation in the South China Sea, where he sees great risk that an incident may get out of hand and lead to a direct confrontation between Chinese and US forces. Goldstein's proposals are more politically realistic than White's. What makes *Meet China Halfway* so valuable is its proposals for a number of relatively small but significant steps that the USA and China can take in order to improve their relationship. Instead of delving too much into the danger of vicious spirals, he suggests the creation of what he calls 'cooperation spirals'. Each of his chapters, whether dealing with history, Taiwan, Korea, economy, climate change, Japan, the South China Sea, or India, is endowed with such a constructive 'cooperation spiral', and the first step in each spiral is always made by the United States. Each first step is also relatively easy, although it carries considerable symbolic significance. Goldstein does not propose a sudden US withdrawal or a big bargain, indeed not necessarily a negotiated agreement at all, only reassuring steps from either side that make the other ready to respond with a step of its own. The cooperation spirals are graphically illustrated and seem ideally suited for being discussed in a constructive unofficial dialogue between American and Chinese opinion leaders. Although some of the steps higher up on the spiral may seem undigestible today, they might become more palatable once the two powers reach that point in the mutually reassuring process. Many of the US steps consist of withdrawing troops and military installations from areas where they might be seen as provocative or threatening by China and are vulnerable to Chinese attacks. Many of China's steps consist of reassuring its neighbours, i.e., by acknowledging their legitimate maritime boundary claims.

Yet events since 2009 are not consistent with the strategic prescriptions from Kissinger, White or Goldstein. Instead of being improved through cooperation spirals, the security of the region has spiralled downwards – although not yet to any military clash. As we have seen, within the realist tradition, there are widely different predictions and recommendations, ranging from John Mearsheimer and Aaron Friedberg's warnings of an inevitable rivalry over Hugh White's proposal for a power sharing deal, to the confident optimism of Andrew Nathan and Andrew Scobell, who think the USA will keep its supremacy, as long as it does not let its economy decline. As for Robert S. Ross, he was relatively sanguine a few years ago but has become more pessimistic.

When reading White and Goldstein, I asked myself: what can Beijing do to facilitate a gradual US withdrawal, which would of course be beneficial from China's point of view. A two-pronged strategy, which nests well into Goldstein's proposals, might be effective: first, acquire the capability to deny access for the US navy to waters near China, while avoiding actions that provoke US military reactions; second: establish various forms of maritime cooperation with the neighbour states while preparing to resolve boundary disputes on the basis of international law. The neighbours would then be dissuaded from inviting US balancing. As White and Goldstein both recognise, China's assertiveness since

2009 – even aspects that were in reaction to moves by other states – has resulted in a strategic backlash against China, of which the Arbitral Tribunal's 2016 award in the Philippines versus China case is just one expression. There has been a demand from inside the region for the USA to affirm and surely not reduce its military presence. The fact that some Southeast Asian states that do not have any territorial dispute with China, like Cambodia, Timor-Leste and Thailand, have chosen a more pro-Chinese line, gives little ground for comfort. However, Vietnam's caution since 2015 and Philippine President Duterte's active wooing of China in 2016 may have given China more faith in its ability to carry out a successful 'good neighbour policy', anchored in aid, trade and investments. From a perspective of grand strategy, it is not in China's interest to split ASEAN. It would be much better for China, in its competition with the USA, to have a cohesive, cooperative ASEAN.

Political Economy Predictions

Authors writing in the Weberian and Marxist sociological tradition also cover the whole spectrum of predictions. In 2009, Martin Jacques, the former editor of *Marxism Today*, the theoretical mouthpiece of the British Communist Party, published the bestseller *When China Rules the World*. He is fascinated by China's challenge to the US-dominated order. China's economy will, he says, surpass the USA in terms of GDP in 2027, and have an economy twice as big as the US in 2050. This will not just allow China to dominate the world economically, but also culturally and politically. In the past, countries such as Singapore, Malaysia, Thailand and South Korea had to Westernise in order to reach modernity. This will not be the case for China, just as it has not been the case for Japan. Japan has its own modernity. Modernisation is not the same as Westernisation: 'My central argument is very simple. Western modernity is not eternal and it is not a universal model ... The West has thought itself to be universal, the unquestioned model and example for all to follow; in the future it will be only one of several possibilities' (Jacques 2009: 144; see also Moody 2009). Just as much as Westerners criticize China for its lack of representative democracy, the Chinese despise the West for its lack of morality. The Western state system founded at the peace of Westphalia in 1648 will be replaced by a Chinese world order, based on tributary relationships in a hierarchical system. The renminbi will challenge the role of the US dollar and the Euro as a global reserve currency. Beijing will become the world's leading capital, and Chinese will replace English as the language of international communication in East Asia. Jacques finished writing his book just as the USA and Europe were hit by the 2008 financial crisis, so he could add as a concluding bravado: 'China's rise will be hastened by the global crisis' (p. 579). Although Jacques' book is full of hyperbole and loosely founded predictions, it deserves praise for having provoked a range of heated debates.

One of the most interesting responses is a coherent and persuasive analysis within the tradition of historical sociology by Hung Ho-fung of Johns Hopkins University: *The China Boom: Why China Will Not Rule the World*. Hung, who grew up in Hong Kong, takes a long historical perspective, doing away with some key myths about China's economic development as he proceeds. China is not as different from the West as Jacques would have it. Its economy was comparable to the British until the turn of the 19th century, but failed to develop an industrial capitalist economy due to the lack of an entrepreneurial class. In the 19th and 20th centuries, the Qing dynasty, the Kuomintang (KMT) and the People's Republic of China (PRC) all tried to replicate the experiences of Germany, Japan, Russia and the Soviet Union: accumulate capital in the hands of the state in order to invest in industrialisation, that is, become developmental states. The Qing dynasty and the KMT failed due to internal turmoil and external intervention, but the PRC succeeded fairly well under Mao, so Deng Xiaoping had something to build upon when he unleashed market economic reforms and integrated China into the global neoliberal order. Hung sees more continuity from Mao to Deng than most historians do. In the period 1979–2008, China had a long boom, and helped the United States to maintain its global dominance by countering the Soviet Union, buying US bonds and taking part in institutions that are central to the US-led world order, such as the International Monetary Fund, the World Bank and the World Trade Organization. China does not challenge the US-dominated order; it depends on it. Beijing does not want to change it, just enhance its own power within it. In 2014, China's economic growth slowed down. The official rate dipped down to 7.2 per cent that year, to 6.9 in 2015, and seemed to end up at 6.7 in 2016. China faces the daunting task of restructuring its economy so it can depend less on exports and more on internal consumption. This will not only reduce its trade surplus, and require a total renovation of its debt-ridden financial sector, but will also require a massive transfer of capital from the state and state-owned enterprises (SOEs) to ordinary Chinese households. Such changes can be expected to meet with resistance from vested interests in the public sector and also from export-oriented private or semi-private companies that depend on cheap loans, public investments and favourable terms of foreign trade. During its period of structural reform, China will have much less growth than it is used to. Hung is sceptical about the ability of China's existing political institutions to survive this needed economic structural transformation. The government may further improve upon its ability to repress protests and opposition, but eventually this will no longer be effective:

> ... there might be an uncontained explosion of social unrest that presents a serious challenge to the authoritarian state. The chaos that this unrest might engender would further repress economic growth, creating a downward spiral of deepening economic crisis, worsening social unrest, and possibly even war if the party-state elite were to try to divert popular anger to aggressive nationalism. (Hung 2016: 177–8)

On the other hand, economic slowdown and multiple crises might also get China to restart its long-suspended political liberalization, which would foster more inclusive political processes. Political liberalization, 'if it unfolds smoothly', would enable the Chinese state and society to weather a slowing economy in a more stable manner. If China can accomplish its economic rebalancing, 'its robust capitalist development will continue for a long time'. While this will not allow China to rule the world, it could 'join the United States, Japan, and Germany as yet another major capitalist power' (Hung 2016: 180).

It is difficult to imagine more divergent predictions than those of the Marxist Jacques and the Marx-inspired sociologist Hung. Where the former thinks China represents a fundamental challenge to the US-dominated world order, the latter claims that China has joined that same order and become its biggest beneficiary. Thus China has no interest in subverting or radically transforming it.

Many scholars have discussed the implications of economic inter-dependence between China and the United States. Does it prevent war between them? Besides nuclear deterrence, mutual economic dependence is the most often cited reason for predicting that China will not use force to challenge the international order. As discussed in the subchapter 'Risk and Interdependence' (see p. 51), the cost of conflict is assumed to be prohibitive.

Dale Copeland, University of Virginia, has launched a whole new theory about the interaction between national security and international trade. What is most important, he says, is not the volume of trade, or the degree of interdependence. What counts most is 'trade expectations'. As long as a government expects to derive future benefits from its trade, it has little interest in disrupting the international order. If it expects to suffer an economic backlash or lose power vis-à-vis its main potential adversaries, there will be more risk that it goes to war (Copeland 1996; 2003; 2015). Scott Kastner, whose corpus will be discussed below, found in 2010 that Taiwan and Mainland China both expect to gain from further integration of their economies, and that this has had a dampening effect on the conflict over Taiwan's status.

Steve Chan, University of Colorado Boulder, who has studied 'enduring rivalries' in several historical periods, is optimistic on behalf of the East Asian Peace. The general trend in East Asia, he says, is toward abating rather than exacerbating rivalries. Territorial disputes are less likely to escalate today than during the Cold War, because East Asian states have shifted to policies that emphasize economic development. This has created a 'synergistic effect that restrains interstate tension and rivalry'. There has been a multilateralisation of ties, with many third parties gaining a vested stake in interstate stability. While China has increased its military capabilities, it has also acquired an interest in preserving regional stability. For its part, the USA faces resource constraints that make it wary of supporting its allies too much. This should work against bipolarization of regional relations. Chan holds that heavy underlying factors create interests securing the peace: 'Economic interdependence and political pluralism promote stakeholders that have a vested interest in stabilizing and expanding foreign ties, and these stakeholders are, in turn, self-motivated to lobby their government to undertake policies that abate rivalry' (Chan 2013: 20). Chan's historical analysis argues that the normal mechanism behind outbreaks and escalation of large wars is that a smaller state in an asymmetric relationship chooses a confrontational behaviour in the hope of gaining support from a patron.

Those with little or no hope of receiving foreign support, and those with a great deal of confidence in their ally's commitment, 'are less likely to initiate such confrontation than those that are in an intermediate position' (p. 186). Given the nature of Sino–American relations, however, no provocation by a smaller state in East Asia is likely to escalate. North Korea cannot count on Chinese support once again if it goes to war, and South Korea, Japan and the Philippines are subjected to US 'escalation control' (p. 82). From the perspective of power balance theory, says Chan, greater power parity between China and the USA should have 'a stabilizing rather than a destabilizing effect' (p. 102). China's rise should stabilize regional relations by 'curtailing any US tendency toward assertive unilateralism'. Chan claims that, 'the last thing Beijing wants to do is to trigger a costly arms race or precipitate forces that will pressure its neighbours to choose between it and Washington' (p. 104).

While Chan's argument seems reasonable, China's behaviour in the last few years does not conform with his expectation. For those of us who tend to take an optimistic view, it is hard to understand why China has decided to antagonize its neighbours by vigorously pursuing its maritime claims at a time when it could have further reduced their quest for US protection through 'good neighbour policies'. If such strategic irrationality is indicative of a lasting inclination among Beijing's decision makers, then the optimism I used to feel on behalf of the East Asian Peace may have been misplaced.

Chan argues that the people and governments of East Asia have turned away from being garrison states to becoming developmental states instead, and that this presents 'the most powerful firebreak against conflict contagion' (p. 135). Only when states expect 'future economic relations to be disrupted or curtailed, they are likely to stop cooperating and might even lash out in war' (p. 149). Hence Chan's optimism depends both on China's strategic rationality and its continued integration in a growing global economy.

In his 2014 book *Unbalanced*, Yale University economist Stephen Roach discusses the risk of a trade war between the USA and China in a world that is no longer characterized by bilateral economic relations but instead by multinational economic interaction in trans-border systems of production and marketing. He sees China as a part of an East Asian 'hub of a massive, integrated, pan-regional export machine' (p. 3) that provides low-cost goods to Europe and America. The integrated countries are 'trapped in a web of co-dependency' (p. ix). In the 1980s–90s, the economic integration of the Chinese and American economies was beneficial, allowing each to draw on the other's strengths, but in the 21st century, the relationship 'morphed into a destabilizing co-dependency' (p. 140). China has built an extrovert economy, with a low level of private consumption, and much of China's current account surplus has been placed in US treasury bonds. This has made it possible to keep down US interest rates so the American consumers can uphold their excessive consumption. The 2008 financial crisis showed that this is unsustainable. Roach sees an urgent need for reform both in China and the United States. He thinks China is more likely than the USA to undertake the necessary reforms. Its savings rate will decline, thus reducing its surplus and diminishing its demand for dollar-based assets. This will make it difficult for a savings-short America to borrow money. US interest rates will soar. Untold hardships will follow and strengthen protectionist impulses. Roach's bad dream is that the USA resorts to trade sanctions against China.

Why does Roach expect China and not the USA to take the initiative in rebalancing the global economy? As we shall soon see, most liberal scholars, with their emphasis on free and open markets, an independent civil society, limited and divided state powers, and the rule of law, are convinced that the Chinese political system prevents structural change. Roach, however, claims that it is the US political system that most inhibits reform. US financial policies are driven by doctrinaire liberalist ideology, while Beijing thinks in pragmatic terms (pp. 58–9). Roach compares the institutions of macroeconomic management in the world's two largest economies. While China's institutions are centralized, have broad responsibilities and are dedicated to maintaining stability, the US institutions are uncoordinated, compartmentalised and operate under a philosophy that allows for 'creative destruction'. Roach expects Xi Jinping to reform the Chinese economy and provide the USA with an opportunity to follow suit: 'China's rebalancing should be seen as America's opportunity, a basis for its long-term resurgence' (p. xiv). The big risk is that Americans fail to realize the necessity of structural reform, use China as a scapegoat for their troubles, and repeat their tragic mistakes from the 1930s: 'America's economic climate is just as precarious today as it was in 1929, if not more so. The same is true of the world economy' (p. 204). As of February 2017, it seems that the new US president, Donald Trump, intends to demand radical changes in the bilateral terms of trade. While many analysts expect Trump to undertake protectionist measures that will damage the world economy, this may be easier said than done since it would lead the USA into serious trouble with the World Trade Organization. One might even imagine Xi and Trump agreeing to carry out win–win reforms instead. China needs to develop its internal market by stimulating consumption and internal demand. This would reduce China's dependence on foreign trade but could also generate more imports from the USA and hence reduce China's trading surplus. However, such rebalancing would mainly benefit the US service sector and hardly allow much re-industrialisation of those US cities that are worst hit by unemployment, so would not satisfy Trump's voters.

Roach's warning against the risk that the USA may succumb to the protectionist temptation was made before anyone could know that Trump would enter the White House. The warning serves as a reminder of Nathan and Scobell's expectation that the main potential driver of an uncertain future would be US decline. A trade war could do tremendous damage. Depending on who is harmed most, it could either foster a resentful and aggressive China or lead to Mearsheimer's scenario of a declining America that uses force to stop China's rise. One of the key contributions from political economists to our understanding of security risk is to underline how governments, in their attempts to reduce the cost of a possible future war, tend to adopt measures to reduce their economic dependence on potential adversaries *before* allowing any crisis with another country to escalate. Wars are therefore often preceded by protectionist measures targeting potential adversaries. This should probably be built into Håvard Hegre's (2013) computerized predictions. If one of the great powers adopts a protectionist policy or seeks to divert its trade and investments away from a potential adversary, this is likely to increase the risk of war. The same may not be said of economic sanctions authorized by the UN Security Council against states (such as North Korea) that violate international law. Such sanctions often serve as substitutes for the use of force rather than as precursors of war. By contrast, Franklin D. Roosevelt's oil embargo against Japan surely contributed to the process that led to Pearl Harbor. Unilateral economic sanctions by one major power against another are destined to exacerbate tension and may well lead to war.

Cultural Predictions

Predictions can also be made on the basis of cultural or constructivist interpretations. David C. Kang of Dartmouth College, USA, and Cathérine Coulomb of Eurasys Conseils, Paris, both work on the assumption that the Chinese culture is uniquely peaceful. In his book *China Rising* from 2007, Kang claims that China's neighbours do not fear China and have no reason to balance against its rising power, because they know that the Chinese do not intend to dominate others. The Chinese culture has never been expansionist. Only in the period of the Yuan (Mongol) and Qing (Manchu) dynasties did the Chinese empire expand through military conquest. In its relations with other East Asian powers, the Middle Kingdom would only demand that they show respect and accept a ritual subordination through the provision of tributary gifts. In return they got real independence. All of China's neighbours know that Beijing respects their independence. Therefore they do not see any need to acquire arms or enter into alliances in order to resist China's increasing power. No one has tried to prevent China's economic development. Instead they benefit from it: 'The East Asian states prefer China to be strong rather than weak because a strong China stabilizes the region while a weak China tempts other states to try to control the region' (p. 4). If US power should recede, the region would not become unstable, because other nations may continue to adjust to China's central position. The East Asian region has its own internal dynamics, shared history, culture, and interactions. If all sides manage their relations with care, 'the future has the potential to be more peaceful, more prosperous, and even more stable than the past' (p. 203). The only factor that could disturb regional harmony would be if the USA misunderstood its role and tried to make trouble. Kang's argument did not seem quite as strange in 2007 as it does now. Since 2008–09, China and its neighbours have acted in the opposite way to what we should expect on the basis of his assumptions about Chinese culture.

Catherine Coulomb's beautifully written book *Chine, le nouveau centre du monde?* [China: the new centre of the world?], also from 2007, goes even further in identifying itself with the virtuous and innately peaceful Chinese culture, its concept of time and space, of the supernatural, of yin and yang, of Taoism, Buddhism and Confucianism, and of its inherent position in the middle of the world. China does not want to dominate or lead the world, but aspires to rediscover its place at the centre of the world and of history. China will shine again and relegate the West to the periphery. The United States, its alliance systems, demography or problems of economic management cannot prevent China from once again becoming the Middle Kingdom. How could the old dragon retain its decency if it were to hide behind the young American eagle?[3] Coulomb's book is a delightful masterpiece of culturally constructivist fiction.

There are some who agree with Kang, Coulomb and Jacques' belief that China will continue its rise and take up a central position in the world, without sharing their enthusiasm. James Mann's *The China Fantasy* (2007) accuses Western leaders of wishful thinking. They close their eyes, he writes, to how China's dictators repress their own population, either because they trust that China's growth will stop someday, or because they think the Chinese will democratize as soon as they can afford it, or when their middle class becomes strong enough to demand it. There is no reason to expect any of this to happen. A rich and powerful China will be just as authoritarian in the future as it is today, and far more dangerous. Mann emphasizes that his book is not about China,

---

3. 'Aujourd'hui, il veut revenir au centre du monde, pas à la tête. Il ne cherche pas à dominer mais à rayonner, reléguant ainsi l'Occident en sa périphérie. ... La Chine est en train de donner naissance au plus grand empire que la terre ait jamais connu. ... Peu de choses peuvent en freiner la dynamique : ni ses tensions sociales, ni le vieillissement de sa population, ni ses limites concernant ses ressources naturelles, ni l'impératif de réduire la dégradation de l'environnement. ... Le vieux dragon peut-il décemment accepter de se situer derrière le jeune aigle américain? ... Le risque de carambolage de l'économie? Un problème de surchauffe que le gouvernement chinois peut aisément résoudre. La Chine n'imposera pas mais elle saura canaliser les énergies vers la compétition avec l'extérieur. ... Prospère, la Chine serait la garantie d'une Asie stable. Mais si elle sombre dans l'anarchie, la tempête secouerait toute la région, et le reste du monde. Ce qui lui confère une grande responsabilité. ... La Chine ayant toujours maintenu des frontières perméables entre l'humain et le divin, les morts et les vivants, le réel et le virtuel, le militaire et le civil, le public et le privé, ne s'est pas laissé emprisonner dans ces schémas mentaux qui aujourd'hui risquent de paralyser l'Occident. ... Puissance responsable et pacifique, la Chine ne fait rien de néfaste, de malintentionné ou d'inutile. Mais elle est en progression, alors que l'Occident est en déclin'. Cathérine Coulomb (2007). *Chine, le nouveau centre du monde?* Paris: l'Aube: 451–460.

but the idea of China in the West. Yet he takes for granted that China is innately authoritarian. US leaders have fooled the American people into believing that China will open up its political system. This is how they have managed to sell their sinophile policy to the public. A backlash will inevitably come when the truth can no longer be hidden. China will never allow itself to be integrated in a Western, liberal order. What is needed, according to Mann, is exactly what Kang says is the only thing that could disrupt the East Asian Peace: the United States must adopt an active policy of promoting human rights and democracy in China.

Stefan Halper's *The Beijing Consensus* (2010) follows Mann in urging the West to contain China, but is more concerned for the rest of the world than for China's own population. Halper expects China to maintain its dramatic growth under authoritarian capitalism, but doubts that China will be strong enough to challenge US military power. The big danger is that other developing countries are attracted to the Chinese authoritarian model. This undermines Western economic and cultural influence. The West needs to mobilize a forceful defence of the liberal world order.

A much deeper cultural analysis can be found in Zheng Yongnian's dense but fascinating book, *The Chinese Communist Party as Organizational Emperor*. Zheng, leader of the East Asia Institute at the National University of Singapore, claims (2010) that the CCP is essentially different from parties in the West. The first Leninist party in China was not the CCP but the Kuomintang (KMT), which built a Leninist structure during 1924–25 under Sun Yat-sen's leadership, simply because that structure suited the Chinese tradition. In the Chinese conception, a party is not an organised group competing with other parties for power in the state. The party represents the whole people and is situated above the state. It replicates the role formerly played by the Emperor. Both the KMT and the CCP conceived of political parties in this way, hence coexistence between them – or between any two Chinese parties – was impossible. Four characteristics of the Chinese imperial tradition are maintained by the Communist Party today: all organisations and institutions represent the Emperor in his relations with the people, not vice versa; the power of the Emperor is superior to that of everyone else, so no division of power is possible; the power of the Emperor has no limits in time or space, since he rules over all under Heaven; and, the power of the Emperor includes all aspects of relations among his subjects as well as their relations with nature. Yet the power of the Emperor is not absolute. It is restrained by rituals (*li*), which set strict limits for what the emperor can do, in ways that have no place in Western thinking (pp. 48–51). The KMT and then the CCP put themselves in the Emperor's place as 'organisational emperor', with the help of Leninist party theory. Although Leninism had been developed entirely outside the Chinese context, it resonated with the Chinese imperial tradition. This also explains how the CCP could survive the fall of communism in the Soviet Union and Eastern Europe.

Zheng has much to tell about the CCP's inner life, how its leadership succession problem is managed, how factions relate to each other, who wields power over whom, and how the party relates to other institutions. In contrast with those who say that the CCP has the 'leading role' in the state, Zheng employs a corporate metaphor, where the party is its owner and the government its managing director. The party is above the government, and in vital issues rules directly. The Chinese government does not control the People's Liberation Army (PLA). Instead the party controls it directly through its Central Military Commission. There are no clear borderlines between party and army. Zheng warns against proposals to place the PLA under the government's control. Without strong support from the party, a civilian government would face great uncertainty in exercising control over the military (p. 117). This is how Zheng explains why all of China's top leaders have sought to chair the Central Military Commission.

Until I read Zheng's concluding chapter, I thought he was constructing a rationale for retaining the CCP's monopoly of power. Based on his reasoning, the party could claim to uphold an ancient tradition, transcend the death of communism, and see itself as a dignified alternative to the chaotic Western pattern of letting two or multiple parties compete for donations, media exposure and votes. To my surprise, Zheng's final chapter instead turns to a class analysis. This century's most important political change, Zheng says, was the CCP's decision to welcome capitalists among its ranks. The CCP has allowed the formation of a new bourgeoisie, which has gained power inside the party alongside the technocrats who used to rule supreme. Accordingly, the middle class does not see a need to revolt. That need has instead re-emerged among the unrepresented and neglected workers and peasants, the social classes that the CCP claimed to represent in Mao's time. The workers lost their right to strike when China adopted its new constitution in 1982, and are not allowed to form independent trade unions. The official union represents the interests of the state, not its members. The position of the peasants is even worse. They have no organization to represent them at all. When they are subjected to land grabs or other abuse, they have no other recourse than ineffective local protests, or suicide – a frequent occurrence.

Now we get to Zheng's prediction. He expects two factors to push the country to democratise itself. One is the leadership succession problem. Since the party leader does not enjoy the same right as past Emperors to appoint a successor, the higher organs of the party have to reach a consensus on leadership succession. If this proves impossible, as it did in 2007, there are two options. Either violence decides or a decision is taken through a vote. In 2007, the second method was used. A fairly large assembly of party cadres took an 'informal' vote, resulting in Xi Jinping's victory over Li Keqiang, although the latter was party leader Hu Jintao's candidate. Something similar may happen in the future. Party factions will fight to win the vote. They will claim to represent larger social groups, and this may give the workers and peasants a chance to make their voices heard: 'When a deadlock takes place, democracy becomes the solution ... the leadership has to, first, legalize factional politics and, second, link factional politics to social forces or interests' (p. 186).

The party will never, according to Zheng, give in to demands for de-mocratisation from groups outside itself. Democracy will instead mani-fest itself as the only orderly way to resolve the party's internal struggles, in turn allowing class interests to be represented. Again Zheng points to history: 'Throughout Chinese history, the regime, together with rich classes, was frequently overthrown by the poor ... If the party does not provide opportunities for the workers and peasants to make their voices heard, the same will happen again' (p. 199). 'We can reasonably argue that democracy is inevitable', says Zheng, if by 'democracy' we mean a form of competition among parties or factions (p. 194).

I am not fully convinced by Zheng's historical argument, but am in-trigued by his prediction. The millionaires, billionaires and technocrats cannot continue to decide China's future by themselves. China's work-ers and peasants will demand a say. Most of Zheng's argument makes sense to me. Yet, so far, the multiple protests organized by peasants and workers have not been coordinated in ways that could make them into a political force. No strong socialist movements exist today that can transform the grievances of the toiling masses into a force for national political change, and liberal critics of the CCP's authoritarian rule are not keen to unleash a movement from below, which could threaten their cherished middle class. Only if a faction inside the CCP should decide to appeal to the workers and peasants for support against another faction, might a challenge emerge against the power of the current alliance of party, state and billionaires.

I include Kang, Coulomb, Mann and Halper in my survey mainly to demonstrate the diversity of approaches to gauging China's future, and their general tendency to extrapolate from current trends. I do not myself believe much in the kind of culturalist explanations that build on ideas of national uniqueness and disregard the ways that most cultural forms can be molded to fit different outcomes. I value Zheng's analysis though, with its combination of historical path dependency, class analysis, and understanding of an authoritarian party's inner dynamics.

Let us now take a critical, almost cynical look at China's foreign policy from a deterministic viewpoint that presents China as a short-sighted autistic power, trapped into self-defeating behaviour by the paradoxical effects of strategic logic.

The Logic of Strategy

Edward N. Luttwak's *The Rise of China vs the Logic of Strategy* challenges most of our conventional wisdom, turning the standard arguments used by proponents of other theoretical approaches upside down. Luttwak refutes the realist school for not being sufficiently deterministic. Instead he claims that a 'logic of strategy' dictates human behaviour and leaves no room for free choice. Luttwak sees little need to be a Sinologist or take cultural differences seriously since 'the universal logic of strategy applies in perfect equality to every culture in every age.' This also obviates any need for agency-based explanations. The intentions of China's and other great powers' leaders are irrelevant, since the logic of strategy dictates actions and reactions regardless of who the decision makers are. The logic of strategy, however, is by no means 'strategic' in any admirable sense of the term, but works in paradoxical ways. Luttwak suggests, for example, that Kissinger's admiration for Chinese strategic culture is totally flawed and serves only to reinforce China's self-delusion. Because big China never had to deal with other states on the basis of equality, it has no deep experience with modern diplomacy, but acts as a short-sighted 'autistic state' with little understanding for the sensibilities of others. Hence there is no reason to be surprised by China's current self-defeating policies (p. vii). Why self-defeating? Because it is a total illusion to think that it is possible for a country of China's magnitude to rise both economically and militarily at the same time without provoking counter-reactions that are bound to defeat it. The only way for China to escape the logic of strategy would be to refrain from military aggrandizement until it gets sufficient economic edge to make resistance futile.

Such military constraint cannot come about as a result of individual agency, but only by an economic slowdown. To wit, the only way for China to save itself is to allow its economy to sputter. Yes, *save itself* – not break up or be dissolved. If China's economy slows down, others will no longer need to mobilize against it. If instead the USA declines, then those who think this will help China are all wrong. The logic of strategy will then work its paradoxical magic: a declining US will be less of a threat to others than it is today. Hence it will be more attractive as a partner for all who fear China's military rise, including India and Russia. If Japan, Vietnam, India, Russia and the USA join forces to stop China, they will prevail. And this is what the logic of strategy forces them to do if China continues to increase its military spending.

Will there then be war? Maybe, but not a big or meaningful war. Luttwak does not think effective warfare is possible in the nuclear age, only limited, localised war, which is meaningless because winning such a war does not necessarily yield a strategic advantage. The coalition that is bound to be formed against China would therefore be wise to adopt a 'geo-economic' instead of a military strategy, aimed at slowing down – but not halting – China's economic growth. This would yield strategic advantage.

Again Luttwak subverts a widespread assumption (which I share) that 'economic warfare' is likely to be followed by a shooting war. Like Navarro, Luttwak sees a geo-economic strategy as a meaningful substitute for rather than precursor to war. The United States, however, finds it difficult to adopt a geo-economic strategy because; according to Luttwak it is a badly coordinated state, pursuing several contradictory policies at the same time. The Treasury does its best to promote China's growth, in complete disregard for the interests of US industry; the US federal government has no Department of Industry. The State Department pursues a policy opposing and criticizing China whenever it violates US values. And the Pentagon is trying to contain China militarily. What holds China back from invading Taiwan, however, is not military deterrence but the fear that the USA might interrupt all trade. This could be done overnight, and would be devastating for China. So this is why the optimal US strategy, if there could be a coordinated approach among its various government branches, is geo-economic.

What fate does Luttwak think awaits China's communist regime? Although only a democratic China can have any hope of continuing its present rise without meeting overwhelming resistance, he does not expect China to democratise. The regime will become more authoritarian (he wrote this before Xi came to power), and risk collapse. Yet it is impossible to predict when the collapse will occur. Authoritarian regimes are often able to predict their own decay and likely downfall, and then act to prevent foreseeable threats. Yet they are unable to cope with sudden events – unforeseen by the regime itself as well as its critics. The predictions Luttwak penned in 2011 conform to what happened afterwards, at least until 2016: more repression of internal opposition, increased military spending, assertive foreign policies, counter-reactions by China's neighbours, a strengthening of US regional influence, and US geo-economic initiatives (TPP) aiming to further integrate China's neighbours into a US-led system, while leaving China outside. This could contribute to the Chinese economic slowdown that Luttwak finds desirable. Luttwak did not predict, however, that TPP would be killed in the USA itself.

In 2016, a confluence of events changed the picture. A pro-Chinese or perhaps mainly anti-American leader was elected as president in the Philippines. An Arbitral Tribunal, set up at the request of the previous administration in Manila, came up with a ruling going so radically against China that its neighbours were afraid to even mention it out of fear of hurting Chinese feelings. And an awkward electoral campaign in the United States, with both major party candidates rejecting Obama's TPP, led to the election of Donald Trump as US president. US participation in the TPP was thus impossible, and a great uncertainty spread in the region concerning future US policies. Luttwak would probably find that the authors of these confusing events were trapped by the paradoxes of the logic of strategy. His book is full of paradoxes, such as his contention that foreign policy is never as totally determined by the logic of strategy as when decision makers suffer from the illusion of having a free choice in the face of conflict.[4]

Foreign Policy Predictions

Before entering into the rich field of liberal interpretations, I shall briefly touch upon the most recent work by David Lampton, an empirically oriented specialist on China's foreign policy who believes in free choice and refutes deterministic logic, be it realist, Marxist, constructivist, Luttwakian or liberal: 'One must inquire into the specific motivations, capacities, and perceptions of individual leaders to anticipate future behavior' (Lampton 2014: 2). His *Following the Leader* draws on 558 interviews with Chinese leaders, and provides historical analyses of their governance, policy making, global policy, anxieties, civil-military relations, and negotiation patterns.

Lampton claims in his previous book (2008) that China had been woven so deeply into the international system that it would be too risky for Beijing to use unrestricted power in its foreign relations. The United States could thus live peacefully with China. He did not exclude the possibility of internal 'convulsions' but considered this unlikely in the short to medium term. His 2014 book is less sanguine. He now sees instability as 'conceivable, perhaps likely' (2014: 44). The biggest challenge for China is to maintain stability with a 'more pluralized and empowered bureaucracy and society' (p. 218). Economic growth will decline over time but remain substantial for a decade or two. Does China accept the existing international system? It accepts, says Lampton, the global economic and social structures and also the UN system but not the US-dominated alliance system. A core question is if the USA and China can develop 'a shared vision of international security architecture, first in

---

4. According to Luttwak (2012: 7), his approach 'is frankly deterministic. Instead of seeing leaders striving to act pragmatically in pursuit of their goals and preferences within the operative political constraints, I see them as trapped by the paradoxes of the logic of strategy, which imposes its own imperatives, all the more so when they retain the delusion of free choice in the presence of conflict'. Much of my summary above is drawn from Luttwak 2012: 248–276.

East Asia and then globally' (p. 231). Just like Nathan and Scobell's 'new equilibrium', Lampton's 'inclusive balance' does not imply any reduction of the US military presence in China's vicinity.

Lampton, an agency-focused foreign policy analyst, arrives at the same conclusion as the defensive realists Nathan and Scobell: if the USA neither declines nor antagonizes Beijing, then China is likely to remain a level-headed actor. Yet it might go through some domestic convulsions. Peace will be preserved because national leaders give priority to economic growth and understand how costly a conflict would be. Lampton thinks peace is enhanced by 'the idea of global interdependence' (p. 3) and puts forward a theory that says: institutional and economic interdependence dampen impulses toward conflict. While not making conflict impossible, economic interdependence provides 'incentives to keep conflict with major partners manageable' (p. 122). There is now a 'struggle for the soul of Chinese foreign policy between the realities of interdependence and the impulses of assertive nationalism' (p. 136). Lampton does not, however, go into a discussion of whether objective or perceived reality has the stronger impact on human decisions.

I appreciate Lampton's focus on agency and I share his belief that leadership counts, but for my taste his work is too short on theory. When reading him, I get the impression that the way to predict the future is to talk with the decision makers and ask them what they want to do. This does not satisfy my need to understand patterns of human behaviour, how decision makers with different kinds of upbringing, experiences, popular appeal and types of power, tend to handle various incentives and constraints. To make predictions we must inquire into patterns of behaviour. Luttwak and Lampton are opposite extremes. One is an avowed determinist, while the other sees nothing but leadership. Our task is to gauge the leverage of agency: which choices are open to the decision makers? And, given what we know about them and the institutions they lead, what are they most likely to do under various circumstances?

I shall now turn to liberal theory, with its emphasis on economic systems and/or political institutions.

Liberal Predictions

Liberals believe that human development and peace are enhanced by market economics, free trade, constraints on state interference in the economy and society, competitive democratic governance, and protection of individual freedoms. There is a difference in liberal thinking between those who think globally and those who look primarily at the national unit. The former tend to assume that China's illiberal, developmental state is being socialized and transformed by inclusion in a liberal world order, while the latter take the view that China's political system is incompatible with a modern market economy and therefore must either give way to a liberal system of governance or prevent China from moving on to a higher stage of development.

G. John Ikenberry, Princeton University, is a leading advocate of liberal optimism on behalf of the world as a whole. He has worked closely with some of the leading Chinese liberal scholars: Zhu Feng of Nanjing University, and Wang Jisi and Wang Yizhou of Peking University (Wang Yizhou is a member of the East Asian Peace programme's Advisory Board). Ikenberry argues that China faces a different type of international order than previous rising states because the United States is a different type of hegemonic power. The order it has built is deeper and wider than any previous one. At the same time, the nuclear revolution has made war among great powers less likely – 'even unthinkable' (Ikenberry 2008: 7).

The world now has 'an open and expansive order built around institutions that bind its members together and which mitigates security competition and rivalry within it'. (p. 14) New great powers do not face established ones in a competition for power, as the realists want us to believe, but grow into an order in which mature political institutions give them a possibility of winning support for their interests and views. If the USA should opt to aggressively contain China, then the other members of the international order would not accept it. So, the United States won't choose this course. While it is not unthinkable that China will seek to change the global order fundamentally, this only makes it more important for the USA and its allies to strengthen that order, with mutual obligations that bind the USA just as much as others. The United States and China are similar in 'their persistent claims of uniqueness and exceptionalism', (p. 114) wanting to be at the centre of world politics while at the same time remaining as autonomous as possible. The more deeply institutionalized the Western order becomes; the greater is the likelihood that China will 'rise up inside that order' (p. 114) – and that the USA will stay inside as well.

Edward S. Steinfeld, Massachusetts Institute of Technology (MIT), whose book *Playing Our Game* (2010) was written against the background of the 2008 financial crisis, goes even further than Ikenberry in speculating that China is inserting itself in 'our' order. He combines the global and national forms of liberal optimism, arguing that China is not just playing the US game internationally but is also changing its internal system of governance in a way similar to what happened in Taiwan during the 1980s–90s. Authoritarianism is 'obsolescing' when a country by its own volition inserts itself in the global system of production and trade, created and designed by 'us'. The Chinese Communist Party might well survive but it is already walking on the same path as the Kuomintang has walked in Taiwan. (At the time when Steinfeld wrote his book, Taiwan was under KMT rule.)

Steinfeld's main argument is based on recent changes in the global system of production. The main driver of change in international affairs is no longer trade but the creation of 'complex global production hierarchies' (p. 22), within which nations insert themselves through engagement with transnational corporations. By contrast to some others (like Japan), China did not do this by first reforming its national institutions to serve its modernising needs but instead just ploughed ahead and opened up the country to international investments. China did not pursue any unique design of its own, but 'defined its new system through worldwide standards handed down, through negotiation, by the World Trade Organization (WTO)' (p. 29). Steinfeld calls this 'institutional outsourcing' (p. 40). This created an abnormal disconnect between politics and economics, and a need to make China's national economic institutions compatible with those of supply-chain leaders. In this way, knowingly or not, China is becoming a 'self-obsolescing authoritarian'. The Chinese party-state has 'promulgated the logic for its own natural end-point' (pp. 45–6).

In his concluding chapter, Steinfeld recounts the end of authoritarian governance in Taiwan, but fails to see how President Chiang Ching-kuo's decision to introduce basic freedoms and open up Taiwan's political system to internal competition were aimed to strengthen his isolated regime's domestic and international standing in its competition with the communist regime in the mainland. Steinfeld interprets Taiwan's reforms as just a necessary adaptation to the global economic order within which Taiwan had inserted itself. This then allows him to speculate that the same thing now happens in the mainland: 'Chinese authoritarianism is currently self-obsolescing in ways that roughly mirror what transpired two decades earlier in Taiwan' (p. 227). On this basis he recommends that his fellow Americans abandon the idea that China represents an existential adversary. It has become a 'partner, an entity that shares with us an increasingly common set of values, practices, and outlooks' (p. 233). When reading Steinfeld, I'm taken in by the ethereal beauty of his counter-intuitive assumptions of benevolent global production hierarchies converting China and the world into players of a game designed by 'us'. Steinfeld is even more Ikenberrian than G. John Ikenberry himself.

The second kind of liberal thinking can be found in the works of Gordon Chang, Minxin Pei, Jonathan Fenby and David Shambaugh. They are not much interested in the global order. Instead they focus on the illiberal nature of China's national political system, which in their view must be unsustainable once the country has reached a certain stage of development. Chang, Pei and Fenby have been unshakable in their conviction that the Chinese party-state cannot adapt itself to new circumstances but needs to be replaced. Shambaugh was long open to the possibility that the party-state could adapt, but then shifted to the view of Pei.

Gordon Chang's *The Coming Collapse of China* (2002) predicted that the Chinese communist regime would collapse by 2010. In 2006, he admitted that this no longer seemed likely, but he still thought it possible. 'Peer beneath the surface', Chang wrote in 2002, 'and there is a weak China, one that is in long-term decline and even on the verge of collapse. The symptoms of decay are to be seen everywhere' (p. xxv). Beijing had a maximum of five years to implement the necessary political reforms. Otherwise the people would carry Mao's corpse away from Tiananmen Square, and the days of the PRC would be numbered. Chang brought a long list of arguments to the table: popular discontent, the CCP's fear of protest movements, unrest among workers, the hollowness of Beijing's attempts to win back Taiwan, the inability to close down unprofitable state-owned enterprises, the uncontrollable nature of internet communication, political interference with private companies, the fact that no Chinese companies go bankrupt except for political reasons, low-standard education, little room for entrepreneurship and innovation, insolvent and debt-ridden banks, a generalised suspicion between the state and the private sector, overcapacity with empty office buildings and hotels, roads without traffic, too much talk about socialism, and above all endemic corruption. If China should try a military adventure, the people would rise up as one and put an end to the communist system. In the epilogue to his 2002 book, he claimed that the Chinese state had already begun to break up.

Minxin Pei's *China's Trapped Transition* from 2006 is a more serious work in the same genre. It builds on a basic truism that penetrates much liberal thinking: economic development beyond a certain level is only possible if a country has an independent judiciary, free media, a regulatory non-interventionist state, and free and fair elections that hold politicians accountable to their citizens. In China, according to Pei, 'the poorly defined boundaries between the state and the market create an environment in which the state is incapable of effectively performing its basic functions – such as enforcing contracts, protecting property rights and policing the marketplace – while simultaneously overreaching into areas where it does not belong' (p. 14). The absence of liberal political reforms has halted the 'transition' that began under Deng. China has been trapped in an uncompleted transition. This must, according to Pei, bring bad governance, corruption and over-investment, and lead China into a long period of stagnation that will eventually break down the Communist Party.

Pei sees neither alternative possibilities nor dilemmas. There is only one way to achieve long-term economic growth. This is through liberal political reforms. Without such reforms, there will be an economic backlash and the communist regime will fall. It is just a question of time. Pei does mention the 'apparent paradox of bad governance and good growth' but finds it 'inconceivable that a developmental autocracy can retain its vigor for long' (p. 208). Pei expects that China, instead of becoming a global economic power, may 'enter a prolonged period of stagnation' (p. 212). He does not have much to say about the political reforms that have been carried out, neither the reforms that to some extent have opened up the system nor those aiming to strengthen the CCP's hold on society. China has actually changed a lot, although not much in a pluralistic direction. Pei concludes by declaring himself in disagreement both with alarmists who perceive China as a military threat against the USA and optimists (like Ikenberry and Steinfeld) who imagine that China is being westernised. Those worrying about war will be relieved and those hoping for more growth will be disappointed. China is about to stagnate (p. 214). Ten years ago, when Pei published his book, his prediction seemed unconvincing. The Chinese economy was still growing at a quick pace. Now, ten years later, when China's economy is slowing down, his theory looks more prescient. Yet this is not necessarily because Pei has been right all along. The reasons for the economic slowdown are not necessarily the absence of liberal political reforms. It may be, however, that if the Chinese leaders had opened up their political system during its period of rapid economic rise they would have been better able to weather the storms they now see coming.

Recently, Minxin Pei published a penetrating study of 260 cases of collusive corruption in China, unveiled by the anti-corruption efforts under Xi Jinping, with the telling title *China's Crony Capitalism: The Dynamics of Regime Decay* (2016). Pei's study shows how a rather decentralized system of power, where power itself on many levels is being bought and sold, has provided room for pervasive collusion between officials and private entrepreneurs in immensely corrupt networks. Pei defines crony capitalism as 'an instrumental union between capitalists and politicians designed to allow the former to acquire wealth, legally or otherwise, and the latter to seek and retain power' (p. 7). China's version of this system does not, like in Russia, have its origin in a once-and-for-all privatization of state owned assets, giving ground for the sudden creation of a group of 'oligarchs'. In China, it is the control, not ownership of companies that has allowed party and state officials to form alliances with private entrepreneurs and amass enormous individual fortunes, particularly in the real estate and mining sectors. The companies themselves have most often not been privatized. Pei is just as convinced now as he was in 2006 that the Chinese Leninist regime is in 'late stage decay' (p. 1). Xi's anti-corruption drive is unlikely to make things better. Instead it has created insecurity and rivalry among elites, thus degrading the political cohesiveness of the regime and 'making it even more brittle' (p. 265). Yet Pei 2016 has shed what optimism he might have felt previously concerning the possible emergence of liberal institutions. He now thinks the CCP's downfall may prepare the ground for an 'opportunistic strongman' to come to power, so crony capitalism will be maintained in just another political form (p. 265).

A less ideological and more empathic analysis of China's internal problems may be found in Susan Shirk's *China, Fragile Superpower* (2007). Shirk accompanied Nixon to China in 1972, and handled US relations with China in the US State Department in the last three years of Bill Clinton's administration. She does not predict the downfall of the CCP or the PRC, but agrees with Pei that the Chinese system is inherently fragile. The main difference between them is that Pei sees this with glee, while Shirk is apprehensive. This is not mainly because she thinks China represents a threat to America:

> Inevitably, as China moves up the economic and technological ladder, it will compete with America and expand its global reach. But a much graver danger is that as China rises in power, the United States will misread and mishandle it, so that we find ourselves embroiled in a hostile relationship with it ... It is China's internal fragility, not its growing strength that presents the greatest danger (Shirk 2007: 64).

The more China grows economically, the more insecure its leaders will feel at home, because they ride so many horses at the same time. Their attitude to globalization is ambivalent. They both need and fear it. The same is the case with nationalism. While the leaders encourage patriotic sentiments among the young, they also strive to avoid becoming the target of nationalist anger. On the one hand, nothing – except the raising of living standards – is more important to the CCP's claim to rule than 'its nationalist credentials ... Nationalism could be the one issue that could unite disparate groups like laid-off workers, farmers, and students in a national movement against the regime' (*ibid*. p. 64). Leaders try to anticipate how an economic downturn might undermine their popular support, and they prepare to defend themselves against succession struggles within their own ranks.

Shirk touches on all the same problems as Chang: insolvent banks, unemployment, increasing inequalities between provinces and social classes, corruption, export dependency, need for investments in education and health, the demographic ageing that will inevitably slow down economic growth. China's leaders know that they have little time, so they try desperately to grow their economy as much as possible while there is still a 'strategic opportunity'. Shirk concentrates her attention on

China's growing nationalism, which has also been the subject of some specialized studies.

One of them, Peter Hays Gries (2004) observes that '... realists are right that the conflicts of material interests between the USA and China are outweighed by a common interest in a stable East Asia'. He adds, however, that the main danger lies in the possible emergence of an 'existential conflict' between the two sides of the Pacific: 'Until Chinese and Americans learn to affirm, rather than threaten, each others' national identities, their mutual benefit from a stable East Asia will not ensure peace in the twenty-first century' (Gries 2004: 150). Christopher Hughes, in his perceptive study of Chinese nationalism, makes a point that is not so often heard: the party state in China uses nationalism as its main rationale for preventing the emergence of a pluralist democracy. Where Gries sees nationalism as a threat against the regime, which may compel it to initiate external conflict, Hughes sees it mainly as a tool used in order to prevent internal conflict (Hughes 2006: 156).

Shirk underlines how the Chinese leadership has tried to put a lid on excessive nationalism by drawing a line between legitimate patriotism and chauvinism. China strives continuously to convince the rest of the world of its peaceful intentions: 'Avoiding international conflicts that could throw the country off course domestically has been the lodestar of Chinese foreign policy in the post-Deng era' (p. 105).

So what we see is a huge difference between the doomsday messages from liberals who focus on the illiberal nature of China's national institutions and optimistic forecasts of those who look at the socializing capacity of the liberal international order. This leads me to consider more closely the work of David Shambaugh, a liberal-minded observer of Chinese politics whose predictions have changed over time.

Adaptive Predictions

As can be seen from Figures 5 and 6 (pp. 86–87), predictions do not just vary from one analyst to another but also over time in response to recent events. In peaceful periods, the future looks peaceful. When there is tension, war seems to loom on the horizon. Are there good reasons for letting predictions be affected by recent events? Well, this depends on theory. The more structural or deterministic a theory is, the less adaptive it will be to shifting circumstances. The more room a theory leaves for human agency, the more capably it can adapt its expectations to the latest events, such as Xi's elevation to 'core leader', the election of Trump, and the contact established between the President of Taiwan and the American president-elect, and whatever may have happened between the time I write this and the time you read it. My own theory of a developmental peace, with its emphasis on the perceptions and priorities of national decision makers, allows for changing one's predictions as circumstances change. The fate of the East Asian Peace may in my view be determined by abrupt changes that are extremely difficult to predict but must be inserted in our predictive models as soon as they occur. Much now depends on whether or not Xi Jinping can consolidate his power during the CCP's 19th Congress, on whether or not he can undertake economic reforms, and on how he handles his relations with Abe Shinzo – and notably with Donald Trump.

David Shambaugh has inspired my devotion to adaptive prediction-ism. He has systematically adapted his future expectations to every shifting trend. In 2005, he held that 'on balance, the USA and China find themselves on the same side of many of the key issues affecting the future of the Asian region', and that this 'augurs well for opportunities for tangible cooperation between the two governments' (p. 42). In the United States, he used to be considered a 'panda hugger' for promoting views such as this. Yet, like Zheng Yongnian, he does not assume that China has a distinct political culture. Shambaugh is fascinated by Leninist parties, by how they break up or survive. His book on the Chinese Communist Party from 2008 does not apply a culturalist or historically path-dependent perspective. For Shambaugh, the CCP is one among several Leninist parties, and he asks if it can keep control of its society when so many others have failed. His answer in 2008 was 'both yes and no', both *Atrophy and Adaptation*. These are two parallel processes. The party has already entered its process of atrophy, yet has managed to adapt itself sufficiently to stay in power.

Shambaugh takes official ideology seriously. Former president Jiang Zemin's theory of 'the three represents' was an expression of a capacity to adapt to new circumstances by recruiting business leaders into the party's ranks. Hu Jintao's promotion of a 'harmonious society' was another attempt at adaptation. How can it be that Leninist parties survived in China, Vietnam, North Korea, Laos and Cuba when they broke up in the Soviet Union and Eastern Europe? Shambaugh looks carefully at the lessons drawn by the Chinese from the dissolution of the Soviet Union. This was such a shock for them that they took a long time investigating what had gone wrong. Gorbachev's main mistake was to separate the party from the state and allow so much internal party democracy that the party itself became uncontrollable (Shambaugh 2008: esp. p. 68).

Shambaugh has also examined what Chinese researchers have thought and said about other political parties with a virtual monopoly on power: the Liberal Democratic Party (LDP) in Japan, Golkar in Indonesia, the Indian Congress Party, the Institutional Revolutionary Party (PRI) in Mexico, and the Social Democratic Party in Sweden. The one that has attracted Chinese analysts the most is the People's Action Party (PAP) in Singapore. In 2005, after having conducted a systematic study of the PAP experience, the Chinese analyst Cai Dingjian noted how it had held on to power by maintaining a highly effective organization and facing the people in elections, where there were alternative candidates. In this way the PAP had been able to regularly test its popular support. This is something the CCP never does. When a party does not regularly face the people in elections, says Cai, it may easily succumb to atrophy.

The reform faction in the CCP has for a long time been inspired by Singapore. Shambaugh (2008) finds it unlikely that China will introduce a pluralist political system of the kind that prevails in Japan, South Korea, Taiwan, the Philippines, Indonesia or Thailand (at that time). A 'Singaporisation' of China is more likely. Democratic reform would come in small steps. New methods would be tested in some localities before being introduced on higher levels. So in 2008, Shambaugh thought China would emulate Singapore. Since then he has changed his mind. Figure 6 above (p. 87) shows how each of Shambaugh's publications adopts a new view. In an article published in 2010, at a time when China was maintaining its high growth through a massive infusion of public financing to overcome the drastically falling demand from Western markets, Shambaugh assessed that '... China's economic growth is likely to continue apace indefinitely. This is not an economy that is going to go off the rails. Not only has China been the major economy that has best weathered the global financial crisis, but as a result it is better poised for more intensive growth in the years ahead'. He expected the country's political system to 'evolve, but slowly and in its own fashion, staunchly resistant to outside pressure' (pp. 222–3).

In 2013, he expanded on the theme of China's inward orientation in a book with the title *China Goes Global*. The title is strange since the book's main message is rather the opposite: China has immersed itself in the global economy without developing a global political agenda. China remains a 'partial power' with a mercantilist approach to trade and investments, and little soft power (pp. 6–7). Shambaugh points out that China's own analysts are confused about their global identity. In 2010, while Hu Jintao was still at the helm, many Chinese intellectuals were asked to propose recommendations for a suitable global agenda. Their advice consisted in a series of warnings: do not confront the United States; do not challenge the international system; do not use ideology to guide foreign policy; do not lead an 'anti-Western' camp (2013: 20). There were hardly any positive suggestions.

Shambaugh holds that the Chinese concept of *anquan* (security) is mainly about security at home: 'internal stability has always been the essence of security' (p. 59). He quotes China's 2011 *White Paper on Peaceful Development*: 'For China, the most populous country, to run itself well is the most important fulfilment of its international responsibility' (p 121). China's role, says Shambaugh, is inhibited by its ambivalence over international involvement, its preoccupation with domestic development, and its focus on protecting 'irredentist interests' in Taiwan, Tibet and at sea (p. 306). All this makes China a lonely power with no real allies. It is a 'narrow-minded, self-interested, realist state' (p. 310). What should the West do about it? As of 2013, Shambaugh saw just one option: continue to engage China, in the hope that it will eventually embrace the existing order. This is 'the best hope' (pp. 312–14).

In a 2015 *Wall Street Journal* opinion piece, Shambaugh abruptly aligned himself with Chang and Pei's prediction of the CCP's imminent collapse. China could not survive as a narrow-minded, self-interested and realist state, but would 'crack up' under the pressure of strong economic and social forces. China's political system, he claimed, is already 'badly broken' and no one knows this better than the Communist Party itself. Xi Jinping's 'despotism' will stress the system and bring it closer to the 'breaking point' instead of, as Xi hopes, reinforcing it. Shambaugh predicted a protracted, messy and violent implosion of the regime, and did not exclude the possibility that Xi will be deposed in a power struggle or coup d'etat.

In addition to Xi's despotism, Shambaugh provides five premises for his 'crack up' prediction. First, the fact that rich Chinese have made themselves ready to flee the country by buying property and educating their children abroad and arranging for their daughters to be in the USA when giving birth so the children will have a right to US citizenship. Second, repression of political opposition in China has intensified. Third, the apparent Party faithful no longer show any energy when defending their regime but feign compliance with official doctrine. Fourth, corruption is pervasive, and Xi's anti-graft campaign is more about targeting the clients of former president Jiang Zemin than actually fighting corruption. Xi is lonely. He has failed to cultivate a group of loyal supporters. Fifth, the Chinese economy is stuck in a series of systematic traps, and Xi seems unable to push through reforms against the interests of state owned companies and local party bosses.

After this assessment of China's situation comes the weaker part of Shambaugh's argument. He claims that the only remedy for all these problems is for the Chinese leadership to carry out political reform, that is, to open up the political system. How a more open political system would prevent billionaires from placing their capital and child rearing daughters abroad, persuade state officials to believe in their mission, overcome corruption, and preclude entrapment in transition, is left just as unexplained by Shambaugh as it was by Chang and Pei. They just seem to assume that liberal reforms will do the trick. The opposite might just as well happen. Luckily, many regimes (such as Sweden in the late 19th and early 20th century, Spain and Portugal in the 1970s, Taiwan, South Korea and a number of Central European and Latin American countries in the 1980s, Zambia in 1991, the three Baltic states after the dissolution of the Soviet Union in 1991, Indonesia from 1998) have opened up their political systems in ways that have preserved the peace, but there are also many examples of liberal reforms that have ended in conflict and chaos, or a return to authoritarian rule (Germany's Weimar Republic after World War I, post-communist Russia in the 1990s, Georgia and Ukraine in the 2000s, Thailand repeatedly, Egypt in 2011–13).

Many CCP members would no doubt welcome a more open political system, but they also want strong, efficient leadership. The most tantalizing part of Shambaugh's new argument is, in my view, that Xi Jinping has failed to be that leader. He is strong in the sense that he has centralized power in his own hands and has weakened his rivals, but not in the sense of being able to carry out economic reforms. He does not seem to trust anyone but himself, which makes it difficult for others to take initiatives. They have to first find out what he wants. This seems to have led to inertia among officials who took quick decisions at a time when the optimal way to obtain promotion was to demonstrate achievements in terms of economic growth. If Xi fails to carry out the reforms needed to deliver further improvement of people's lives under far more difficult international circumstances than previously, gets China into trouble internationally, and fails to gain sufficient support for his One Belt One Road initiative, he may, as Shambaugh says, be deposed. However, this would not necessarily lead to any crack up or major crisis for the party state. Someone else, who would also want to keep up the party state, would most likely replace him.

Shambaugh's *Wall Street Journal* article was published while he worked on his most recent book, *China's Future*. By the time of its publication in 2016, Shambaugh had already backtracked, now claiming that readers had misunderstood his op ed. He did not want to predict an imminent collapse, just a 'protracted decline' (p. 134). *China's Future* presents four scenarios, based on an assumption of a '*direct linkage* between politics and all other aspects of China's future'. Each is based on a strategic choice: continued hard authoritarianism, a return to totalitarian authoritarianism, a return to soft authoritarianism and a soft democratization that emulates Singapore (his dominant scenario from 2008). Like myself, Shambaugh posits that China's future will be determined primarily by the strategic choices of its leaders, not by economic, external or structural incentives or constraints. He now finds that Xi's most likely strategic choice will be to maintain 'hard authoritarianism', although this does not provide any solution to China's need for structural reform and furthermore will meet with considerable resistance from social forces that have become more complex and open during China's long period of economic growth. This is why he predicts capital flight, elite emigration, unsuccessful economic rebalancing, low economic growth, factional struggles and Xi's possible downfall. Shambaugh asserts that if the party leaders decide to either return to soft authoritarianism or soft democratisation, then they will 'enhance their chances of staying in power, and launch China onto another three-decade wave of growth and development' (p. 54). However, if they opt for hard or totalitarian authoritarianism, 'then the economy will progressively stagnate, frictions will germinate throughout society, and the regime will progressively atrophy' (*ibid.*). This is a bold statement of the primacy of politics over economy.

Shambaugh's four scenarios make sense, but the main weakness of his argument, in my view, is its assumptions concerning the likely effects of each possible choice. He thinks totalitarian authoritarianism will lead to economic failure, chaos and war. Hard authoritarianism will prevent the needed structural reforms and thus bring sclerosis or atrophy, and could unleash armed conflict internally as well as externally: 'The possibility of war is not to be discounted. It is, in fact, a distinct possibility (the probability is not insignificant)'. (2016: 112) A return to the soft authoritarianism of the kind practised in the 1998–2008 period however, will be conducive to economic reform, peace and stability. And the best results from every point of view would be achieved through Singaporisation. It would secure the peace, thinks Shambaugh, as he acknowledges the continuing relevance of the 'democratic peace' thesis: democracies do not fight each other, so if China democratises, there will be no war.

Quite strangely, when presenting the likely outcomes of his four scenarios, Shambaugh refers to Ian Bremmer's J curve, which shows that if an authoritarian regime opens up, loosens its social controls, allows more political competition, and fails to nip threats to its authority in the bud, its stability will make *a sharp downturn* before – if it survives – it can rise again, this time to a much higher level of stability than it had at the outset. This is why Bremmer (2008) suggests that developed nations should work to create the conditions most favourable for 'a closed regime's safe passage through the least stable segment of the J curve'. It is dangerous for an authoritarian regime to open up. The democratic system, however, once established and consolidated, is the least unstable system we know. (I still dare to say this after Brexit, the election of Rodrigo Duterte as President of the Philippines, and Donald Trump as US president.) Shambaugh, however, has succumbed to the doctrinaire logic of Minxin Pei's 'trapped transition' theory, and sees only the positive long-term effect of softening up an authoritarian regime, not the short-term risk (Shambaugh 2016: 11). Bremmer emphasizes that unstable states can achieve stability by moving in either direction of the J curve, and the quickest way is to reinforce authoritarian rule.

In *The Dictator's Dilemma* (2016), Bruce Dickson of George Washington University fully grasps the first part of Bremmer's J curve. Dickson (2016) concentrates on the risks entailed by democratization but pays scant attention to the long term stability that may be obtained through the formation of democratic institutions operating under the rule of law and with respect for basic human rights. Dickson situates himself in the 'authoritarian resilience' tradition, building on the work of Nathan (2003) and the earlier work of Shambaugh (2008). His work is based on surveys of public opinion in a sample of fifty Chinese cities, and he finds that the regime has a 'remarkable degree of popular support' (loc 212). People think – or say they think – that China is already democratic and expect their lives to continue to improve under the party's rule. Dickson (2006: loc 6004) sees China as 'a paradigmatic case of authoritarian resilience and durability'. Official appointments are increasingly based on merit and professional accomplishments, and the regime is able to adapt itself to change in ways that maintain basic political stability. This relies on costly and effective repression, in conjunction with co-optation and legitimation (consultation without accountability).

Dickson cites multiple reasons for doubting that China will open up its authoritarian regime to political competition, transparency and accountability. Experiences from elsewhere do not seem to yield much confidence that such opening allows for stability. The Chinese leaders have observed the troubling events in Russia after the demise of the Soviet Union, in the Middle East in the wake of the Arab Spring, and in Asian countries like South Korea, Thailand and the Philippines. The Japanese democracy has been stagnating economically for more than two decades so it can hardly serve as a model, and India's political system does not seem conducive to effective economic management. Recent elections and referendums in Europe do not inspire confidence in pluralistic political systems. In Taiwan and Hong Kong, open elections have undermined support for the One China principle. If China allows a more pluralistic system internally, then this could facilitate ethnic separatist mobilisation in Tibet and Xinjiang, and undermine Beijing's control over other parts of the country as well. So while the party has clear incentives to mix repression with co-optation and consultation in order to maintain popular support of its rule, it must see it as dangerous to allow the formation of any organized opposition.

Based on public opinion surveys, Dickson refutes the accepted wisdom that an economic slowdown will lead to dissatisfaction and hence to demands for democracy. People will remain basically satisfied as long as they expect their household incomes to improve, and such expectations, Dickson assumes, may well survive a slowdown of economic growth. He sees some threat to the regime, though, in the possible emergence of powerful elites outside of the party's control (loc 265). Thus it is important for the party to co-opt social elite groups through various kinds of institutionalized consultation, yet not too much since this might provoke a 'revolution of rising expectations' (loc 5741).

Although he does not see regime change as likely, he discusses how it might happen, singling out three modes: a state-led transformation, which he finds unlikely for the reasons mentioned above; a pacted transition, which he finds even less likely, since there exists no opposition movement to negotiate a pact with; and finally a society-led revolution. This third possibility is the one he finds least unlikely although it would need to be triggered by a traumatic event, like another Cultural Revolution or an exogenous shock, such as a defeat in war or an economic recession.

Although I agree very much with Dickson's analysis I think his first option, a state-led transformation, remains quite possible, although not soon. There is now an international trend away from democratic governance in all of the world's core regions. Xi Jinping'a authoritarianism is a part of that trend. Democratisation comes in waves. If the East Asian Peace survives, then China might join the next wave, and then the Singaporean or even the Taiwanese model may again seem attractive, because they allow a combination of democratization and stability.

Dickson does not mention a fourth possibility: factional struggles inside the party might become so intense that disagreements can no longer be hidden from the public view. Faction leaders may then try to mobilize popular support for competing views or visions through media outlets that sympathize with their views. This would open up the media to open political contestation. In order to avoid violent power struggles, the party leaders might then pragmatically decide to let their differences be resolved through votes in the Central Committee or the Congress of the Communist Party, notably in connection with the election of new leaders. This could further enhance the possibility of open political debate.

A scenario of this kind might lead to the establishment of democratic procedures for resolving political differences, not because of any ideological commitment to democratic values but due to a shared pragmatic wish to avoid violent internal struggles for power. One underlying force behind such a process might be increased attention to the enormous inequalities that have developed between China's social classes. As Zheng Yongnian predicts, sooner or later, the workers and peasants are likely to finds ways of organizing a movement that demands a more just society. It is difficult, however, to assess the likelihood that anything like this might happen, because it would require insight into not only popular sentiments but also the secret world of intra-party politics.[5] At present, when Xi has been confirmed as 'core leader' and seems likely to receive a strong mandate from the 19th Party Congress in autumn 2017, there does not seem to be much need for taking votes. Party members are not free to form any factions. Xi must continue to consult, but for the time being, the 'dictator' decides.

It is amazing how differently the various scholars perceive China's realities. Jean-Luc Domenach, an astute observer of contemporary China, sees a much less satisfied or optimistic Chinese population than the one Dickson has found in his surveys. Domenach's *La Chine m'inquiète* (China Worries Me) from 2009 was translated, updated and revised with the help of George Holoch under the title, *China's Uncertain Future* (2012). Domenach is worried by the growing inequality, pollution, cultural destruction and abuse of workers and women in capitalist China, and is struck by the lack of optimism among average Chinese citizens. He agrees with Zheng Yongnian (2010): when the Communist Party falls apart, there may be a chance for democratisation, as the various party factions try to resolve their differences. Yet he has no more faith than Dickson in any lasting democracy in China: just as in Russia, de-

---

5. A source of such insight is Li (2016). He talks more about pressures for reforms to strengthen the rule of law than about political competition.

mocracy – if introduced – would soon give way to a new authoritarian nationalism, not necessarily totalitarian, but perhaps a new version of Chiang Kai-shek's Kuomintang. This would be consistent with one of Bremmer's points about the J curve: a stable democracy is not achieved overnight, but needs to be built over time; in order to regain short-term stability, many unstable democracies have reverted to authoritarian rule.

The Perfect Dictatorship (2016) by Stein Ringen, Oxford University, conveys a pessimistic, almost indignant image of China's development without, however, predicting that the party-state falls apart. Where Domenach sees an uncertain future, Ringen is sure that China will remain a 'relentless, determined, and unforgiving, sophisticated' dictatorship (loc. 100), using all the means at its disposal to control its citizens. China has not introduced capitalism but remains a state-led and state-dominated economy, which is not as strong as most people believe. Real growth in China has been much lower than its inflated GDP figures indicate, and the growth has led to immense inequality. China has failed to introduce a welfare system in time. Now it is too late, says Ringen, since the poor who would benefit from it are now a minority; the middle class will not want to spend resources on social welfare that it does not need for itself (loc. 776–84).

Ringen compares China negatively to South Korea, whose 'modernisation is the greatest development story ever told' (loc. 793). It has managed to make the jump from a low-income to a high-income country. China remains just a middle-income country. It pursues an uncompromising foreign policy towards its neighbours, and may well end up in a war (loc. 395–6; 4167). Ringen does not see this as highly probable, however. In his concluding chapter, he discusses several Chinese scenarios: muddling through, utopia, democracy, demise, or 'the perfect fascist state'. Until Xi revealed the level of his ambitions, Ringen thought China was likely to continue on the same path as before, muddling through as it were. Then he realized that Xi was different, a man with a vision, more resembling Mao, and found that the most likely scenario for China's future was 'the perfect fascist state' (loc. 4207) based on unity of party, state and security forces, a high level of thought control, and a cult of the omnipotent core leader: *Xi Dada*.

Contra Ringen, I do not see Xi as engaged in an ideologically motivated, perfectly successful fascist enterprise. I assume that Xi understands the urgency of new market economic reforms, but has become a prisoner of a perceived need to secure his own power within the party before he can overcome the expected resistance against such reforms. There is a purpose behind his concentration of power, and the purpose is not just control in itself. He craves to be respected by the great powers, notably the USA, but he also sees a need to secure his own legacy by generating continued economic growth. He does not want liberal political reforms. Xi is as far from a liberal as can be. But he must create the foundations of a thriving domestic market, so China can reduce its dependence on foreign export markets. The key goal in his China Dream is to achieve precisely what South Korea has achieved, namely a high-income society. A high-income country of China's size will overcome its vulnerabilities and become a secure and respected world power. The problem, as I see it, is that Xi is likely to fail. The magnitude of his failure, the time it takes for others to discover that he has failed, and the way they react when they understand, will have a decisive impact on China's future.

My speculation is of no greater value than Shambaugh's or Ringen's but I think Ian Bremmer's J curve provides a clue to the dilemmas faced by Xi and his entourage. He and his advisors have studied the process leading to the dissolution of the Soviet Union. Xi does not want to be China's Gorbachev. Yet he does not want to be a Brezhnev either, upholding a decaying system. Xi is likely to see his predecessor Hu Jintao as a Brezhnev type. Hu's time in power was a time lost for reform. Xi may resemble Yuri Andropov, who could perhaps have saved the Soviet Union if not for his untimely death in 1984. But Xi also has Vladimir Putin as a possible role model. Putin was too junior in the 1980s to save the Soviet Union, but from 1999, he got his chance to save Russia from the wreckage of its much-too-hasty neoliberal reforms, managed to overcome the power of the corrupt oligarchs, and built a highly personalized, authoritarian regime with solid popular support, not least because he dared to stand up against the West. However, as Shambaugh demonstrates, Xi's chosen course is fraught with danger. In order to rebalance the Chinese economy, restructure its system of finance, boost domestic consumption, close down unprofitable enterprises, stimulate innovation and open up shielded sectors to competition, he needs an insulated bureaucracy of hard-working and incorruptible officials on every level of decision-making, each with the confidence and authority needed to overcome resistance from vested interests. Instead, what Xi has obtained so far, with his anti-graft campaign and by immersing himself in every field of decision-making, is to spread fear among China's cadres, leading to inertia and tacit resistance. If Xi proves unable to trust his subordinates, he will be unable to achieve much, and then one day his failure will become evident. As mentioned above, this would not necessarily lead to Shambaugh's 'crack-up' or Ringen's 'demise' scenario. The party state could survive under a new leader.

On 26 February 2016, *China Daily*, the English-language mouthpiece of the Chinese Communist Party, may have sent an oblique signal to Xi by publishing the following extract from a classic seventh century text[6] under the title, 'The Way of a Leader':

> One of the bigger problems about a leader is when he spends too much time on minor details and not enough time on what is really important. He can be too concerned about immediate issues but lack foresight to plan for the future. History has shown us that such a leader will certainly bring forth destruction.

If we believe, as I do, that leadership can – under the right circumstances – decide between war and peace, then predictions must be adapted to the most recent political changes, yet not to the extent of overlooking the structural incentives and constraints that successive decision makers are compelled to take into consideration. I find it interesting that even the proponents of structure-based theories have changed their predictions over time – and vary so much in their expectations. I find Shambaugh's work particularly interesting because of his boldness in making precise predictions and his frequent changes of view. It is extremely difficult to predict abrupt change. At the time of writing this book it seems likely that Xi Jinping will get the support he needs at the CCP's 19th Party Congress, and fill the seven-member Standing Bureau with loyal supporters. This would further increase his powers, but given his failure so far to carry out economic reforms, it is unlikely that he will suddenly turn into a true reformer. Yet this remains uncertain. It is possible that Xi will meet with resistance in the run-up to

6. *Qunshu Zhiyao,* or *The Compilation of Books and Writings on the Important Governing Principles,* curated by Wei Zheng and Yu Shina under commission by Emperor Tang Taizong (599–649) during the Tang Dynasty.

Table 3: Independent variables affecting China's future

	International stability	China's internal stability
Power relative to the US	Enhances risk if approaches parity	Increases domestic urge to demand respected status
Nuclear deterrence	Leads to restraint in acute militarized crises, except if not credible	Helps regime stability by instilling national pride; enhances domestic support for restraint when there is risk of a nuclear exchange
Existing alliance pattern	Confirms US dominance, reassures its allies, provokes a sense of insecurity in China	Instils fear of isolation, strengthens Japanophobia
Climate change, pollution	Drives cooperation, but also struggle over costs	Stimulates protests, increases need for effective reforms
Demographic ageing	Confirms US dominance since it has a balanced age structure	Reduces economic growth; shifts political focus to health and pensions
Economic crisis	Exacerbates tensions and/or generates reforms	Undermines popular support for the government unless it is seen to take effective action
Middle income trap	Confirms US dominance; obviates others' need to counter China's rise	Undermines public support, necessitates reform
Capacity for financial and economic reforms	Drives proposals for revising the global order	Alienates vested interests, while generating growth, hence also popular support
Nationalism	Exacerbates tension	Enhances domestic support
US–China power sharing	Alienates US allies	Enhances domestic support
US–China contact intensity	Enables crisis management	Undermines public support if seen as preventing China from realizing its interests
Xi's concentration of power	Enables summit diplomacy	Could lead to admiration if he succeeds, but otherwise resentment, fear and bureaucratic inertia

the Congress and be forced to accept a compromise, with other factions being represented in the Standing Bureau. If there are serious factional struggles, then this could open up the political system in ways that might either disrupt China's internal stability or eventually allow the creation of a more legitimate political system.

The state of China's foreign relations is also now more difficult to predict, given the election of Donald Trump as US president. If Trump, as seems likely, initiates a conflict over trade, then there could be either a damaging trade war, which might escalate, or a healthy adjustment of the economic relations between the world's two largest economies along some of the lines suggested by Stephen Roach (2014). Xi, on his side, might utilize the uncertainties created by Trump's election to forge closer economic and political relations with the traditional US allies in the region (South Korea, Japan, the Philippines, Singapore, Malaysia, Thailand) and thus enhance China's further development. On the other hand, he is likely to once again miss an opportunity to gain the trust of China's neighbours, and instead get into more trouble both with them and with an erratic US president.

If predictions about war and peace shall become more accurate and reliable, then they must be sensitive to shifting circumstances, including unforeseen choices by key decision makers. A computerized prediction model must be continuously fed with new data, so it can update its predictions each time something happens that the model had been unable to foresee.

For the prospects of internal peace, it may be possible to learn from a comparison between regimes that have managed to generate long-term stability, and regimes that have failed to do so. The party-states in China, North Korea, Vietnam and Laos may be compared across the various dimensions of regime stability: factionalism/consensus; individual/collective leadership; soft/hard repression; aggressive/assertive/moderate nationalism; consultative capacity; popularity; rule of/by law; meritocracy/corruption; regulating/engaging in commercial activities. When there is gradual or abrupt change along one or more of these dimensions in one or more of these polities, this can be used to predict the likelihood of continued internal peace in others as well.

Let me make one rather safe prediction: What happens in 2017, with Donald Trump in the White House and Xi Jinping succeeding or failing in his bid to fill the CCP standing committee with loyal followers, will lead us to once again change our China predictions.

Conclusion

If I may now return to Håvard Hegre's model for predicting the incidence of armed conflicts in the world, I would suggest including some of the factors that have just been discussed. A number of independent variables may influence the prospects for continued peace and stability in China's internal and external relations.

The list of variables in Table 3 reflects the factors discussed above. They are difficult yet not impossible to operationalize in a prediction model. Except for Luttwak's deterministic logic of strategy, and the liberal argument that only a pluralist system of governance can allow a country to get out of the middle income trap so China must either stagnate or democratise, most of the cited predictions are indeterminate or probabilistic, allowing for alternative outcomes. This applies regardless of whether they adopt one or the other theoretical approach. The general form of most arguments is: if $x + y + z$, then p (peace) or w (war) or c (collapse) is a likely but not necessary outcome.

A key challenge for the predictive enterprise is to establish precise theories concerning the interplay of long- and short-term factors: under which structural conditions will a certain political choice by a certain government increase the risk of internal or external armed conflict, and how much will it increase the risk? Political choices and events need to be fed into the model immediately as they happen – or preferably before – so theory-based calculations can be made of the likely outcomes before a bad choice is made.

The China watchers tend with good reason to underline the personal role of Xi Jinping. He has changed China's political system by centralizing power. As 'core leader' he now holds more personal power than any of his predecessors since Deng Xiaoping. Mao and Deng held greater authority than Xi does today, and used it to generate more radical change, but they had neither capacity nor personal inclination to immerse themselves in day-to-day affairs. When Deng came of age and took over as China's leader, he took up Mao's practice of staying away from daily decision-making. The nitty-gritties of reform and management were left to his younger protégés, Hu Yaobang and Zhao Ziyang. Xi Jinping is different from Mao and Deng. Instead of delegating responsibilities, he has made himself chair of all the main Leading Groups in the party (within the CCP there are so-called Leading Groups for each policy area, and they are far more powerful than the government ministries) and has alienated scores of powerful people with his anti-graft campaign. It was hard to predict, when Xi was elected to lead the Chinese Communist Party, that he would act so differently from the cautious Hu Jintao. It is hard to gauge what the long-term impact of Xi's leadership will be. As mentioned, Nathan and Shambaugh both worry that Xi may provoke dissent, opposition and factional struggles. While this seems possible, we may also still imagine that Xi will use his power, if reconfirmed at the next Party Congress, to push through with structural reforms.

Xi has spent considerable time on China's foreign relations and has successfully managed China's international crises without losing control. An independent variable that must be accounted for in predictions for China's future is the ability of its top leaders to work with each other. If Xi is allowed to lead the Party through both of his five-year terms, and there is no internal revolt, a big question is whether he respects acquired custom and manages his own succession through a collective decision-making process, or tries instead to perpetuate his rule, select his own heir and create a new position for himself as a superior advisor.

Another key independent variable is of course the fate of China's economy. Those who say that economic dependence may both inhibit and drive conflict are right. It raises the cost of conflict but does not necessarily prevent it. The key factor may not be economic dependence per se, but economic expectations. If the leaders of a nation believe in a bright future, they are likely to avoid excessive risk. If they have reason to think their nation is in relative decline – as Putin's Russia – they are more likely to take risks. On the other hand, a trade war with the USA could give impetus to Chinese structural reforms. Any loss of market access in the USA would do great damage to the Chinese economy but at the same time it could make it possible for Xi to overcome internal resistance against reforms aimed at boosting the domestic market. He could blame all economic problems on US hostility and argue that it makes reforms indispensable.

In conclusion, let me repeat that predictions based on statistical modelling are likely to become more reliable when more precise data are fed into them. Yet, for a long time they will fail to forecast the most surprising changes. What is most important to predict, is the unpredictable. Predicting the global incidences of armed conflict can only be done with some degree of certainty if China is predictable. And accurate predictions are possible only if analysts incorporate variables such as the disposition of a country's leaders and the style of their decision-making into their models. While it does not seem to matter much if those who make predictions are realists, political economists, culturalists, constructivists, strategic logistics, foreign policy analysts, liberals or Leninist party watchers, it does matter whether or not they are open to the possibility that China's future may develop in ways that are not consonant with Western liberal expectations. Those who believe in just one form of modernisation, which is liberal, tend to expect a coming collapse or war, while those who think there are several roads to modernity have more confidence in continued peace.

Former Swedish ambassador to Vietnam and China, Börje Ljunggren, is a member of our Advisory Board and has followed and supported our programme throughout. He affirms, 'China has the capacity to shape or undermine the East Asian Peace' (Ljunggren 2015b: 56). Until Donald Trump's election to the US presidency, I saw three main ways in which this shaping or undermining might unfold.

The first scenario is a continuation of the present. China avoids war with other states through a combination of diplomacy, deterrence and display of force, and accedes to a new stage of sustainable economic development within the global system of trade and finance. It continues to repress political opponents, curtail civil liberties, use sophisticated information technology to keep its population under control, and uphold its established intra-party mechanism of orderly transition of power from one leader to the next (in 2022, 2032, 2042, etc.). Thus the East Asian Peace continues more or less in its present form. This seems like a plausible scenario if China can uphold a reasonable level of economic growth, e.g. at least five per cent annually. However, this will require drastic economic reforms and astute weathering of US attempts to change the terms of trade.

The second scenario was an internal political crisis in China, caused by an economic backlash and/or factional struggles inside the communist regime. This could lead to internal turmoil as well as adventurous policies abroad, or provoke outside powers to intervene one way or another. This was my most dangerous scenario, although radical change in China would not necessarily lead to either internal or external armed conflict.

The third, most optimistic scenario was one with genuine détente and cooperation between China, Japan and the United States. The defunct Trans Pacific Partnership (TPP) could be used as inspiration for other multilateral initiatives without US participation at the outset, but with China as a partner. The United States and Japan would be invited to join the Asian Infrastructure Investment Bank (AIIB) and decide, eventually, to back up China's One Belt One Road (OBOR) initiative. If supplemented with other initiatives, this could pave the way for a gradual transition to an East Asian security community, based on 'good neighbour' policies, respect for international law, commitment to the UN and other global and regional organizations, diplomatic management and resolution of international disputes, and mutual respect for national sovereignty in the tradition of the Five Principles of Peaceful Coexistence.

Under such circumstances, national elites in China and other countries might feel sufficiently secure to reform their systems of internal governance, uphold human rights, develop mechanisms that hold the government accountable to its citizens, and provide a basis for the development of a popular culture based on values of tolerance and gender equality. None of these values are essentially Western. They are already firmly established in some Eastern countries.

This third scenario seemed idealistic and less likely than the first two, at least in the short term, but if the East Asian nations continue to avoid war among themselves, and also continue to allow their economies to be integrated, it did not seem unreasonable to expect that conditions would change over time, so the regional peace could take hold for real. This would, however, require military restraint, arms reductions and confidence building measures between the various national armed forces. If the current military build-up were to continue, this third scenario becomes impossible.

The election of Donald Trump in November 2016, his declared intention to slam China with protectionist measures unless it agrees to changes in the terms of trade, his acceptance of a congratulatory telephone call from the unrecognized Taiwanese President Tsai Ing-wen, certain statements made by Trump or members of his new administration before the presidential inauguration about China's role in North Korea and the Chinese artificial islands in the South China sea, and notably the appointment of Michael Flynn, Stephen Bannon, Peter Navarro and other proponents of confronting China to central positions in his administration, radically increased the risk of a Sino–US reckoning. As of February 2017, I therefore have to follow what I said above about the need to adapt predictions to unforeseen events. Although there are many possibilities, a crisis scenario seems more likely than before, and I do not then talk about mere 'incidents.' The Trump administration could perhaps be paralyzed by internal chaos and resistance from Congress and US public opinion, giving China an opportunity to enhance its regional and global influence. Yet it seems likely that Trump will get a chance to try out his counter-Chinese strategy and provoke an acute crisis. Xi Jinping is unlikely to back off easily, so the result may be either a grand bargain or a full-scale war, or more likely a Cold War type confrontation, with the USA seeking to contain China's power, and China answering with a number of different means, including cyber warfare. A dramatic reduction in cross-Pacific trade and investments would follow, and probably a backlash against the global economy as a whole. In turn, this would represent a huge challenge for Xi Jinping's leadership. He would be faced great dangers externally but also huge opportunities to impose domestic reforms and enhance China's standing in many parts of the world.

Part III

A Viable Peace?

I n the rest of the book I seek to defend myself and my theories against critics both outside and inside the East Asian Peace programme (sometimes just from inside my own brain), while trying to learn from the criticism. While my research has focussed on explaining the relative peace since the 1980s, and the question of China's future, many of my colleagues in the research programme have questioned the very concept of the East Asian Peace on the basis of more demanding definitions of peace. In order to have peace, it is not enough to avoid armed conflict, they argue. Disputes need to be resolved. The many unresolved militarized interstate disputes in the region show that there is no genuine peace. How can one say that there is peace in the Korean peninsula when its two states constantly prepare for war against each other, and watch each other from either side of a zone filled with landmines? The Korean peninsula is no more peaceful today than Europe was during the Cold War.

A genuine peace cannot rely on military deterrence externally and violent repression internally. Today's absence of war between the states in East Asia relies on military deterrence rather than trust or cooperation, and internal peace is in many cases obtained only through harsh repression. To call North Korea 'peaceful' just because there has been no war there since 1953 goes against any reasonable understanding of the word peace. A truly peaceful society does not prepare for war by building weapons; it renders the option of war implausible by building secure, peaceful relations with other nations as well as among its own people. The state must respect basic human rights as well as the rights of ethnic minorities. There must be rule of law, gender equality, and the children must learn peaceful values. My colleagues are thus concerned by the extent to which the so-called East Asian Peace is not really peaceful, which is easy to see from the low rank obtained by most East Asian countries on the Global Peace Index (Table 4, overleaf).

Table 4: East Asia by rank in the Global Peace Index 2015 and 2016 (out of 162 countries, USA, India and Russia for comparison)

Country	Rank 2015	Rank 2016	Country	Rank 2015	Rank 2016
Japan	8	9	USA	94	103
Singapore	24	20	Cambodia	111	104
Malaysia	28	30	China	124	120
Taiwan	35	41	Thailand	126	125
Laos	41	52	Myanmar	130	115
South Korea	42	53	India	143	141
Mongolia	43	50	Philippines	141	139
Indonesia	46	42	Russia	152	151
Vietnam	56	59	North Korea	153	150
Timor-Leste	58	56			

Source: Institute for Economics and Peace (2016). Global Peace Index, 2016. pp 10–11. Published online by IEP: http://static.visionofhumanity.org/sites/default/files/GPI%202016%20Report_2.pdf. Last accessed 26 October 2016.

I meet these objections with several arguments in favour of a narrow conception of peace. A first argument is normative. Absent better options, most people would prefer a life that is nasty, brutish and long to one that is nasty, brutish and short. It is of tremendous value for people to be free from the scourge of war. North Korea has been a much better place to live since 1953 than during 1950–53, and it has been infinitely better to live in China since its authoritarian communist regime shifted to a course of Peaceful Development in the late 1970s. The suffering of previous generations during the battles, massacres and famines of the 'war after war period' are almost unimaginable for today's young Chinese. My second argument is also normative: The East Asian Peace – in spite of its deficiencies – has allowed tremendous improvement in people's lives through economic development. Just look at Table 5, showing the increase of average life expectancy at birth for people in the East Asian countries from 1981 to 2013. Every country has seen an increase, including North Korea (although its subjects now live shorter lives than South Koreans). See also how the countries that have seen the most radical increase are those that were at war in 1981, most notably Cambodia, where the average life expectancy has gone up from 35 to 66 – almost reaching the same level as in North Korea.

Table 5: Population (millions) and average life expectancy at birth by country, 1981 and 2013/14 (World Bank)

Country	1981 population	1981 life expectancy	2014 population	2013 life expectancy
Japan	117.6	76	127.1	83 (+7)
Hong Kong SAR	5.2	75	7.2	84 (+9)
Singapore	2.5	73	5.5	82 (+9)
Macao SAR	0.3	73	0.6	80 (+7)
Taiwan	18.0	72	23.2	80 (+8)
Brunei Darussalam	0.2	71	0.4	79 (+8)
Vietnam	54.7	68	90.7	76 (+8)
Malaysia	14.2	68	29.9	75 (+7)
China	993.9	67	1,364.3	75 (+8)
South Korea	38.7	66	50.4	81 (+15)
North Korea	17.6	66	25.0	70 (+4)
Thailand	48.3	65	67.7	74 (+9)
Philippines	48.7	62	99.1	68 (+6)
Indonesia	151.0	60	254.5	69 (+9)
Mongolia	1.7	57	2.9	69 (+12)
Myanmar	35.3	55	53.4	66 (+11)
Lao PDR	3.3	49	6.7	66 (+17)
Timor-Leste	0.6	36	1.2	68 (+32)
Cambodia	6.8	33	15.3	68 (+35)
Total NE Asia	1,193.0		1,600.7	
– % of E Asia	76.5		71.9	
Total SE Asia	365.6		624.4	
– % of E Asia	23.5		28.1	
Total East Asia	1,558.6		2,225.1	

Source: World Bank Indicators, 2015: http://data.worldbank.org/indicator/SP.POP.TOTL/countries?page=6.

My third argument is more academic: If we apply a wide definition of peace, we may not be able to discover East Asia's transition from widespread and intense warfare in the years 1839–1979 to a period of no war between states and little internal armed conflict since then. The peace/war dichotomy is a useful heuristic device. It allowed us to discover the scholarly puzzle that motivated our East Asian Peace programme: How could East Asia make its transition from intense, widespread warfare to much fewer and less intense armed conflicts? My fourth argument is purely academic. We need narrow definitions in order to carry out a precise causal analysis. For the explanatory part of the East Asian Peace programme, it continues to be essential to know exactly what we try to explain: a reduction in armed conflict, measured primarily in battle deaths (serving as dependent variable).

My fifth argument is an attempt to meet my critics on their home turf and find a conceptual path allowing me to combine my narrow peace definition with an active interest in the limitations of the East Asian Peace. My suggestion is to focus on the *viability* or *sustainability* of a peace (narrowly defined as absence of armed conflict) instead of using dichotomies: negative/positive, shallow/deep, artificial/genuine. I shall try to transform the various arguments directed against the concept of an East Asian Peace into an exploration of its likely viability.

In accordance with our original plan, the question of the depth or quality of the East Asian Peace has drawn serious attention within our programme. It is common among peace researchers to see peace as a continuum from 'negative' to 'positive', shallow to deep, artificial to genuine, or low-quality to high-quality peace (Wallensteen 2015a, b; Davenport, Melander and Regan forthcoming). Among these rival concepts I prefer the low–high quality continuum advocated by my deputy programme leader, Erik Melander. Yet I see it as a problem that the criteria used for defining the 'quality' are so many and contested. They are derived from a quest for common human values instead of being related directly to avoiding armed conflict or violence.[1] I wish to link my continuum to war avoidance and this is what I manage to do by focussing on viability. Hence factors such as gender and social equality, human rights protection, rule of law and participatory democratic governance move peace towards the right side of the continuum only to the extent that they enhance its viability.

---

1. Another stimulating way of relating the continuum directly to violence is Johan Galtung's distinction between 'peace with peaceful means' and 'peace with unpeaceful means'. This distinguishes peace obtained through cooperation from peace obtained through threats. Galtung's distinction would converge with mine to the extent that cooperation is more viable than threats.

A prominent and influential example of quality continuum thinking is the one that goes into the Global Peace Index (GPI). As mentioned in my Introduction, the GPI builds on a loose definition of peace and a hodgepodge of 22 indicators, some of which are based on real statistics, while others are assessments made by expert panels (of for example a country's level of corruption). On the 2016 index, only one East Asian country is among the ten most peaceful nations in the world: Japan. Nine are ranked among the upper half (more peaceful than the United States). They are Singapore, Malaysia, Taiwan, Laos, South Korea, Mongolia, Indonesia, Vietnam and Timor-Leste. The remaining six (Cambodia, China, Thailand, Myanmar, the Philippines, and North Korea) have a very low ranking, along with great powers such as Russia (which often resorts to the use of force in its foreign relations) and India (where, in addition to low scores on other variables, there are several ongoing internal armed conflicts).

If Kivimäki, Svensson and I had relied on the GPI back in 2009, we would not have discovered East Asia's transition to peace. Reductions in battle deaths have only a limited impact on the ranking. Instead of letting multiple indicators go into the definition of peace, I want to know how those indicators affect the viability of peace as it is narrowly defined. They will then be considered as independent variables, which may or may not affect peace, measured in battle deaths (as dependent variable). In our programme we have to some extent explored the relationship between matters such as demography, justice, reconciliation, equality, freedom, democracy, human rights and capacity for conflict management or resolution with the reduction or absence of armed conflict, although not always through clear causal reasoning. To establish causality, I see it as important to treat these various issues as independent variables (with appropriate proxy values), not as parts of the dependent variable (peace). I wish to know how they affect transitions from war to peace, and how they influence the viability of peace once it has been established.

Kivimäki hits the nail on its head as he explains why the Short Peace in the 1950s ended so soon, while the Long Peace of East Asia still remains in force. If the Long Peace should end tomorrow, it will still make sense to discuss how it could last so long. Duration is the simplest and most direct measure of viability. Yet it is not of course a sufficient

Table 6: Duration of peace in East Asian countries (as of 2015)

Country	Peace years 1946–2015	Years since last armed conflict
Japan	70	70
Mongolia	70	70
South Korea	65	62
North Korea	65	62
Taiwan	66	57
Brunei	69	53
Vietnam	50	40
China	49	27
Laos	43	25
Timor-Leste	52	19
Indonesia	25	12
Cambodia	26	4
Malaysia	47	2/34
Thailand	41	0
Philippines	13	0
Myanmar	3	0

Source: derived from UCDP Data. See http://www.ucdp.uu.se/gpdatabase/gpregions.php?regionSelect=11-Oceania. Last accessed 26 October 2016.

Note: Explanation of Malaysia 2/34: On 11 February 2013, a group of 100–200 armed men arrived by boat from the Philippines to Lahad Datu in Sabah, East Malaysia, leading to a three-week standoff with the Malaysian army, whereafter it defeated the insurgents in bloody fighting. This had more to do with internal conflict in the Philippines than with Malaysia, although the incompatibility between the conflict parties was related to the Philippines' formal claim to Sabah, based on the fact that historically it was a part of the Sulu Sultanate. The clash happened on Malaysian territory. This is why Malaysia's last conflict in the table was in 2013. If the incursion had not happened, it would have been 34 years since Malaysia had its last armed conflict meeting the UCDP definition.

indicator. A long peace may be based on temporary factors such as the longevity of a king or lifetime president, or rapid economic growth. A viable peace must be able to survive leadership successions and economic downturns. The various factors that sometimes enter into definitions of positive or quality peace (justice, equality, democracy, etc.) are best considered as independent variables, which may have an impact on peace viability. This links the two questions of our research programme together. A convincing explanation for regional peace must account for both the transition from war to peace and for the duration of the narrowly-defined peace.

I shall now look into a number of independent variables that have been explored within the programme in order to test or undermine the East Asian Peace proposition, and which may have an impact on peace viability: militarized disputes, unhelpful ceasefires, demographic ageing, masculine honour, state repression, aggressive public opinion, historical wounds and lack of reconciliation.

Militarized Disputes

In the early phase of our research programme, my fellow Norwegian historian, Geir Lundestad, who served as the director of the Nobel Institute and secretary of the Norwegian parliament's Nobel Peace Prize committee, commented with a heavy stroke of sarcasm on the Swedish decision to grant several million dollars to a research project about something that might not exist tomorrow. I replied that if war should break out in East Asia tomorrow, it would still be of interest to find out how it could be so relatively peaceful for a period of three–four decades. And then we would also be able to explore the reasons why it broke down.

Luckily, there have been many tomorrows since that conversation took place, without any East Asian war. Yet there is no way of denying that the East Asian states as well as the USA have been preparing for war and have failed to resolve their militarized disputes; that there have been dangerous incidents and much international tension. East Asia has not moved in the direction of a 'security community'. Quantitatively oriented researchers focussing on Militarized Interstate Disputes (MIDs) instead of armed conflicts (as defined by the Uppsala Conflict Data Programme) have found no evidence of an East Asian Peace.

Throughout the programme period 2011–17, I have followed with apprehension the proliferation of arms in the region, the disputes over North Korea's nuclear weapons programme, about islands and maritime zones in the East China and South China Seas, about trade, freedom of navigation, about history, and the status of Taiwan. I have looked in vain for national leaders seeking to resolve any of those disputes in a way that could make the regional peace more viable. At the same time, I have been relieved to see that in spite of all the tension, incidents have not been allowed to escalate, and the East Asian governments have continued to allow their companies to integrate their business with other regional economies in ways that enhance economic co-dependence. There has not been enough trust to avoid incidents and tension – and certainly not enough to forego military expenditures and exercises – but there has been enough trust to allow functional economic integration. This has convinced me that we are not likely to soon see an outbreak of interstate war, and I consider this immensely important.

The great powers are concerned about the risk of escalation and are aware of how much they stand to lose economically. This combination of security and economic risk may be enough to keep governments away from the brink, at least as long as the Chinese, Japanese and US political regimes are reasonably secure at home and none of the great powers suffer from a deep economic crisis. This remains a valid assessment even if China's relative power, including its military strength, should continue its rapid relative rise. The great powers will follow the situation on the Korean peninsula as well as in the Taiwan Strait, and do what they can to minimize the risk of local allies pulling them into an open conflict. For this reason, as well as in response to concerns for their economic interests, Taiwan, North Korea, Vietnam and other East Asian states remain likely to abstain from initiatives leading to war.

At our annual conference in Singapore 2015, Scott Kastner presented an illuminating paper on risk in the Taiwan Strait,[2] a follow-up to his much-acclaimed 2010 book on the subject. Kastner sees a continuum of possible solutions to the dispute over Taiwan's status that ranges from formal independence to full national unification. In between is the status quo, under which a de facto independent Taiwan enjoys no international recognition. Somewhere between status quo and independence is Beijing's red line. If Taipei crosses the line by weakening the One China principle, Beijing will use force. China's red line may change its position on the continuum, depending on circumstance and on who is in power. The red line could even move to the other side of status quo, in which case Taipei would need to accommodate some Chinese demands in order to avoid war. This could mean moving close to Taiwan's red line. Both parties can only guess where the other side's red line is – and Kastner makes guesses about both. His main research question is not

---

2. A revised version of the paper was subsequently published by *International Security* (Kastner 2016).

where the red lines are situated, but how the risk of war has been affected by burgeoning cross-strait economic integration, including direct flights, tourism, and direct investments. It has certainly heightened the economic cost of a confrontation, and has fostered a business sector with a vested interest in peace. Kastner finds good reason to think that economic integration acts as a constraint that should make Taiwan less likely to test the PRC's red lines. Meanwhile, however, the Taiwanese population has acquired a more uniquely Taiwanese identity, a factor behind the massive victory of Tsai Ing-wen in the January 2016 presidential election. Hence, as Rex Li (forthcoming) has pointed out, there is nothing to indicate that economic integration has led to more popular support for rapprochement across the strait, and there is even less support than before for national unification. If Li is right that the viability of the cross-strait peace depends on the social contestation of the meaning of national identity in China and Taiwan and how this impacts on policy, the peace does not seem viable. The national identities on either side of the strait are moving apart.

In my view, the risk of a Taiwan crisis must be higher now than it was when Ma Ying-jeou was president (2008–16), in particular after president-elect Trump accepted a 2 December 2016 phone call from Tsai Ing-wen. While Ma was principally in favour of One China and often referred to a consensus which is said to have been established between Taiwan and mainland China in 1992 that both the mainland and Taiwan are part of 'the same China', Tsai leads a party with a long-term aim of independence, has been reluctant to declare allegiance to the 1992 consensus, and does not enjoy Ma's level of trust in Beijing. The Kuomintang party, with its Chinese identity, is now in shambles. While economic interdependence may not in itself prevent a clash, it may serve as a conflict barometer. If it is allowed to deepen, then the danger is low. If President Tsai takes tough initiatives to reduce cross-strait interdependence, the danger will increase.

In my view, however, the main factor is not the economic dependence as such, but how it is perceived and handled politically. Politicians who promote or allow growing interdependence are unlikely to exacerbate conflicts. Those who see a compelling need to reduce their dependence on others may put the peace in danger. In the case of Taiwan, the US is crucial for maintaining status quo. The United States is ambiguous as to whether it will intervene militarily if Beijing attacks Taiwan. It might or might not launch a pre-emptive strike against the thousands of land-based missiles in China's Fujian province if a Chinese missile attack against Taiwan were seen as imminent. Without such pre-emptive action, Taiwan could be defeated before there was time to retaliate. If both Taipei and Beijing think the USA may be ready to pre-empt a Chinese attack this way, then they are likely to avoid a crisis, and allow further economic integration in the hope that this will strengthen their own relative power.

Together with Yin Zhengshi, East Asian Peace programme research associate Wang Dong of Peking University has examined China's capacity to deter Taiwan from declaring itself independent. They conclude (2016) that China's use of conventional deterrence, including deployment of missiles and other capabilities, has been effective. However, they also find that such deterrence is only efficient up to a certain threshold, which was reached around 2007–08. Beyond that point, any further strengthening of the deterrent capacity may be counterproductive, adding nothing to the deterrence but provoking fear in Taiwan that China actually intends to use the force it has deployed. They hint that China may have lost an opportunity for making progress with cross-strait talks by continuing its arms build-up beyond the threshold, and that this played a role in paving the way for Tsai Ing-wen's victory at the polls in 2016. At any rate, the presence of Chinese land-based missiles and the (perhaps unrealistic) expectation that the US might be capable and willing to destroy them are now the foundations of non-nuclear military deterrence in the Taiwan Strait. The days when Taiwan could expect to keep an amphibious invasion at bay long enough to allow US reinforcements are gone. China has deployed so many missiles across the strait that it can destroy Taiwan's defensive capabilities and basic infrastructure before any invasion is launched.

What can we learn from the situation in the Taiwan Strait about the viability of peace? The existing peace is not based on mutual trust or rapprochement, but on calculated restraint on either side due to the risks involved. In this sense, the peace does not seem viable. On the other hand, strong economic co-dependency and the priority given both in Beijing and Taipei to their national economies allow us to estimate that, in spite of the deterioration of the relationship after the January 2016 election of Tsai Ing-wen as Taiwan's new president and the contact she was able to establish in December 2016 with US president-elect Donald Trump, the peace in the Taiwan Strait would only be seriously threatened if the US decided to change its Taiwan policy dramatically, and encourage the Taiwanese government to make moves in the direction of formal independence.

Sadly, the same does not apply to the relationship between the two Korean states. There is virtually no trade any longer between them. None of the big South Korean conglomerates invested in the Kaesong industrial zone in North Korea during the time when it was in operation (2002–16). In February 2016, South Korean President Park Geun-hye took the controversial decision to close down the zone completely and withdrew all South Korean staff. (North Korea then liquidated the South Korean private property in the zone.) President Park's decision was motivated by a perceived need to respond dramatically to North Korean provocations. However, her disregard of both the economic loss and the loss of useful contact channels between the two Korean regimes proved costly. Now, there is no economic interaction and very little contact between Seoul and Pyongyang. Hence there is no economic interdependence that can prevent a confrontation, and no business sector lobbying for peace. The main business leaders in South Korea are generally hawkish as far as North Korea is concerned. So the only factors that now prevent war in the Korean peninsula are deterrence and North Korea's economic dependence on China. China may still have some restraining influence in Pyongyang. The United States wields a heavy influence on its South Korean ally, and the US military presence in South Korea represents a deterrent against any North Korean attack on the South.

In a 2015 review essay, I presented a theory of how the combined effect of nuclear deterrence and economic interdependence affects Sino–US relations, arguing that there can be no war between them as long as both factors apply. As Robert S. Ross (1999) has pointed out, a pacifying order was created in the 1980s by Sino–US cooperation and Soviet retrenchment. China was allowed to dominate the East Asian continent, while the USA would continue to dominate East Asia's maritime rim with superior naval power, bases and alliances. Under this order, states in the region could safely set export-driven economic growth as their top national priority. As trade grew, so did the economic risks for everyone.

At a seminar in Oslo in 2005, John Mearsheimer suggested that a theory combining nuclear deterrence and mutual economic dependence might be the best rival to the one he laid out in his now-classic 2001 work, *The Tragedy of Great Power Politics*. I took up the challenge, arguing in 2015 that while neither nuclear deterrence nor economic interdependence can be relied upon to prevent the outbreak of war between China and the United States, but the combination may be sufficient, because each then has to calculate with both a high security risk and a high economic risk when deciding how to manage a dispute. Assuming both sides have an effective, centralized command structure, the risk of escalation will prevent them from going to war. However, if steps were first taken by either side to reduce their economic interdependence drastically, the danger of war would rise since the perceived cost of war would be reduced.

Bates Gill, our Advisory Board member, a former director of SIPRI and now professor at the Australian National University, gave a lecture in Singapore in January 2016 in which he looked at US–China relations and underscored the constraints on conflict between the two. In addition to deterrence and interdependence, he added a 'geo-demographic' constraint, arguing that the combination of an enormous population and a huge territory with long borders has historically served as a constraint on Chinese power projection that demands a largely inward-looking strategic perspective on the part of the country's leaders. This has three main consequences. The first, restraint in relationships with other countries promotes peace. The second, a high degree of sensitivity concerning foreign intrusions in what China considers to be its own territory, such as Taiwan and a number of small islands. The third, a tough policy to prevent internal dissent may yield stability but can also backfire and stir up rebellion. Gill remains relatively optimistic regarding future peace and cooperation between China and the United States, but worries about the course that China's domestic policies have taken under Xi Jinping.

In recent years, the political commitment to economic development has been reduced in the region. Classic 'old-fashioned' goals relating to status, regime security and assertive nationalism have become more prominent. This change may accelerate if there is an economic downturn. Development is more difficult to prioritize when there is little prospect of success, and when one's level of prosperity is already high.

China and the USA are not protectionist powers, at least not yet. They are both members of the World Trade Organization (WTO). It is still worrisome that China's pet project is a Eurasian infrastructural development scheme (OBOR) that does not include Japan or the United States, while the thrust of US economic diplomacy during the Obama administration was geared towards concluding the Transatlantic Trade and Investment Partnership (TTIP) and the Trans Pacific Partnership (TPP), neither of which included China or Russia. Yet this was much less threatening for China than Donald Trump's intention to completely redefine the bilateral terms of trade, in order to protect American industry. The WTO's Doha Round has long been at a standstill, and little progress has been made in the Asia Pacific Economic Cooperation (APEC). Yet it does not seem impossible that economic integration in the Japan–China–US triangle maintains its momentum, driven by transnational companies and their investment in competitive production chains. The main danger sign would be if one or more of the great powers see this as a big enough problem to resort to sanctions or outright protectionist policies. Then leaders may turn less sensitive to economic risk, and only military deterrence will remain to keep them off the brink.

The main danger now, of course, comes from President Trump's declared intention to reduce US imports from China. Another sign of danger, however, is that Asian leaders are so focused on their domestic and international security that they may become selective in their choice of trading partners, boost their military expenditures, and give more political power to their militaries. The most extreme example of this tendency is North Korea, but it can also be seen in several other countries, including China and Japan, the only great powers in the world whose armed forces have no combat experience. The increased focus on security has already gone so far that some, including Ljunggren (2015b) have spoken of a transition from an 'economy Asia' to a 'security Asia'.

Unfortunately, North Korea is not alone in making the East Asian Peace fragile. It does not rely on strong regional institutions or shared democratic values. ASEAN and its various consultative frameworks (ASEAN Regional Forum, ASEAN+3, and East Asian Summit) are no substitutes for genuine institutional cooperation. East Asia's peaceful economic integration has not been matched by institutional security guarantees. Instead, a pattern of alliances remains from the Cold War.

The San Francisco system has not been superseded by a regional system of collective security.

Also, since the national political systems in the region are so diverse, the East Asian Peace cannot rely on shared political values. Some, like Japan, Taiwan, South Korea and Indonesia, are liberal democracies. Malaysia and Singapore have semi-democratic political systems, dominated by one party. And North Korea and Brunei are outright dictatorships. China, Vietnam and Laos are capitalist Communist Party states. In Thailand and the Philippines civilian governments have never gained control of their armed forces or built capacity as developmental states. Thailand, which holds the world record in frequency of military coups, has been living under a military dictatorship since 2014. Struggles over democratisation characterize Myanmar as well as Hong Kong. Myanmar seems on its way into a political situation that is similar to the one that has characterized Thailand in its periods of civilian governance: a public civilian face (represented by Aung San Suu Kyi) and a military 'deep state' that imagines itself to hold a mandate to preserve national unity (represented by the commander-in-chief, Min Aung Hlaing).

The biggest danger to the East Asian Peace comes from crises or tension in Sino–Japanese and Sino–US relations. As David Shambaugh (2016: 139) says, 'As long as the rivalry exists and the relationship is dysfunctional, Asia as a whole is strategically unstable.' The strange fact is that in the last two decades, Chinese and Japanese political cultures have returned to the memory of their murderous past and reignited historical grievances instead of appreciating the peace they have enjoyed for so long. It is as if no reconciliation had ever occurred. Japan's main conservative leaders reinterpret not just Article 9 but also the history of the militarist period. They want new generations to be proud of their history and stop making endless apologies for Japan's past mistakes. On its side, the Communist Party of China has abandoned communism in favour of a classic, assertive nationalism – the same ideology that used to be held by Chiang Kai-shek's Kuomintang Party. It emphasizes China's long struggle to resurrect its past glory after the humiliations it suffered from the European powers and Japan. Today the Kuomintang Party is in shambles, but the Chinese Communist Party carries much of its ideological baggage further.

The underlying premise for Xi Jinping's China Dream is that the nation was humiliated in the 19th–20th centuries by Europe and Japan. Now China is about to become strong enough to make up for its past humiliation by entering the world stage as a great, respected power in a New Type of Great Power Relations, where there is room for Russia, the USA and perhaps the EU and India to also play a role as great powers, but not Japan. China has drastically modernized its armed forces. Deng Xiaoping's downsizing of the People's Liberation Army was followed by an upgrade under Jiang Zemin and boosted dramatically under Hu Jintao and Xi Jinping (although the 2016 budget, largely due to financial constraints, had less growth in military expenditure than before). And China has engaged itself in assertive demonstrations of its excessive maritime claims. China's new assertiveness has instilled fear among its maritime neighbours, notably the Philippines, Vietnam and Japan, where it has paved the way for yet another attempt to empty Article 9 of its pacifist content.

As argued in Part I, Article 9 is deeply embedded in the process that led to and continues to buttress the East Asian Peace, but its role has never been fully recognized or appreciated in the region and deserves greater scholarly attention. Japan's political left supported it, but the Japanese left now hardly exists any longer. The Buddhist Komeito party and the Soka Gakkai religious organisation used to support Article 9 staunchly, but since Komeito entered into a coalition government with the Liberal Democratic Party, it has compromised its pacifist principles. An attempt to generate Sino–Japanese political cooperation and understanding, and alleviate the region's reliance on US security guarantees and military bases, failed miserably under the governments of the Democratic Party of Japan during 2009–12. Instead came a new and vigorous attempt by the government of Abe Shinzo (2012–) to do away with Article 9 and clear a path for implementing Japan's sovereign right to so-called 'collective defence', meaning that it can take part in the wars of its US ally if a threat is perceived to Japan's survival. Abe Shinzo is now trying to achieve what his grandfather, Yoshida Shigeru's conservative rival Kishi Nobusuku, tried unsuccessfully in the 1950s. Kishi's elder brother, the pragmatic Sato Eisaku (who was even less of a pacifist than Yoshida), got the Nobel Peace Prize in 1974. At that time, Article 9 had protected Japan against having to send troops to Vietnam. Instead it was once again able to make money on a US war. Sato Eisaku had stuck to Article 9 and stated in 1970, at a time when the USA had begun to look for ways to extricate itself from Vietnam, that the Japanese Constitution made 'foreign service impossible'.

Yet Article 9 had already then been reinterpreted several times, and its reinterpretation has continued. Japan has built a modern and well equipped Self-Defence Force, although this was always difficult to reconcile with the wording of the constitution: 'land, sea, and air forces, as well as other war potential, will never be maintained.' Yet this one limit has remained until now: the Self-Defence Force could be used only to defend the homeland. Japan would not take part in US wars in any other parts of the world. The US–Japan security treaty of 1960 obliged Washington to defend Japan in case it came under attack, but the reverse was not the case. Japan was not obliged by the security treaty to take part in defending US security in Korea, Vietnam, the Middle East or Afghanistan. In fact, it was prohibited by its constitution from doing so. In 2015, when the Abe government issued a new interpretation of Article 9, and a new Security Law was adopted by the Japanese parliament, although some restrictions still apply and the majority of the Japanese public is opposed to taking part in wars abroad, the road was opened to the possibility that Japan may still become a 'normal nation', with a similar inclination to take part in US wars as have several European members of the NATO alliance.

When Abe's government first made its decision in July 2014 to exercise Japan's right to collective self-defence, it argued that

> No country can secure its own peace only by itself, and the international community also expects Japan to play a more proactive role for peace and stability in the world … In particular, it is essential to avoid armed conflicts before they materialize and prevent threats from reaching Japan by further elevating the effectiveness of the Japan–United States security arrangements and enhancing the deterrence of the Japan–United States Alliance for the security of Japan and peace and stability in the Asia-Pacific region. ('Cabinet…' 2014)

So the full emphasis here is on Japan's contribution to the deterrence capacity of the US–Japan alliance. Japan shall no longer have its own particular profile, but shall act on an equal footing with its US ally in preventing war through deterrence.

In 2014, Kazuhiro Togo, director of the Institute for World Affairs at Kyoto Sangyo University, and grandson of Japan's wartime Minister of Greater Asia, explained that

> the 'excessive pacifism' that Article 9 commanded has long become [a] pain in the minds and hearts of some politicians and government officials, including myself. The idealism of Article 9 could not change the reality of international politics: power balancing is the key to sustainable peace. Japan's failure to help ensure a balance of power made Japan an ego-centric country that cared only for its own peace. The toll of this 'one-country irresponsible pacifism' was sharply felt in the first Persian Gulf War in 1990–91, but the explosion of the Senkaku issue in 2012 and increasingly erratic North Korean behavior under Kim Jong Un made such irresponsible pacifism an unsustainable policy. (Togo 2014)

The reasoning of Abe and Togo contradicts the main argument in this book: Article 9 has played a role not just in giving peace to Japan, but also in spreading it to the region. Researchers and analysts pay too much attention, in my view, to Japanese politicians' quest for identity as a normal nation. What matters most, in a regional context, is not Japan's quest for a new identity, but the role its current identity has played in facilitating regional peace. Article 9 has hugely contributed to East Asia's pacification by reducing the sense of insecurity among Japan's neighbours and creating a model of Peaceful Development. To protect and respect Article 9 is not a self-interested Japanese enterprise, but a regional and global concern.

Togo's argument that Japan must play its part in classic power balancing seems reasonable at first sight. Nonetheless, the argument is actually problematic. Since the United States is the world's dominant military power and sees itself as responsible for upholding world order through the use of force whenever needed, with or without basis in decisions by the UN Security Council, a Japanese pledge to play its part in upholding the regional balance of power could lead Washington to expect that Japan takes upon itself a helping role in policing the world. This is particularly worrisome in light of the fact that Japan's big neighbour, China, is undergoing a parallel change in the direction of exercising its right to actively defend its interests and principles – in its region as well as globally. Since 1988, China has refrained from engaging in any armed conflict outside its own territory and has upheld a purely defensive military doctrine. More recently, the Chinese government has realized the extent to which its interests abroad have expanded. There are those within the People's Liberation Army who see a need for acquiring combat experience if China shall be able to cope swiftly with future challenges. Japan and China are thus both moving away from their defensive military doctrines, stimulated by each other's example and threat, and could end up on a collision course. To prevent this dangerous scenario, the United States will need to be more vigilant in checking or guiding Japan's foreign policy, just as it does with regard to Taiwan.

The increasing integration of US and Japanese security policies was confirmed and boosted by new Guidelines for Japan–US Defence Cooperation (Ministry 2015). They gave ground for the following comment by Yoji Koda, a former commander-in-chief of the Japanese Self-Defence Fleet:

> It is crystal clear that, in theory, any military should be able to operate in any area on this planet in order to protect its own country or national interests. Of course, in the actual execution of operations, an objective area such as 'the region surrounding Japan' will be set for practical purposes. However, when taking into account the global nature of Japan's national interests and the operational characteristics of our alliance partner's forces, the attempt by the Government of Japan to remove the geographical limitations should be viewed positively. This will provide the Government of Japan with more flexibility to make vital security decisions. (Koda 2015)

Unless Japan's Supreme Court decides that the two security laws adopted by the Japanese parliament on 19 September 2015 are unconstitutional, Article 9's positive role in the East Asian Peace may have reached its end. When Japan is ready to exercise its right to collective self-defence, it may feel compelled to take part in US military operations wherever in the world they happen, if only they are seen to represent a threat to Japan's survival. Thus Japan can no longer reassure or inspire others as a 'peace nation'. Some other countries, such as Russia, China and North Korea, will see Japan's military forces as a threat to themselves and take this emotionally and rationally into account. Then – in addition to economic interdependence – the remaining pacifying factors in East Asia will be the deterrent capacity of the US–Japan alliance, and Chinese restraint.

Japan's increasing integration with the US system of command makes it unlikely that Japan can undertake military operations that have not been fully endorsed or requested by its ally. The risk of war in East Asia will remain limited as long as the USA maintains a working relationship with China. This is a dilemma for Japan's decision makers. The more successful they are in removing constitutional constraints on their armed forces, the more they must be prepared to accept interference by the United States in their policy making.

Beijing of course knows, and will continue to know, that Tokyo depends on its big ally in times of crisis, and may therefore play tough with Japan whenever it feels certain that the United States does not want a confrontation. Yet Beijing is also aware that if a crisis escalates into an armed confrontation, then China will have to face the full combined force of the Japan–US alliance. This may not be enough to prevent assertive Chinese behaviour at the initial stage of a Sino–Japanese crisis but is likely to deter China from actually using force if a crisis escalates. While this may preserve the East Asian Peace, fear and crisis management undergird the security dynamic, not trust or cooperation. Japan's special role in allaying other countries' fear and inspiring them to worry less for their security, and more for their economic development, may already have ended.

Johan Galtung has made a distinction between 'peace with peaceful means' (diplomacy, consultation, cooperation, confidence building, conflict management and resolution) and 'peace with unpeaceful means' (coercion, deterrence, power balancing, alliances, shows of force). Article 9 has been a peaceful constituent of the East Asian Peace. The 'unpeaceful' or coercive nature of the peace is now being accentuated.

Yet we should remember – and perhaps celebrate – the historical role of Article 9 and the Yoshida doctrine. Yoshida was not just an instrument of contemporary circumstances, although he would never have come to power in 1946 if he had not met some 'stuctural prerequisites': the US occupation authorities needed someone who had remained close to the Emperor without having been responsible for the government's wartime decisions. As Prime Minister, Yoshida seized his chance to personally shape Japan's future and made choices of historical significance for his region. He led Japan in a direction that would not necessarily have been chosen by someone else.

The Yoshida doctrine consisted of three main elements: economic primacy, accommodation of the USA, and a slow and unthreatening rearmament only for self defence. This combination, and the balance Yoshida struck between the three elements, set Japan on its course to peaceful rise, allowing it to use its resources mainly for civilian purposes, prevent the men with guns from unduly influencing politics, and stay completely out of armed conflict at a time when most countries in its neighbourhood continued to be consumed by war. Although the Yoshida doctrine might now have been eclipsed, it deserves to be remembered. East Asia would not be where it is today without it.

Another factor contributing to undermining the East Asian Peace is the regional proliferation of arms. In recent years, the East Asian countries have invested heavily in expanding and modernizing their military forces, with new logistical technology and weapons systems. This is something we have left out of our research in the East Asian Peace programme. Highly respected research is undertaken at the Stockholm International Peace Research Institute (SIPRI) and other renowned institutions. We have perhaps naïvely presumed that arms expenditures have limited impact on regional peace, and that their rapid increase reflects the growth of government revenues more than changes in the security environment. Yet this is just a part of the story. Rising military expenditure is both a sign and a cause of mounting perceptions of threat. If this should lead to an arms race, we would be in real danger.

Fears for internal stability may fuel perceptions of external threat. A regime challenged by opposition movements may exaggerate the intensity of external threats in order to bolster its cohesion and appeal. That said, none of the states in East Asia seem so fragile that one would envisage a Syrian scenario. Even states with ongoing separatist struggles (the Philippines, Thailand, and Myanmar) are unlikely to fall apart. What could most dramatically transform the region would be a collapse of the Chinese Communist Party. This would not necessarily lead to war; the Communist Party of the Soviet Union lost power more or less peacefully, and Russia's later wars have been limited. The Soviet scenario, however, is precisely what the Chinese Communist Party is prepared to do its utmost to prevent. If Beijing should change tack and introduce liberal reforms, the communist leaders would no doubt seek to monitor the process closely from above, and institutionalise a new order while clamping down on anything resembling a 'colour revolution'.

Unhelpful Ceasefires

The history of the East Asian Peace is full of ceasefire agreements, which have often not led to any genuine peace agreement, and have allowed armed adversaries to keep troops indefinitely on the same national territory. But is ceasefire peace? Situations where several armies live side by side and use their arms to extract taxes from the local population while at the same time exploiting local natural resources, have given ceasefires a bad name. This is notably the case for Myanmar's many ceasefire agreements from 1989 onward. They are seen to have created a 'no war no peace' situation, with little concern for the needs and aspirations of the local population. Since I have defined peace as absence of armed conflict, I am compelled to say that a ceasefire, to the extent that it is respected, equals peace. Yet understanding the limitations and deficiencies of such agreements is crucial to gauging the prospects of peace viability. Ceasefires are meant to be part of or a stepping stone to a genuine peace agreement, but are often either broken or lead to a drawn out rivalry between two or more armed groups. Many ceasefire agreements have been flawed, leading only to a temporary halt in the fighting. Such defective ceasefires are much criticized, not just because they are not designed to last, but also because they do not remove the 'root causes' of conflict by satisfying the demands or main interests of the contestants, or because they do not build trust. Yet such agreements often save lives. This is not to say that it is always advisable to agree on a ceasefire. A truce can break down faster than it took to negotiate it. The Paris agreement of 1973 allowed the US forces to withdraw from Vietnam while the local belligerents regrouped in preparation for the final onslaught, so in a sense the ceasefire was peaceful only for US troops.

In Aceh, a ceasefire agreed upon in 2000 broke down in 2002. In 2005, against the background of the 2002 failure and after the 2004 tsunami that took perhaps 180,000 lives, the Finnish mediator Martti Ahtisaari told the Indonesian government and the Free Aceh Movement (GAM) that he was not interested in mediating a ceasefire. He would accept the request he had received to serve as mediator only if the parties aimed for a full peace agreement. His gamble worked. Not many lives were lost in the fighting that went on while the peace talks were held, and a full agreement was signed, including not just ceasefire, but withdrawal of government forces, disarmament of the GAM, and creation of an autonomous state with free and fair elections. This resulted in a more viable peace than would likely have happened if the parties had started with a ceasefire while deferring the main issues.

The Aceh peace can be contrasted with the Sri Lankan tragedy. A Norwegian-brokered ceasefire between the government and the Tamil Tigers (LTTE) saved lives for many years, but did not create a viable peace. Instead the war ended in a military victory for the government, which used massive force to inflict an intentionally humiliating peace on the Tamil Tigers. The defeat of the deeply authoritarian LTTE successfully deterred the formation of new armed groups, but instead led to a resurgence of non-violent Tamil politics as well as a political reorientation among the Sinhalese population, leading to defeat of the Sinhalese war party at the polls. The Aceh–Sri Lanka contrast contributes to the unsettled and disquieting topic in peace research as to whether victories or peace agreements lead to the most durable peace. All of us feel it must be peace agreements. Yet we are not so sure.

The ceasefires signed in Myanmar from 1989 onwards between the government and many of the country's non-state armed groups have saved many lives, but have also allowed the signatories – both the national Army (Tatmadaw) and the ethnic militias – to regroup and attack non-signatory groups. Since 1989, Myanmar's experience of repeated ceasefires, interspersed with fighting, and accompanied by the plundering of natural resources and abuse of local populations, has led some to question the peace-generating value of ceasefires. In some circles, Myanmar's past ceasefires are held in disrepute.

This is notably the case in Kachin State, where a 17-year ceasefire from 1994–2011 is seen to have allowed an inter-ethnic amalgam of corrupt elites, some of whom negotiated the ceasefire, to enrich themselves through exploitation of the local resources. Although the new outbreak of armed conflict in 2011 seems to have happened at the initiative of the Union Army, many Kachin Independence Army (KIA) sympathizers looked at the resumption of armed struggle as a moral renaissance for the Kachin people, who had been deceived by their old leaders. The argument is often heard that the ceasefire did not bring peace (see Sadan 2016, for instance). I would argue that the main deficiency of the 17-year ceasefire was that it did not last longer. If it had not broken down in 2011, then the opening up of Myanmar's political system might have contributed to an environment conducive to a more sustainable peace. The Kachin Independence Organization (KIO) could have formed a political party of its own to contest the 2015 elections and be in a much better position today to fight non-violently for the interests of the Kachin people. By utilizing the freedom of association and opinion introduced in Myanmar in 2011, political parties and civil society organizations in Kachin State could have exposed the crimes of the Myanmar army at a time when it was no longer protected from public criticism. And they could have pursued effective, non-violent strategies to reclaim their rights to natural resources that had not yet been so rapaciously extracted. In addition, many lives would have been spared. Thousands of internally displaced people would not have been forced to leave their villages, and food prices would not have differed enormously between the areas held by the government, those held by the KIA, and the contested zones between them.

The two ethnic parties that won the strongest position in Myanmar's 2015 elections were those that had for a long time emphasized unarmed means of struggle, Rakhine State's Arakan National Party (resulting from a 2014 merger of the Rakhine Nationalities Development Party and the Arakan League for Democracy, which split up again in 2016–17) and the Shan National League for Democracy in Shan State. Although the anti-Muslim posture of the winning Arakan National Party gives ground for worry, its victory at the polls is likely to have created a less dangerous situation than would have been the case if there had been armed fighting in Rakhine State and the Arakan National Party had been unable to take part in the elections. Unfortunately, however, an Arakan Army has also been reconstituted and retrained, first by the KIA and later by the United Wa State Army. The fact that the Arakan National Party has not been given a strong say in the government of Rakhine State, and that the growing Arakan Army has been denied a seat at the table in the national ceasefire process, have contributed to deepening the crisis in Rakhine, where some 150,000 Muslim Rohingya have lived in camps for internally displaced persons (IDP camps) since the communal violence of 2012. In

October 2016, armed fighting broke out in northern Rakhine state when an Islamist group attacked Myanmar's border forces. The Tatmadaw responded with an extremely brutal clampdown on the local Rohingya population.

All of this is meant to say that although an armed 'ceasefire peace' is often deficient and unsustainable, we should not heap scorn on cease-fires as possible precursors for a viable peace. In order to increase the likelihood that they have a lasting impact, ceasefire agreements need to include a code of conduct, a clear demarcation of the territories con-trolled by the parties, solid monitoring arrangements, and institutional mechanisms for initiating talks aimed at a lasting settlement. When both sides see that the other intends to uphold the ceasefire, seeds of trust can be sown that provide a basis for a comprehensive peace agreement, including reforms that, together, satisfy some of the demands of all sides, and allow military forces to be withdrawn or demobilized. At any rate, a ceasefire is only an 'armed peace'. Whether or not it leads to a viable peace depends primarily on how it is followed up. In Myanmar, the government of president Thein Sein (2011–16) made it a matter of priority to arrive at a national ceasefire agreement before the elections of 2015. When the Kachin Independence Army (KIA) and its ethnic allies decided not to sign because the government refused to invite a number of smaller groups into the process (and because they had not had enough time to consult their grassroots), the government went ahead with a public ceremony, although only a minority of eight ethnic armed groups were ready to sign.

When new fighting broke out in several places during and after the ceasefire signing ceremony, both between the Union Army and non-signatory groups and between signatory and non-signatory groups, the national ceasefire also came into disrepute. Indeed, the agreement had several deficiencies. The main flaw, as mentioned, is that it was signed only by some groups. Another was the exclusion from the preceding talks of some small but significant groups – such as the Kokang, who had been defeated by the Army and driven across the border to China in 2009 at a time when the military government tried in vain to persuade all ethnic armed groups to transform themselves into Border Guard Forces (BGF) under the Union Army's command. In early 2015, the Kokang engineered a well-armed return, which led to heavy fighting and hundreds of casualties. Another flaw in the national ceasefire was that it strengthened the military position of some of the eight signatory groups, who were not just in conflict with the Army but also with other ethnic armed organizations. This was the case for the Shan State Army-South, which allegedly used the ceasefire as a cover for occupying territories previously controlled by others, thus provoking an exodus of villagers toward hastily set up IDP camps. In 2016, after Aung San Suu Kyi came to power, the situation got even worse, with military offensives and counter-offensives between the Union Army and what came to be known as the Northern Alliance of armed groups in northern Shan State and Kachin State. No new groups signed the national ceasefire, and the government made clear that only those who had signed could take part in the national political dialogue at the so-called 21st century Panglong conferences.

The 2015 'nation wide' ceasefire agreement is supposed to be followed up with development aid to the ceasefire areas, in great part provided by external donors. As conceived this good idea could provide a basis for sustainable development and local participation in decision-making. However, since Aung San Suu Kyi's government insists that the funding scheme must be aimed only at areas controlled by the ceasefire groups and not those held by non-signatory groups, it may actually do harm by privileging some groups over others and by failing to reach out to the most vulnerable population groups. Despite the intentions of the agreement, participation rights are perceived to be granted as a political reward, which further strengthens the general distrust among the ethnic minorities of the central authorities. In spite of these flaws, which do not seem to have much prospect of being repaired, the national ceasefire agreement has yielded some genuine good in the areas where only signatory groups are present. It consolidated the ceasefire that was reached in 2012 between the Myanmar government and the Karen National Union (KNU), and might thus pave the way for peaceful development in Kayin State (previously called Karen State) and neighbouring areas. However, this demands collaboration not only between the KNU and the government, but also between the various Kayin factions. The KNU, the local government and the companies investing in the area may have much to learn from the failures of the 17 year long ceasefire in Kachin State 1994–2011. The most important lesson is probably a need for transparency concerning the exploitation of natural resources, and that a substantial part of revenues from such exploitation must be used for the benefit of the local communities.

A succession of democratically elected governments in the Philippines have negotiated unsuccessfully for many years with the country's communist rebels in the New People's Army (NPA), who did not end their armed struggle at the end of the Cold War, not even when the 1986 People Power uprising in Manila led to the reintroduction of basic freedoms and electoral democracy. The elected governments failed to carry out any radical land reform, so the distribution of land in the Philippines remains unequal and thus not conducive to economic development. The big landowners have few incentives to invest, and those who till the land have neither money to invest nor property to use as collateral. So the NPA has continued to recruit fighters among the impoverished rural populations, often ethnic minorities, and subject them to direction from doctrinaire political leaders who live in exile in the Netherlands.

The Philippines government has also negotiated with two rival Muslim Moro organizations in Mindanao. In 1997, after a failed experiment under which leaders of the Moro National Liberation Front (MNLF) were allowed to govern with relative autonomy, the central government arrived at an agreement for general cessation of hostilities with a new rival rebel movement, the Moro Islamic Liberation Front (MILF). Formal peace talks followed in 2000, but were quickly interrupted when President Joseph Estrada ordered all-out war against the MILF, leading to heavy fighting and approximately 1,500 battle deaths. After Estrada had been ousted as president in January 2001, peace talks were resumed and an agreement was signed in Tripoli (Libya). The ceasefire continued to be broken, however, with reciprocal accusations of responsibility. Yet there were also periods when the cessation of hostilities agreement was generally respected (notably in 2006 and 2010).

Rapid progress was made in new peace talks after President Benigno Aquino Jr made this a priority for his government in 2010. In July 2012, a Framework Agreement for Bangsamoro was signed and, in March 2014, after 19 years of negotiations, with help from Malaysian mediators, a comprehensive agreement was signed between the MILF and the government. It included a Basic Law for a new autonomous

Bangsamoro province in western Mindanao. However, opponents of the Basic Law took their battle to the legislature, where they procrastinated and managed to delay a ratification vote. The agreement was further weakened when fighting between the Army and a new breakout group from MILF, the Bangsamoro Islamic Freedom Fighters (BIFF), broke out in January–February 2015. Hence, when the Philippines elected Rodrigo Duterte as its 16th president in May 2016, the Basic Law had not yet been adopted by the Senate, and Duterte put it aside while insteading beginning to work on his vision of a federal Philippines. A huge negotiating effort thus ended in failure, and there is now a risk that the moderate MILF may be superseded by more radical groups. There is little doubt that the cessation of hostilities agreement from 1997 was conducive to peace, although it was often broken. The negotiations continue to depend on trust between the parties, so it is no surprise that progress was mainly made in the periods when both sides avoided hostilities. It takes a long time to gain trust, but it can be quickly lost.

An example of an extremely long-lasting and life-saving ceasefire, despite not being followed up by a peace agreement, is the armistice signed by the Chinese, North Korean and UN forces in Korea on 23 July 1953. The South Korean government did not accede to it, and North Korea has sometimes declared that it will no longer abide by it. Yet both North and South have mostly complied in practice, and the provisions of the armistice remain in place. For 63 years it has contributed to preventing a new outbreak of war in the Korean peninsula. This is a peace upheld with military deterrence and a Demilitarized Zone that totally separates the two parts of the country. Attempts at rapprochement in 1972 (between South Korean president Park Chung-hee and North Korea's leader Kim Il Sung) and 2000–08 (under South Korean presidents Kim Dae-jung and Roh Moe-yun, and North Korean president Kim Jong Il) both failed. Yet the 1953 armistice may have saved hundreds of thousands of lives that could have been lost if the Korean War had not ended or had broken out anew. In the Korean case, a new war could also have brought China and the United States into direct conflict. Indeed this risk has been a major factor in upholding the 1953 armistice, since neither Beijing nor Washington have wanted to see it broken. Even the fragile peace in Korea must be seen to have great value. It allowed an economic miracle in South Korea and its democratic transition. The

Korean armistice is still at risk, however. Its historical role would be even more positive if it could be superseded by a peace agreement between the USA and North Korea, denuclearization of the peninsula, and a political settlement between the two Korean states.

If we were to use a quality peace concept, we might be overwhelmed by the many deficiencies of ceasefire agreements. The absence-of-armed-conflict definition allows us to see the lives that were spared, and does not prevent us from realizing how fragile a ceasefire peace may be, and how human rights may continue to suffer even as all parties adhere to the ceasefire terms.

In spite of all that I have said in defence of defining peace as absence-of-armed conflict, its accentuation of battle deaths has been felt as a straitjacket by most researchers in the East Asian Peace programme, also by myself. It has forced me to consider that some of the world's most violent societies have peace. The most extreme example is North Korea, which is near the bottom of the Global Peace Index.[3] Both Koreas spend enormous resources on arms. US troops are permanently stationed in South Korea, and there are no diplomatic relations between Pyongyang and Washington. North Korea has developed nuclear weapons. The totalitarian nature of the regime is upheld through a sensation of being permanently threatened. Basic human rights are constantly trampled upon.

There have been numerous violent incidents between North and South Korea over the years. Yet none of them has satisfied the Uppsala definition of armed conflict either because they have not yielded as many as 25 battle deaths in one year or because it has been impossible to establish with certainty who the perpetrator was.[4] My narrow definition of peace obliges me to see the Korean peninsula as an integral part of the East Asian Peace. Although this is strange from a normative point of view, it is not meaningless. The puzzle of explaining the East Asian Peace cannot be resolved without determining how and why war has

---

3. To see the 2016 Global Peace Index report as well as engage with an interactive presentation of the Index's 23 variables as applied to all countries, see http://www.visionofhumanity.org/.

4. The sinking of the South Korean warship Cheonan in 2010 would have been included in the statistics if it could be proven that the ship was hit by a North Korean torpedo. The number of sailors who drowned (46) exceeded the UCDP's 25 battle death threshold for an armed conflict.

been avoided on the Korean peninsula for well over sixty years. This has therefore been a part of our explanatory endeavour.

Jong Kun Choi (2016) wonders if the situation in the peninsula has changed since the 1950s, from 'crisis stability' to 'general stability'. Crisis stability is defined as a situation where neither side attacks because it knows that the other is able to respond in kind, while general stability denotes a situation where both sides prefer to keep the peace regardless of whether they could win a war or not. Jong concludes, unsurprisingly, that there is no general stability on the Korean peninsula. The security order in Northeast Asia remains precarious. Yet he claims that seeds have been planted for a transition to general stability. South Korea could get into a situation where it rejects the option to attack the north, even if it is certain of victory. This is partly because South Koreans have become so prosperous that they don't want to pay for unification, and partly because the young generations are accustomed to being South Korean, have little interest in national unification, and do not want any violent disruption of the peace. The same is not the case, however, in Pyongyang. North Korea avoids war because it cannot win, not because it abhors war. The North Korean regime does everything in its power to uphold a feeling of pride in its armed forces.

I have argued above that ceasefires equal peace (when respected) but that a 'ceasefire peace' is often unsatisfactory and non-viable. One of my examples was the North Korean armistice of 1953, which must be seen as non-viable although it has been enforced for well over sixty years. Instead of letting the failures and deficiencies of ceasefire and peace agreements compel me to give up my definition of peace as absence of violence, I have drawn attention to the viability or sustainability of peace narrowly defined. This has allowed me to take into account the criticism made of the many ceasefires and peace settlements that have not resolved key conflict issues.[5] I have done this by addressing the question of how the criticism affects the viability of the East Asian Peace, and although many border agreements and also some peace agreements have contributed to a lasting peace, the many unresolved disputes or conflict issues have forced me to doubt that the East Asian Peace is viable.

---

5. Key conflict issues are often referred to with the biological metaphor 'root' causes. This is unfortunate since conflicts are not trees with causal roots but disputes between individuals or organized groups over certain issues.

Demographic Ageing

One variable explored in our programme is the age composition of the East Asian populations. The viability of a regional peace may be affected by the age of its population. As can be seen in Table 6 (p. 152), the average life expectancy in East Asia has increased dramatically. One country after another has gone from a situation where a combination of high fertility and reduced infant mortality created a 'youth bulge' to a phase in which a dramatic decline in fertility leads the former youth bulge to become a bulge of elderly.

The total population of East Asia increased by 43 per cent from 1981 to 2013, and the average life expectancy improved in every single country. This was most dramatic in the poorest countries, and in those that still suffered from war in the 1980s: Cambodia, Timor-Leste, Laos and Myanmar. North Korea, whose famine in 1997–98 cost hundreds of thousands of children's lives, shows the least progress. The growing gap between North and South Korea is startling. In 1981 the average life expectancy was the same in the two parts of Korea: 66 years. In 2013 newly born South Koreans could expect to reach the age of 81 while a North Korean baby could only expect to live for 70 years. Yet this is not low from a historical perspective. If life expectancy were to be seen as a key measure of quality peace, then the East Asian Peace would be of a high quality.

However, the dramatic increase in life expectancy through East Asia is not primarily due to the absence of war, but to improved health and better nutrition. These factors have led to higher life expectancy all over the world, even in areas with deep and protracted warfare. The Global Peace Index shows the relative 'peacefulness' of countries, but does not reflect the tremendous strides toward reduced mortality that have been taken in almost every country on the planet. When speaking of relative improvements, what sets East Asian demographic developments apart from other developing countries is a higher median age due to low fertility. East Asia shares this trait with Europe, including Russia, which faces a bleak future due to a rare combination of low fertility and high mortality – particularly among men.

The demographer and peace researcher Henrik Urdal (2017) concludes from a study within our programme that the ongoing demographic changes are likely to be conducive to a viable peace in East Asia, and that ageing may lead to a shift away from military to social spending. He joins those (including Haas 2007) who call this a 'geriatric peace'. When a country or region has a young population – a 'youth bulge' – both national and rebel armies may find it easier to recruit soldiers and fighters. Disgruntled young people more readily engage in conflict. Education does not always help, and may in fact lead to more rather than less dissatisfaction, if it creates expectations the labour market cannot satisfy. However, when the young are offered education *and* employment opportunities, the youth bulge may contribute to peaceful and perhaps dramatic economic growth instead of conflict. This happened in East Asia. The region benefited economically from a youth bulge that no longer exists, except in the poorest countries (Timor-Leste, Laos and Myanmar). Even in China, the young are now getting old. The number of working-age people has peaked, so, in the next few decades, China shall enter a situation similar to that of Japan, with a quarter or third of its population depending on support from a diminishing workforce. This of course creates a heavy need for pension funds and makes it difficult to maintain huge military budgets. In China, there were 13 people of working age for every elderly person in 2009; by 2050, forty per cent of the population will be above working age so the ratio between the working people and the elderly will be just 2:1. In China this is known as the 4–2–1 problem: each adult person who is a one child will have to care for two parents and four grandparents (Dickson 2016, loc 1482). This should not create much incentive for him or her to engage in war as a soldier or rebel fighter.

Yet we cannot be sure to see a 'geriatric peace'. China's economic slowdown could challenge the government's ability to care for the elderly and lead it to emphasise priorities other than the economic progress on which much of its legitimacy is based. Japan, for example, has increased its military expenditures despite the needs of its ageing population. This demonstrates that a combination of demographic ageing and economic slowdown does not necessarily lead a government to move in the direction of more peaceful policies.

Masculine Honour

When designing the Uppsala programme, we wanted to study the role of gender in the East Asian Peace but were at first not certain of the most fruitful way forward. The regional context presented a challenge in that there were too few countries for cross-sectional time series studies to yield robust statistical results, but too many countries for in-depth qualitative analysis. Following Hudson and den Boer (2004), we discussed how the practice of aborting female foetuses might influence peace, by creating a surplus of young men without families, who might form violent gangs. On the other hand, we imagined that the Chinese one-child policy might induce parents to prevent war in order not to lose their only child.

I asked my colleagues why women play a more prominent role in the Philippines – in business, politics, government – than in other East Asian societies, without this leading to a reduction in the country's level of violence. We did not find much previous research on these matters, so our first gender project, carried out by Erik Melander and Elin Bjarnegård (2013), is a straightforward statistical study that assesses the extent to which gender equality is statistically associated with peace, with a special focus on East Asia. It supports the claim that countries with higher levels of gender equality are also more peaceful narrowly defined (avoiding armed conflict). However, when looking at East Asia only, a widely used indicator – representation of women in parliament – does not correlate with national peacefulness. Using the proportion of women in parliament as a measure of gender equality gives countries with communist regimes an excessive impact on the results since their focus on formal equality leads them to have comparatively many women in their legislature assemblies, while they have also efficiently avoided armed conflict. Yet representation in communist assemblies offers little information about a country's actual gender equality, because these elected assemblies hold little power. One has reason to be sceptical about gender equality in countries where party politburos and central committees remain dominated by men. Finally, Bjarnegård and Melander (2013) argue that the peace in these countries was at least in part achieved by effective repression. While the global relationship between different measures of gender equality and peace holds also when controlling for the communist regime type, they find it impossible to discern any statistically significant association between gender equality and peace when confining the analysis to East Asia.

Bjarnegård and Melander decided that a different approach was needed to get at the role of gender in the East Asian Peace. They harnessed survey data concerning popular *attitudes* to gender roles – and to ethnic, religious and sexual minorities. Here they found significant statistical association. Norm changes among men and the meaningful inclusion of women in setting political agendas revealed themselves as far more important for a turn to peace than formal political representation. In other words, if we want to explore the relationship between peace and gender, it seems that we should focus on a society's values and norms concerning gender equality, rather than the sex of individual political representatives.

The group decided on this basis to use Thailand as a focus country and carry out a special survey there, led by Bjarnegård and Melander and with Karen Brounéus contributing psychological expertise. The survey shows a clear association between attitudes favouring inequality between the sexes and participation in political violence. Inequality values are also positively correlated with personal experiences of violence, both as victim and perpetrator. While working on the survey, Melander and Bjarnegård (2014) developed the proposition that, in Thailand, a militarized masculinity culture with a deeply held concept of honour may facilitate violent conflict, while a cultural emphasis on equality between the sexes and tolerance toward minorities is more peaceful. Every statistical or other formulation of these questions yielded results that support this thesis.

When comparing their survey results from Thailand with surveys undertaken by others elsewhere in East Asia, Bjarnegård and Melander have found some stark differences, which could indicate that peace viability may also vary from one place to another. Some kinds of attitudes can threaten the peace in one place, while other kinds of attitudes threaten it in another. There are different kinds of animosities. Among China's Northeast Asian neighbours, there is considerable resentment against China, and the Chinese feel a similar resentment towards Japan. Survey results from Thailand, Malaysia and Singapore show much less resentment towards China, also less than in the Southeast Asian countries bordering China (Vietnam, Laos and Myanmar). In several Southeast Asian countries, there is a noticeable lack of tolerance towards certain religious minorities, indicating a pervasive risk of communal violence. This is not the case in Northeast Asia.

In Northeast Asia, instead, gender discrimination is pervasive. In China and South Korea a widespread practice of sex-specific abortion has led to a skewed gender composition; many excess males have remained single or have imported a partner from abroad. China and South Korea also used to have the world's highest rate of homicides on new-born girls but this now seems to be changing (*The Economist* 2010; 2017). While we do not have evidence to indicate that this has had any impact on the propensity to engage in armed conflict, it is in itself a form of extreme violence. When excluding infanticide, Bjarnegård and Melander (2014: 20–5) confirm that East Asia has a comparatively low rate of registered homicides among its adult population, but the level of non-lethal domestic violence is difficult to measure since most incidents are likely to go unreported. One survey found that a majority of the Chinese condone domestic violence, both against wives and children. Over 50 per cent of Chinese men reported that they themselves had perpetrated physical or sexual violence against their partner, and only 22 per cent thought it was never justifiable to beat a child (the comparable figure in Japan was 80 per cent).

In order to gauge the role of meaningful inclusion of women in peace processes, Bjarnegård continues to follow the peace process in Myanmar, where women have been systematically excluded from participation. They are, however, affected by conflict in very particular ways, something Bjarnegård outlined in a chapter in the *SIPRI Yearbook 2015*. On the basis of deeper exploration of their data set, Melander (2015: 40–5) claims, using a wide definition of peace as not just absence of armed conflict but also of other kinds of physical violence, that a strong continued adherence to honour ideology makes the East Asian Peace fragile and unlikely to reach the realm of the private home. Domestic violence makes life insecure for women and children and passes on attitudes to new generations that are detrimental to the development of a resilient peace. The assumption here is that a society with a high level of domestic violence is more likely than a less violent society to engage in armed conflict.

I have been intrigued by Melander and Bjarnegård's findings. If gender-equal values have the side effect of perpetuating a narrowly defined peace, this provides an additional impetus for the struggle for gender equality. My inclination is to imagine that gender-equal norms, in and of themselves, are perhaps not highly significant motivators of people who prevent a militarized dispute from escalating or who find ways to terminate a war. The role of gender-equal values enters into the equation mainly at a stage when a society no longer has armed conflict and sets about to reduce all forms of violence. Peace may become truly viable when all use of violence is thought of as dishonourable.

State Repression

North Korea represents the most acutely felt challenge to my narrow concept of peace. Since 1953 it has not been engaged in armed conflict either internally or externally, if we rely on Uppsala University's definitions. Yet absent a peace treaty, in a formal sense it remains at war. North Korea spends a much greater proportion of its national income on the military than any other country in the world, and the regime's rhetoric is highly aggressive.

The incredible discipline of the North Korean population and its willingness to endure untold hardships probably depend on its sense of being threatened by the United States and South Korea. If people did not believe that North Korea is under threat, much of what the regime does would not make sense. The North Korean regime subjects is population to harsher repression and control than any other regime in the world, with systems of dividing the citizens in accordance with their perceived loyalty to the regime. North Korea thus strongly challenges the relevance of peace defined as just absence-of-armed conflict. This is all the more important since, to some extent, the same is the case for other East Asian nations, many of which are ranked lowly on the Global Peace Index (Table 4, p. 148).

We have discussed the question of whether peace within states can be viable when it is obtained through authoritarian governance, repression of political opponents and disrespect for human rights. Kivimäki has explored an interesting concept of peace that does not just require absence of active armed conflict, but an absence of certain kinds of repressive violence as well, such as arrests, imprisonment, torture, killings and executions. He asks what it takes to remove the *fear* that people have for their lives. Fear may be caused by a government's repressive violence and also by criminal violence. He finds that the occurrence of repressive violence is relatively high in East Asia (China executes more people than any other country in the world) but the available statistics indicate that repressive violence has been reduced in the region during its period of peace (Kivimäki 2014: 49–50). One may therefore assume that people have less reason to fear for their lives now than before.

Liselotte Odgaard, a programme research associate based at the Danish Defence College and her colleague, Thomas G. Nielsen, have studied the Chinese government's counterinsurgency strategy in Xinjiang and Tibet. They find (2014) that while the civilian branches of government seek to integrate ethnic minorities in programmes of economic development, the military and police often resort to harsh methods of repression. This may create order in the short term, they surmise, but at the same time exacerbates ethnic grievances that continue to represent a long-term threat to national unity and Communist Party rule. Their research indicates that China's harsh and ill-coordinated modes of repression in the ethnic minority areas is not viable, and is likely to lead to more conflict down the road.

In the programme core group in Uppsala, Kristine Eck has undertaken detailed research on repression, using both historical source material and contemporary evidence. A key premise is the realization that effective, viable repression requires accurate intelligence. Massive, blind repression may be effective in the short run when it provokes a sense of paralyzing fear, but in the long run is more likely to provoke resistance since it leads to anger and calls for revenge. Systematic repression, built on accurate information, may help stabilize a state. In a study she has made of the Myanmar army's cooperation with independent militias, Eck (2015a) finds that the army may engage in such cooperation when it has purged officers in a certain area from its ranks, and therefore no longer has access to local information. The militia steps in because it has the best knowledge of local conditions. This demonstrates the importance of intelligence.

Eck works on two projects that may influence the way we understand the East Asian Peace. One evaluates qualitatively distinct inheritances from various European colonial powers. While Singapore, Malaysia and Brunei could take over and perfect the British system of repression – and the Philippines the American one – this was not the case for Indonesia, Laos, Cambodia and Vietnam – although the Vietnamese communists learned much from their decades of struggle against the French *Sûreté*.

It was also not the case for Myanmar, which made a cleaner break with British colonialism.

Eck distinguishes between hard repression, which involves violence, and soft repression, which consists of suppressing civil liberties. The aim of both is to impede opposition, but the argument posits that states revert to hard repression only when they lack capacity to make soft repression effective. In the book manuscript she is working on, which looks at how divergence in these repressive strategies occurs, she suggests that one explanation may lie in states' historical trajectories. Eck posits that variations in experience with armed opposition prior to independence may help explain the different paths that states take in preparation for or response to threats of armed opposition. Experience affects decisions state leaders take regarding what level of surveillance and security preparations are appropriate.

Eck's other project, undertaken in cooperation with Chris Fariss of Penn State University, compares respect for human rights in East Asia with the situation in the rest of the world (Eck and Fariss 2015). They do not look primarily at harsh methods of repression, such as extra-judicial killings, torture, disappearances or political imprisonment. Instead they focus on the softer kinds of repression that may render direct violence unnecessary, such as violations of civil liberties and political rights. While violations of physical integrity rights have been on the decline in East Asia, the evidence collected so far suggests that this may not be the case for violations of civil rights. If this hypothesis is confirmed, it may have significant implications the viability of the East Asian Peace. If conflict is suppressed through systematic violations of civil liberties, then peace is built on a foundation of human rights violations. Eck's general proposition is that a peace bought at the expense of human rights is fragile.

Pavel Baev, a Russia expert at the Peace Research Institute Oslo (PRIO) has engaged with me in a joint project on Russia and China's strategic partnership and its importance for the East Asian Peace (Baev & Tønnesson 2015; Baev & Tønnesson 2017; Tønnesson & Baev 2017). We have asked ourselves why semi-democratic Russia often resorts to direct violence both at home and abroad, while the Chinese communist regime has shown restraint in its foreign relations and a greater capacity for keeping opponents under control with less use of hard repression.

Some of our Chinese interviewees have claimed that the West tried to orchestrate 'colour revolutions' both in Kiev (orange) and Hong Kong (jasmine). They allegedly succeeded in Kiev because the Yanukovych regime was poorly organized and could not act on the basis of accurate intelligence, while China was better equipped to meet the challenge in Hong Kong.

My inference from Eck's work, from my own observations and from reading Dickson (2016) and Ringen (2016) is that an authoritarian peace is viable as long as a regime remains cohesive at the top, maintains hierarchical control of all branches of government – notably the armed forces – and has an efficient system of gathering and processing intelligence. If there is also some leeway for expressing grievances and political opposition through strikes, petitions, critical media or multi-party elections – like in Singapore and Malaysia – an authoritarian peace may well be viable. The big question for the future of the East Asian Peace, as discussed in Part Two above, is whether China can continue to uphold its repressive peace.

Aggressive Public Opinion

I already touched on the role of public opinion in the section on 'Rulers, Citizens and Democratic Peace' above. Rulers are influenced by their understandings of public opinion, and leaders can frame public opinion, particularly with regard to foreign policy. Allan Dafoe of Yale University and Jessica Weiss of Cornell University have undertaken an experimental project (2015) within our programme, during which they asked Chinese audiences to express their preferences about how their government should act in several hypothetical and real life disputes (about the East China Sea Air Defence Identification Zone). They look at the willingness of the Chinese public to support the use of force in the context of disputes about rights of transit in the East and South China Seas, and aim to find out what kinds of events are most likely to tie the hands of the Chinese government. They fielded their surveys to coincide with the US freedom of navigation operations in 2015 and 2016, thus recording the reactions of the respondents to these operations.

Dafoe and Weiss' main finding is that Chinese public opinion is sensitive to what happens during a crisis, and to what their government says. Events presented as US or Japanese provocations tend to increase public calls for resolve. Provocations include insults from foreigners, escalation of disputes by foreigners, actions that are perceived to harm China, and blatant rejections by foreigners of Chinese claims, such as the US freedom of navigation operations in the South China Sea. The evidence suggests that such events and the way they are presented to the public in Chinese media make it harder for the government to show restraint, and if the Chinese government expresses a commitment to fight, the public follows suit and backs it up. On the other hand, Dafoe and Weiss also find that Chinese leaders can mitigate disapproval by framing inaction as a policy of biding time: avoiding conflict with the United States or Japan until China gets stronger. To the extent that such framing is effective, China's leaders may reduce public disapproval of government restraint, though perhaps at the cost of reinforcing popular expectations for a more aggressive Chinese behaviour in the future.

All of this suggests that the East Asian Peace is only viable to the extent that Chinese and foreign leaders manage to avoid incidents that could create a sense of being provoked. If an incident occurs in which personnel are killed or property damaged, and no apology is offered, the Chinese public will demand a vigorous response; this provides an incentive, beyond realpolitik or regional considerations, for the Chinese government to respond resolutely. Given current developments in the South and East China Seas, Dafoe and Weiss find that governments that are not sensitive to the nature and trajectory of Chinese public opinion might engage in actions that are met with a more violent response than they imagined. Once such an escalatory process begins, predicting its course is difficult indeed.

This risk is exacerbated by the fact that the maritime disputes around China are not just about sovereignty, islands, fisheries, oil and gas, or naval power. They are highly symbolic remains from China's 'century of national humiliation'.

Not Much Reconciliation

It is no wonder that the many wars in the period 1840–1979, and the horrible crimes that were committed, continue to haunt the present. What is remembered are mainly the crimes committed by others against oneself: the Opium Wars (against China), the Nanjing massacre (against China), the comfort women (against Korea), Hiroshima and Nagasaki (against Japan), the Taiwan massacre 1947 (against native Taiwanese), My Lai 1968, Agent Orange, and China's 1979 destruction of the Pac Bo caves (against Vietnam).

Nationalist narratives have a fixed structure:

- a glorious past
- decay
- defeat
- victimhood and humiliation
- renaissance
- rejuvenation and rise
- greatness restored

A condition for a victim to regain one's rightful place is that the perpetrator is punished or forced to apologize and pay an indemnity. The story told in Chiang Kai-shek's *China's Destiny* from 1943 is strikingly similar to the one that penetrates Xi Jinping's 2014 China Dream. Both are about a greatness to be restored, as is Donald Trump's campaign slogan: 'Make America Great Again!' When history is used to underpin a nationalist ethos, some facts are distorted or inflated, while others are left to oblivion.

Unfortunately, the same is the case when well-meaning advocates of reconciliation try to establish a shared narrative of past conflicts. Conciliatory peace history is unscientific and rarely successful. In my view, the best way to approach the past is to let historical sources be explored and discussed from diverging perspectives by trained historians who respect the rules of source criticism and stimulate historical debates among free intellectuals who use past events as argumentative resources. As I have pointed out (2016a), the Taiwanese debate surrounding the 70th anniversary of the end of the Second World War was exemplary. It allowed a Kuomintang narrative, a Communist account, a more separate Taiwanese version, and also a pro-Japanese story to be debated within the same polity, with only verbal skirmishes.

John Dower (2014) has described how Japan's separate peace of 1951 delayed the process of Japanese reconciliation with Russia, China and Korea. This delay may be part of the reason why the so called 'history struggles', between Japan on the one side and China and Korea on the other, remain so emotional today. The 'history struggles' concern

Japan's colonization of Taiwan and Korea, the way the 1937–38 Nanjing massacre is treated in Japanese textbooks, the Japanese army's use of Korean and Chinese 'comfort women' during the 1937–45 war, the repeated visits by Japanese cabinet ministers to the Yasukuni shrine in Tokyo, where convicted Japanese war criminals are being honoured, and the failure of the Japanese Emperor to apologize for what Japan did to China and Korea in the past.

During the Cold War, the history of Japan's past misdeeds was frozen; it was not the subject of any discussion between Japan and the communist countries, since they were ideological adversaries. The historical wounds were thus still open when the Cold War ended, and have since remained inflamed. In Korea and China, the historical grievances against Japan are linked emotionally to the disputes over sovereignty to the Takeshima/Dokdo and Senkaku/Diaoyu islands.

Do history struggles threaten the East Asian Peace? Holly Guthrey, our programme co-ordinator in Uppsala, who has studied the failure of East Asians to reconcile and acknowledge their own past wrongdoings, thinks they do: 'Peace is teetering on the brink of renewed violence due to continued grievances and mistrust' (Guthrey 2015: 34). She may be right. Yet quarrels about history are perhaps not enough to generate armed conflict. The problem is that the history struggles between Japan and its neighbours fuel territorial disputes and contribute to blocking Japan from realizing its dream of being recognized as a normal great power through permanent membership in the UN Security Council.

Ryu Yongwook, a programme research associate based at Australian National University, has pointed out (2015) that the sense of a regional 'we feeling' in East Asia is weak, with only a rudimentary development of a regional community. What has made it difficult to form a meaningful community is the emergence and salience of the history problem. Attempts by conservative intellectuals to portray Japan's past aggression and colonialism in a positive light have provoked strong reactions in China and Korea. What is at the heart of the issue, says Ryu, is the clash of national identities. The national identity of Japan envisioned by today's conservative nationalist groups contradicts the modern national identities of China and Korea that emerged out of their struggles for independence. Hence, the effort to describe Japan's past role in China and Korea in a positive light clashes with the founding myths of the Chinese and Korean republics – both the Republic of China (ROC) and the People's Republic of China (PRC), both the Republic of Korea (ROK) and the Democratic People's Republic of Korea (DPRK).

Yet the history problem was not as acutely felt in the first decades after 1945 as it is today. Paradoxically, Ryu's 2013 analysis of newspaper articles in the Chinese *People's Daily* reveals that China's perception of Japan as a malign threat emerged in the mid-1980s, just as the East Asian Peace began, and increased thereafter. This trend is puzzling because it coincides with China's economic modernization, which eventually put China ahead of Japan in terms of GDP. The history problem turned up in earnest only during China's successful rise. Paradoxically, the cycle of Chinese denunciation and Japanese denial that characterizes the history struggles has gained intensity in the period of regional economic integration. The apparent linkage between regional economic integration and intensifying nationalism needs to be further explored.

Does peace require reconciliation in order to be viable? Holly Guthrey studies reconciliation and truth commissions, and has done fieldwork in the Solomon Islands, Timor-Leste, Indonesia and Taiwan. She finds (2015a, b; 2016) that there have been fewer elaborate attempts at reconciliation in East Asia than in other world regions. The preference in East Asia is either to try to forget the past (with amnesties) or to use memory as ammunition in history struggles. Amnesties can be beneficial in the short term, but only cover up the wounds of conflict without healing them.

Guthrey regrets this since, in the words of former president of the United States Institute of Peace (USIP) Richard Solomon, sustainable peace 'requires that long-time antagonists not merely lay down their arms but that they achieve profound reconciliation that will endure because it is sustained by a society-wide network of relationships and mechanisms that promote justice and address the root causes of enmity before they can regenerate destabilizing tensions' (Quoted in Guthrie 2015b: 32). Policymakers who are interested in pushing East Asia toward a viable long term peace would be wise to meditate on these words, written by one who played a part in reconciling the USA with the People's Republic of China under President Richard Nixon in the early 1970s, and also in negotiating the 1991 Paris agreement on Cambodia.

Guthrey finds that the countries with the greatest surge of violence during the East Asian Peace are also those that have issued the highest number of amnesties and shown the least interest in reconciliation. These are Thailand, the Philippines and Myanmar, the three countries in the region where internal armed conflicts are still active. My work with Elin Bjarnegård (2015) supports this insight. We find that a key reason why the Thais have not achieved peace is a lack of state capacity and of civilian control over the armed forces. The armies act on their own volition and enter into cycles of violence with non-state armed groups.

In the years 2008–11, Thailand did not just suffer from internal armed conflict in the south and debilitating political struggles in Bangkok, but was also involved in an interstate armed conflict with Cambodia, the first armed conflict ever to be registered between two members of ASEAN. For this reason we have singled it out for a special study, which is undertaken by Thitinan Pongsudhirak of Chulalongkorn University in Bangkok. His initial findings tend to demonstrate the weakness of ASEAN. At the time of the Thai–Cambodian skirmish in May 2011, Indonesia tried to harness its influence as chair of ASEAN to mitigate and mediate but failed. This led to calls for the UN to intervene, but it was also ineffective. The only great power with enough leverage to bring the two sides in line was China, which chose not to do so.[6]

Pongsudhirak points out that the Preah Vihear temple is central to national imaginings both in Cambodia and Thailand, which makes it vulnerable to political exploitation. Real interests, however, are also at stake. Cambodian strongman Hun Sen aligned himself with Thai leader Thaksin Shinawatra after the 2006 Thai military coup. The yellow faction in Thai politics used the Preah Vihear dispute to stir up trouble for pro-Thaksin governments.

Puzzlingly, however, when the Thai army deposed Thaksin's sister Yingluck in May 2014, and again established military rule, Hun Sen was conspicuously accommodating. Hence the conflict has not flared up again. This has two reasons: first, Cambodia depends on the Thai economy (Goldsmith 2013 uses the Thai–Cambodian conflict as a case to illustrate how a high volume of trade may prevent a conflict from escalating). Second, Hun Sen's domestic hand weakened as the political opposition gained ground in Cambodia. So even though he remained pro-Thaksin, he had to bow to his survival instincts. All of this serves to demonstrate a point made above: there are strong interlinkages between

---

6. Personal communication with Thitinan Pongsudhirak.

interstate and intrastate conflicts. In this case, internal conflicts in both Bangkok and Phnom Penh have had a decisive impact on whether or not there is fighting at the border.

The Malay Muslim insurgency in Thailand's southernmost provinces is linked to the relationship between Thailand and Malaysia. Until 1989, Malay communist rebels were operating from sanctuaries in Thailand. Thailand put an end to that in 1989, and in return Malaysia did not provide sanctuaries or support to the Malay Muslim rebels in Thailand, although the Malay Muslims are in fact a trans-border community with family connections, constant trans-border traffic, and a memory of the historical Patani Sultanate that they share with their brethren across the border. We have studied the situation in Thailand's southernmost provinces, benefiting hugely from the networks of Prince of Songhkla University's Srisompob Jitpiromsri, who has been a guest researcher in Uppsala. Together with Magnus Andersson, our research associate, Anders Engvall of the Stockholm Business School has mapped (2014) the geographical coordinates of all violent incidents and checked them against other geographical data, convincingly demonstrating that the conflict is not about religion or economic grievances but about the status of the Malay language, culture and tradition.

Several members of the programme core group, including myself, have visited the conflict-affected region and continue to be impressed with the strength of the local civil society, which helps victims of the violence and tries to establish foundations for dialogue between Malay Muslims and Thai Buddhists, and also with the police and armed forces. The fighting coincides with intense efforts towards reconciliation on the level of civil society, so if a ceasefire could be reached, the existing organizational base could be harnessed to the goals of inter-ethnic cooperation.

We had planned to do research in the Philippines, and recruited Professor Miriam Coronel-Ferrer of the University of the Philippines, as a research associate. She presented an excellent paper to our first annual conference in Uppsala 2011, analysing the reasons why the Philippines had been unable to achieve internal peace. Then Coronel-Ferrer was appointed by the Philippines government as a member and, on 7 December 2012, as leader of its negotiation panel with the Moro Islamic Liberation Front (MILF). She remained in touch with us but concentrated fully on the task of negotiating the 2015 agreement between MILF and the

Philippines government, (which was not implemented since the Senate failed to pass the required Basic Law).

In November 2015, Coronel-Ferrer delivered a keynote address to our conference in Singapore, in which she emphasized the key importance of trust and called for more research on trust building (Heldmark & Wrangnert 2015). At the time of writing, it remains unclear if President Rodrigo Duterte will allow an autonomous Bangsamoro to be set up in accordance with the agreement made by his predecessor, or if he will delay the whole matter until he can realize his grand plan of federalizing all of the Philippines.

The three East Asian countries that have not achieved internal peace are Thailand, the Philippines and Myanmar. Several members of our programme, not least myself, have conducted fieldwork in Myanmar and monitored its momentous transformation since the establishment of a constitutional government in 2011 to the victory of Aung San Suu Kyi's National League for Democracy (NLD) at the polls in November 2015. We concluded our 5th annual conference in Singapore on Myanmar's Election Day, so I could fly into Yangon that evening and stand among the crowd that cheered and celebrated The Lady's success. I was also in Yangon in February 2016, when the parliament elected her close confidant Htin Kyaw as Myanmar's new president. She could not be elected herself because of a provision in the constitution prohibiting someone whose spouse or children have foreign citizenship to serve in the country's highest office, so she instead took up a new position as State Councillor, which made her the country's top leader in all but name. Yet the military continued to control matters in the broad area of national security, because of certain constitutional provisions. Hence, Myanmar now has two leaders operating side by side in an uneasy collaborative relationship. One is State Councillor Daw Aung San Suu Kyi. The other is commander-in-chief of the armed forces Min Aung Hlaing.

Our main research in Myanmar has been directed toward understanding the ongoing ethnic armed conflicts in Shan State and Kachin State, the communal violence against the Muslim Rohingya, the crisis in northern Rakhine State from October 2016, the failed attempt to arrive at a nationwide ceasefire, and efforts to establish a national political dialogue aiming at a federal solution to the range of ethnopolitical challenges Myanmar continues to face. Although Myanmar has avoided armed conflict with other states, it is now the poorest and least internally peaceful of all East Asian countries. The populations of few countries (if any) suffered more than the people of Myanmar during the Second World War, and armed fighting has been going on somewhere on its territory continuously since independence from Great Britain in 1948.

Ashley South, a researcher affiliated with Chiang Mai University in Thailand as well as with our programme, has followed the peace process in Myanmar and is finishing a book that extends work published together with Christopher M. Joll in 2016. He sees questions of legitimacy as central to the peace process: the country's many Ethnic Armed Organisations (EAOs) derive their legitimacy from decades of armed struggle; Aung San Suu Kyi's new government regards its legitimacy as a result of participation in democratic elections, and does not necessarily see ethnic armed groups as acceptable partners. In areas where ethnic armed groups have de facto governance authority, and in areas where both armed groups and the government tax the population, extract natural resources, and provide some services, it is difficult to arrive at an agreed division of revenues and responsibilities, even when there is an effective ceasefire.

In the ceasefire areas, unarmed civil society actors may have an important role to play, through participation on joint monitoring committees and processes of political dialogue. Nevertheless, many civil society actors remain highly sceptical of the peace process. The Union Army has a decades-old reputation for being untrustworthy. Trust can develop gradually through cooperation in resolving issues of concern to the local populations, but this will take time – and in the meantime there are widespread concerns around land-grabbing and natural resource extraction in ceasefire areas. Nevertheless, many conflict-affected communities have enjoyed significant benefits during the ceasefires. There are numerous challenges to implementing a credible national political dialogue, notably the fact that most armed groups are not included because they have not signed the national ceasefire. The non-signatory groups have demanded an 'inclusive peace process'. This demand has been rejected, and from October 2016, the armed conflict resumed in full in northern Shan and Kachin State between the Union Army and the Northern Alliance, consisting of the KIA (Kachin Independence Army), the Kokang MNDAA (Myanmar National Democratic Alliance Army), the Palaung TNLA (Ta'ang National Liberation Army) and the Arakan Army (receiving training and arms in this area although its 'homeland' is Rakhine State on the west coast). In December 2017, the Shan State parliament adopted a resolution calling the Northern Alliance terrorists. The term 'insurgent-terrorists' was also used by the commander-in-chief in his 2017 New Year message. This seemed to preclude any widening of the national ceasefire to include new groups. Aung San Suu Kyi appears unwilling to challenge the Union Army, opting instead to pretend that the peace process remains on track. The Union Army's identity and interests remain, in Ashley South's and my own view, a grave threat to the peace process.

Aung San Suu Kyi faces the daunting challenge of running a government she does not formally lead, one in which the Union Army retains constitutionally defined prerogatives such as the right to manage its own internal affairs, nominate key ministers and disobey governmental orders with impunity. The army also dominates the National Security Council, which can declare a state of emergency under which the army could once again declare itself the sole repository of political power. At the same time as endeavouring to uphold the combined process of widening the ceasefire agreement and initiating a national political dialogue, State Councillor and Foreign Minister Aung San Suu Kyi must navigate internationally between her sympathy for Japan, the UK and the USA on the one hand, and her awareness of China's importance on the other. And the people expect her to improve their livelihood through economic development. If Myanmar should prove able to meet these challenges under Aung San Suu Kyi's leadership, and create its own version of an inclusive developmental state, it would make a strong contribution to the viability of the East Asian Peace.

Part IV

Conclusions

A s has been shown above, our programme has brought to light many reasons to be pessimistic regarding the viability of the East Asian Peace. The region continues to be challenged by unresolved militarised disputes, skyrocketing arms expenditures, increased tension, ongoing civil wars, human rights abuse, authoritarianism, masculine honour culture, domestic violence, history struggles and failed attempts at reconciliation. Our research into these issues has forced me to conclude that much change is needed in order to make the East Asian Peace sustainable. I shall now sum up the main *structural weaknesses* that threaten sustainable peace, analyse with a critical eye some of the *troubling trends* that lead many analysts to imagine that the regional peace is doomed, evaluate *changing priorities* among the region's national leaders, and then observe some *sources of optimism* that, in spite of everything, may offer reason to imagine that the peace can be sustained. As a peace researcher, with a mission to make the world more peaceful, I shall end the book with *ten proposals* for how to make the East Asian Peace viable.

Structural Weaknesses

Bruce Russett and John Oneal (2001) claim that a viable peace among nations has three cornerstones: economic integration, strong international institutions, and similar systems of democratic governance. East Asia has so far just one: economic integration. Most regional governments are members of the UN and other international organisations, but institutional cooperation on the regional level remains limited. Systems of governance vary greatly among states in the region. As Choi, Kivimäki, Odgaard, Eck, Bjarnegård, Melander, Guthrey, Scott and Zou have underlined in their publications from our programme, what Karl Deutsch calls a 'security community' – a group of people who take their peace for granted – is still a distant prospect.[1]

---

1. Karl Deutsch et al. (1957) defines a security community as a group of people with a sense of community and 'institutions and practices strong enough and widespread enough to assure for a 'long' time, dependable expectations of 'peaceful

Many states uphold internal peace by breaking fundamental human rights. Domestic violence, capital punishment, torture, and extra-judicial killings are tolerated or even supported by public opinion in several countries, as we saw in the 2016 case of Philippines President Duterte. Equality between the sexes remains a distant dream, and masculine honour culture retains its influence. The conflicts of the past have not been reconciled. East Asian governments have not on their own initiative apologized for what their nation did in the past. Instead, groups claiming to represent the victims raise demands for apologies, which are sometimes met and sometimes not. The rule of law has become a respected ideal, and the volume of legislation and depth of knowledge of legal rights have improved. Yet neither national nor international laws are sufficiently respected or enforced to generate confidence in a long-term peace based on a legal foundation. Although most national borders have been fully agreed, some heavily militarized territorial disputes remain: in Korea, over Taiwan, at the Sino–Indian border, and at sea. There is no way to avoid the conclusion that the region still lacks solid cultural, normative, institutional and legal foundations for a viable regional peace. Yet a peace defined as absence of war and armed conflict somehow has prevailed since the 1980s. Some new factors, however, have recently arisen that could disrupt the peace.

Five Troubling Trends

Since the financial crisis of 2008, tensions have grown worse in the region. The deterioration of interstate relations has been driven by five troubling trends.

The first is an apparent acceleration of the long-term transition of power from the United States to China, resulting from the fact that the 2008 financial crisis hit the USA and Europe hard while China maintained its rapid growth. China's economy is today two and a half times bigger than Japan's, measured in nominal GDP, and could surpass the USA within a decade. If measured in purchasing power parity, the Chinese economy is already the world's number one. Yet the level of income *per capita* remains fairly low in China, and – as discussed in Part 2 on Predicting China – it is by no means certain that China can trans-

---

change' among its population.' Such communities could exist within just one state or within a territory consisting of several states.

late its economic power into overall global power in the way the USA did in the previous century. Stephen Brooks and William Wohlforth (2016) argue rather convincingly that the United States will remain far ahead in terms of weapons technology well into the second half of this century. It takes time to develop sophisticated weapons systems. China will therefore not be able to challenge US global military dominance for a long time.

What China can do and is already trying to do is to gain preponderant military power in its own neighbourhood, meaning the area within the so-called 'first island chain' from Japan over Taiwan to Luzon and Palawan, and over Borneo to Singapore (see map, p. xv). From 1945 until recently, the US Navy held sea control in these waters, which include the world's busiest shipping lanes. US vessels and aircraft could sail and fly undisturbed along China's territorial sea, and submarines could venture undetected right up to the Chinese coast. This is no longer the case. China has deployed thousands of land based missiles along its coast, developed more sophisticated anti-ship missiles than even the United States has, and has purchased and later built a great number of submarines, fighter aircraft and surface vessels, including one aircraft carrier so far and soon several more. This makes it risky for US ships and aircraft to approach the Chinese coast and has led many analysts to conclude that it will be impossible for Taiwan, even with full US support, to defend itself against an invasion from the mainland. Nowadays, neither China nor the US–Japan alliance has 'sea control' in either the East or the South China Sea. These have become 'no man's seas', ripe for rivalry among not just the US and Chinese but a range of national navies.

The change in military capabilities has given ground for strategic competition between the USA and China. Beijing opposes any US interference in China's regional neighbourhood, and its laws say that foreign military reconnaissance and exercises cannot be conducted in China's EEZ without prior permission. Washington defines freedom of all kinds of navigation, including the right to conduct military reconnaissance and exercises, as one of its main foreign policy interests. This legal dispute, backed up by naval power on both sides, entails a risk of clashes either directly, as when the US Navy operates near China's coast or artificial islands, or indirectly, if the United States is drawn into a standoff or incident between China and Japan, China and the

Philippines, or China and Vietnam. Since the Second World War, the USA has dedicated its naval dominance to ensuring free passage of all commercial ships (except those suspected of contributing to the proliferation of weapons of mass destruction), and this has benefited all states – not least the United States itself. However, behind this dominance has always been the threat that a US president had the capability to cut off such free passage. By breaking US naval dominance, China reduces this potential threat.

If it could secure its own naval dominance not just in its near seas but also along the sea lanes through the Indian Ocean to the Gulf region, then China would remove the threat altogether and thus protect its interests. However, by trying to do this, China itself offers a parallel threat to the other coastal states in the region. What happens if China chooses to use its capability to pursue a non-free-trade policy? China has offered no evidence that it intends to pursue such a course (indeed it is the US Trump administration that now leans in that direction), but China's ability to do so demands that all countries consider the possibility. Preparations in this regard can challenge the East Asian Peace even if China in fact uses its naval power to ensure free trade for all.

The second trend is a partial return to the dominant pattern of great power alignments in the 1950s–60s, during the Korean and Vietnam Wars. At that time, China, the USSR, North Korea and the Democratic Republic of Vietnam were allies in a revolutionary struggle against a US-dominated alliance system that included the French and British colonial domains, Japan, South Korea, Thailand, ROC Taiwan and the Philippines. This bipolarity gave way to a more stable system when China and the Soviet Union fell out with each other in the 1960s. Their schism made it possible for US Presidents Richard Nixon, Gerald Ford, Jimmy Carter and Ronald Reagan to cooperate with China against the Soviet Union and Vietnam. And in the second half of the 1980s, after the Soviet Union decided no longer to sustain communist movements and regimes abroad, East Asia's security concerns could be addressed without being much affected by global power plays. In other words, China's pivot toward the United States in the 1970s–80s contributed to a negotiating environment in which outstanding issues could be resolved. In many cases, they were. Sino–American strategic cooperation stabilized East Asia and made it possible for the local states to consolidate their power, give priority to their economies, and trade with each other despite ideological divides.

Since 1989, however, this trend has reversed itself. China and the USSR began to cooperate again, but when the Soviet Union collapsed shortly afterward, Deng Xiaoping rejected suggestions that China should take over as leader of a socialist camp, and instead made his later so famous statement that China should bide its time (*taoguang yanghui*). While maintaining a cooperative relationship with the USA, Beijing did not spare any effort to forge good relations with Russia and the Soviet Union's Central Asian successor states. In 1996 it agreed on a Strategic Partnership with Russia, and in 2001 – the same year that it joined the WTO – China institutionalised its cooperation with the Central Asian countries in what would become the Shanghai Cooperation Organization (SCO).

In 2000, when Vladimir Putin was elected as Russia's president, he expanded Russia's partnership with China, which he viewed as a crucial component of a range of policies aimed at restoring Russia's great power status. This led inevitably to friction with the West. Since the early 2000s, China and Russia have been united in a growing opposition to US hegemony. The rivalry is not as intense or ideological as it was in the Cold War, and this time neither China nor Russia wants to form any formal alliance. One may not speak of two opposite and mutually exclusive 'camps' as in the Cold War, since trade and other forms of communication between China and the West have continued apace. Yet there is mutual suspicion across the Pacific, and active preparations are made on both sides for the eventuality of a future war.

If China should be inspired by Russia's recent behaviour in Ukraine and Syria, annexing territories (Crimea/Taiwan) by force, intervening abroad, and bombing countries far away, it would disrupt the East Asian Peace. However, China did not support the Russian annexation of Crimea and consistently emphasizes that its strategic partnership with Russia is not a military alliance. Beijing is in fact opposed to formal alliances as a matter of principle. Moreover, the two countries' socio-economic trajectories are completely different. Russia is a strong military power with a weak, retracting economy and a social crisis, while China derives its growing power mainly from its huge economy. The Chinese can expect to become more powerful tomorrow than they are today if they continue to avoid conflict with other big powers. Russia will be weaker tomorrow than it is today under virtually every scenario. We can therefore probably count on a certain level of restraint in China's foreign policy also in the years ahead (Tønnesson and Baev, 2017).

The third troubling trend is a dramatic build-up of military capabilities in several countries. This reallocation of resources has already shaken the power balance. I do not refer primarily to the build-up of deterrent capacities, but to weapons systems that may be used in limited warfare. Weapons that enhance the idea that war, even cyber war, may remain limited when being fought between great military powers, are dangerous. A war that from the outset is meant to be limited may just so easily escalate. Virtually every state in East Asia is devoting an increasing share of its huge export revenues to investment in modern weaponry. This is as much the case for the US allies and partners (Japan, South Korea, Taiwan, Singapore and Malaysia) as for Vietnam and China. The result is that the number of states that claim the ability to influence through force of arms the direction of regional rivalries has increased, thus rendering the whole situation more volatile.

Volatility in itself increases the risk of incidents in the air or in the sea as more and more aircraft, warships, drones and submarines navigate the same disputed zones. Washington could one day decide to reduce its presence in the vicinity of China and play a more backstage role as an offshore balancer. This might indeed be desirable: a more distant US presence would be seen as less threatening and more reassuring to China. Yet Japan and South Korea might not feel sufficiently reassured by an offshore balancer to uphold their close co-operation with the United States. They want a more direct US presence and, if deprived of that presence, could decide to develop offensive capabilities of their own – including nuclear weapons. If the United States becomes just an offshore balancer, Japan and South Korea might even opt to manage crisis situations in ways aimed at forcing the United States to intervene. This would be tempting if they began more seriously to doubt US will or ability to protect them in a war with North Korea or China.

The fourth menacing trend is growing nationalist sentiments in combination with conflicts about history and disputed islands. Chinese nationalism is directed against both Japan and the West, both of which humiliated China during 1839–1945. Korean nationalism, both North and South, is directed more against Japan, the former colonial overlord, than against China, although South Korea and Japan are both US allies with US military bases on their territory. There is also a groundswell of ill feeling towards the USA in parts of the South Korean population. Paradoxically, in spite of all the suffering inflicted by the United States on Vietnam during the Vietnam War, Vietnamese nationalism is in no way directed against the United States, which retains a high level of popularity among the Vietnamese people. Vietnamese nationalism is primarily directed against its historical adversary, China, fuelled by histories of several northern invasions and by memories of the 1979 invasion and the fighting at the border during 1979–87. Yet as communist party states, Vietnam and China are united by their fear that liberal ideas from abroad might fuel internal opposition.

In Myanmar, many ethnic nationalisms live side by side and stimulate each other, and there is much suspicion of foreigners in general, be they American, European, Chinese or Indian. The Japanese enjoy more trust. They are fellow Buddhists who helped Myanmar liberate itself from British colonialism in the Second World War, and have for a number of years helped Myanmar build up its infrastructure.

For all those who thought that the strength of nationalist ideology would weaken with growing prosperity and globalization, the renewed assertiveness of Asian nationalisms has come as an unpleasant surprise. Many believed that travel, the internet, the social media and studies abroad would shape cosmopolitan identities and fellow feeling of a kind that removes the temptation to use violent tactics in political conflicts. This has not so far been the case. Instead, although less effectively in East Asia than in some other parts of the world (Ryu, 2017) nationalist movements are using new communication technologies to rally and mobilize like-minded people, wherever they live, in support of their otherwise-local struggles.

The fifth troubling trend is a slowdown of economic growth. In 2015 the world economy was in recession for the second time in less than a decade. From 2008–09, as an effect of the global financial crisis, world GDP fell from 63.1 to 59.8 trillion USD. Growth resumed during 2010–13, but from 2014–15, mainly due to the European crisis, the world economy fell again from 78.4 to 73.1 trillion USD.[2] East Asia

2. http://data.worldbank.org/indicator/NY.GDP.MKTP.CD

did better than the rest of the world, largely due to a continued robust growth in China: 6.7 per cent in 2016 (although this is the lowest official growth rate since 1990). Reduced demand from the European and American markets has contributed to weakening the Chinese economy. Its persistent growth has depended on an expansive financial policy with huge investments in infrastructure and rapidly rising debts, primarily corporate debts. Some analysts see a risk that the Chinese economy is heading for a hard landing while others fear that it may suffer the same fate as Japan: long term stagnation. And the typical Chinese citizen continues to enjoy a much lower level of prosperity than exists in Japan.

By contrast to Japan, South Korea and Taiwan, which managed to advance from middle to high-income status during their booms, China risks falling into what Rajat M. Nag (2011) calls 'the middle income trap' and be stuck at a transitional stage from poverty to prosperity. China suffers today from enormous overcapacity in key sectors, and faces adverse reactions from other countries – notably Trump's USA – if it dumps its products on their markets. Drastic reforms will be needed in order for China to advance to its next stage of development, including huge investments in research and innovation, the introduction of an efficient system of bankruptcy for non-profitable enterprises, and measures to stimulate domestic consumption. If China should fall into 'the middle income trap' and enter into a long period of slow growth or stagnation, then this could lead to political convulsions as household incomes suffer.

More broadly, if Europe and North America do not regain their capacity to import more and more products from Asia, then the entire Asian developmental state project may be called into question. The leaders in the region may then no longer give top priority to their economies but concentrate on other goals, such as anti-terrorism, securing regime survival, taking control of 'lost' national territories, or preventing immigration or influence from abroad.

Changing Priorities

Decisions about war and peace are not taken by structures or computers, but by presidents, prime ministers, commanders-in-chief and rebel leaders. Peace depends on their constraints and incentives, motives and priorities. Since the financial crisis of 2008–09, the national leaders in

East Asia have not done much to make regional peace more viable. The financial crisis led to uncertainty about the stability of the global order; instead of unleashing joint initiatives to adjust or stabilise that order, nations became more vigilant in defending their narrow interests. They accentuated disputes over rocks, islands, history and status, and took steps to prepare themselves for possible future wars.

The Obama administration tried to relieve itself of heavy commitments in the Middle East in order to focus more on East Asia. Secretary of State Hillary Clinton announced this intention in an article in *Foreign Policy* in October 2011, and President Obama followed up on 17 November in a speech to the Australian parliament, which became known as his 'pivot to Asia' speech. Budgetary constraints, however, and the wars in Syria, Iraq, Afghanistan and Ukraine, made it difficult for Washington to push through with the rebalancing. Yet the White House and State Department took pleasure in noticing how well its announcement of reinforced engagement with Asia was received by some of China's neighbours.

The Chinese themselves saw the pivot as an attempt to contain their rise and prevent them from regaining their rightful position at the centre of their region. Beijing accentuated its strategic partnership with Putin's Russia and took steps to demonstrate its claims to islands, reefs, rocks and resources in the East China Sea and South China Sea. In violation of the UN Convention on the Law of the Sea (UNCLOS), which China has signed and ratified, it claimed to have historic rights in most of the South China Sea, including areas close to other countries' coasts. China issued unilateral fishing bans in areas claimed by other states as their Exclusive Economic Zone (EEZ), built artificial islands on submerged reefs sitting on what the Philippines rightly claims under UNCLOS as its continental shelf, issued oil concessions in parts of Vietnam's continental shelf, and wrested control of Scarborough Shoal, a tiny island surrounded by rich fish resources, from the Philippines.

China's increased maritime assertiveness provoked strong reactions in the Philippines and Vietnam, which sought closer ties with the United States, although President Duterte pivoted back to China when he took power in Manila in August 2016. China's fishing activities also led to incidents with Indonesia east of Natuna Island. The Chinese themselves saw this assertiveness, reflecting their growing maritime capabilities, as following logically from claims that had been made long ago and by both the ROC Taiwan and the PRC. They saw the new assertiveness as a reaction to the fact that the Philippines, Vietnam and Malaysia had long occupied islands belonging to China, and as a response to claims made by Malaysia and Vietnam in 2009 to an extended continental shelf that covers much of the Spratly area. While the USA remained neutral as far as the question of where sovereignty to islands lay, it engaged itself more actively from 2010 onward by insisting that the disputes over maritime zones must be resolved peacefully on the basis of the law of the sea, offering its good services, and accentuating the principle of the freedom of navigation.

Meanwhile, the Obama Administration, instead of giving top priority to rebalancing its all-important bilateral economic relationship with China, negotiated a comprehensive Trans-Pacific Partnership (TPP) with eleven states, among them Japan and Vietnam, but failed to get the US Congress to ratify it before the 2016 presidential elections, after which the whole project was scrapped by the incoming Trump administration. China also took major economic initiatives that may have more lasting effect, including the ambitious One Belt, One Road (OBOR) project, which seeks to boost trade and infrastructure between the two sides of the Eurasian continent while effectively excluding the United States and Japan. While both the TPP and OBOR could be considered peace-promoting initiatives in the sense that they would further integrate national economies, they were both conceived in a way that would at least initially exclude the world's two most important bilateral relationships: China–USA and China–Japan. The TPP, which was a forward-looking free trade agreement with heavy emphasis on services and flows of investment, may conceivably be continued by its remaining partners and could eventually be joined by China, although this is hardly acceptable to Japan. OBOR will also meet some huge challenges, linked among other things to the rivalry between Pakistan (which takes part) and India (which remains outside).

Many aspects of Xi Jinping's policies worry Japan and the West. He concentrates powers in his own hands, uses his fight against corruption to remove political rivals, seeks to rein in the media and curtail the activities of independent lawyers, continues China's rapid build-up of military capabilities, and actively pursues maritime irredentism, yet has failed so far to carry out much-needed economic reforms. The intended US pivot and the tightening of the Japan–US alliance worry China. These mutual worries could lead to a dangerous spiral.

Consolation may be found, though, in the fact that Japan and China (and perhaps the USA) continue to cooperate in many areas (notably climate policy) and also in China's tendency to show restraint whenever there is risk of a direct confrontation. China methodically seeks ways to push its territorial claims to the maximum without provoking a military clash. It used fishing boats and well-armed surveillance vessels, not warships, to push the Philippines out of Scarborough Shoal in 2012. In August 2014, it withdrew its huge oil rig from the continental shelf of Vietnam when the protests from both the government and population in Vietnam became stronger than anticipated. It sent fishing boats, which serve as a coordinated maritime militia force, and maritime surveillance vessels into the territorial sea of the Senkakus (Diaoyu) but not warships. This policy of restraint was further demonstrated in June 2016, when a Chinese naval frigate passed through the contiguous zone just outside the territorial sea of the Senkakus but did not move inside (Stashwick 2016) and, in December 2015–January 2016, when China's first aircraft carrier (the *Liaoning*) sailed all the way around Taiwan, conducting naval drills in the Spratly area while on its way, but stayed well outside of Taiwan's territorial sea at the same time as Taiwan's president, Tsai Ing-wen, stopped over in Houston and San Francisco in connection with a visit to Central America.

When US naval vessels conducted 'freedom of navigation operations' near Chinese-held artificial islands in 2015–16, China protested but did not try to prevent them. It continues to negotiate with ASEAN with the aim of reaching a code-of-conduct agreement for the South China Sea. Rhetorically, Xi Jinping upholds his predecessors' Peaceful Development doctrine, and China has only occasionally resorted to economic warfare, as when it suddenly halted exports of rare earth minerals to Japan during the 2010 Senkaku crisis, and when it curtailed banana imports from the Philippines through new regulations during the 2012 standoff at Scarborough Shoal.[3] China has not undertaken any move to reduce its dependency on global flows of trade, finance and technology.

---

3. When the Philippines president, Rodrigo Duterte, visited China in October 2016, the markets in Beijing were suddenly full of fruit from the Philippines.

As for Japan, it reluctantly joined the TPP project, and many Japanese felt relief when it was scrapped by Trump. Prime Minister Abe Shinzo (2006–07 and 2012–) has two competing priorities. One is to get Japan out of its long period of economic stagnation through 'Abenomics'. The other is to make Japan a 'normal nation' by reinterpreting or revising Article 9 of its constitution so it can strengthen its capability to meet threats from North Korea, China and anywhere else in the world where it (or its ally, the USA) sees threats (Tønnesson, forthcoming). The Yoshida model is no longer a source of inspiration. After Prime Minister Koizumi Junichiro (2000–06) tried to raise Japan's profile as an independent but US-friendly nation, the Democratic Party of Japan (DPJ) governments of Hatoyama Yukio, Noda Yoshihiko and Kan Naoto made futile attempts to build trust with China. Their attempts were frustrated by the DPJ's domestic challenges as well as negative Chinese reactions, and therefore contributed to the resurgence of the Liberal Democratic Party (LDP) under Abe's leadership, with its emphasis on military deterrence.

Linus Hagström and Ulv Hanssen have compared the way Japanese politicians described the Japanese 'peace nation' in 1972 (the year Japan normalized its relations with the PRC) and 2010 (the year of the first serious Sino–Japanese incidents in the Senkakus). Their study shows how the word 'peace' can change its meaning in a national discourse, even within a single political party. The LDP was undefeated at the national level from 1948–96 and now again dominates Japanese politics. In 1972, foreign minister and later LDP Prime Minister Fukuda Takeo declared: 'Japan has Article 9 of the constitution. There is also a consensus among the people never again to wage war. Our economic power has grown tremendously, but we will never again become a military great power.' In 2012, a statement by leading LDP member Imazu Hiroshi, provided a rather different conception: 'Japan must play a part in deterring China. Only by properly strengthening our defence forces will we be able to defend our nation's safety and sovereignty and this, I think, will lead to peace in Northeast Asia.'

Hiroshi's ideas have become Japanese policy: under Abe, peace has come to equal deterrence. Abe Shinzo's government and the Japanese parliament have emptied Article 9 of most of its content by allowing for 'collective defence'. This means that, for the first time, the Japanese government is legally entitled to take part in a war outside of its own territory. Many Japanese suffer from the illusion that this is just a formality, and that they will not be called upon actually to fight. Yet, in view of how often the United States intervenes abroad, how eager it has been for Japan to contribute, and its declining capacity and willingness to carry the burden of intervention alone, the request for Japanese troop contributions is bound to come. When that happens, Tokyo will no longer be able to shelter itself behind Article 9.

One driver of Abe's interest in developing independent Japanese military capabilities is North Korea's nuclear programme and its frequent tests of missiles that can hit targets in Japan. In 2000, President Bill Clinton was on the verge of going to Pyongyang when George W. Bush won the US presidential elections. Bush, and also his successor Barack Obama, were unwilling to engage directly with North Korea unless it first halted its nuclear programme, and instead asked China to put pressure on Pyongyang. In 2009, however, Kim Jong Il pulled North Korea out of the Six Party Talks that China had initiated in 2003. Since 2011, when Kim Jong Il died and his youngest son Kim Jong Un took over, the relationship between China and North Korea has gone from one crisis to the next. North Korea has carried out no fewer than five nuclear tests. In addition, it has test-fired numerous short-, medium- and long-range missiles whose trajectories were surely intended to provoke. North Korea may now be able to produce nuclear warheads, mount that weapon onto a missile, guide that missile to its target, and perhaps even reach targets on the US west coast.

Kim Jong Il and Kim Jong Un have caused their people to pay a hefty price for their nuclear ambition. UN sanctions have further hindered the prospect of the North Korean people benefitting from economic development. North and South Korea no longer trade with each other. The special economic zone and tourist area that were opened at the time of South Korean President Kim Dae-jung's Sunshine Policy in the early 2000s have been closed. At a time when eighty per cent of North Korea's foreign trade is with China, Beijing is strongly opposed to North Korea's nuclear weapons programme, which could threaten China itself and moreover serves as a reason for the USA to deploy weapons systems and conduct exercises that may also threaten China. Beijing has thus voted in favour of UN sanctions.

As of late 2016, almost five years into Kim Jong Un's reign, he has not yet visited any foreign country; in August 2015, when Xi celebrated the 70-year anniversary of the Allied victory over Japanese militarism, he did so in the company of the South Korean president, Park Geun-hye. When Kim Jong Un's Korean Workers' Party held its 7th Congress on 6 May 2016, the first since 1980, there were hardly any prominent foreign guests.[4] North Korea most likely aims to be tacitly accepted as a de facto nuclear state on a par with India, Pakistan and Israel, and intends, once that goal has been achieved, to increase policy emphasis on its economy. But it will take a long time before South Korea, Japan or the USA are ready to engage diplomatically or commercially with a nuclear-armed North Korea. President Park Geun-hye, who was originally elected on a platform of so-called *Trustpolitik* vis-à-vis North Korea, presided over a loss of any trust that might have remained between Seoul and Pyongyang during 2014–16 before she herself lost the trust of her people, was impeached and suspended from office.

The presidential elections in Taiwan in January 2016, which brought the Japan-oriented Tsai Ing-wen of the Democratic Progressive Party (DPP) to power, demonstrated once again the vitality of the Taiwanese multi-party system but also increased the risk of new crises between Taipei and Beijing. With the Kuomintang in the doldrums so shortly after its leader, Ma Ying-jeou, held a historic meeting on 7 November 2015 with CCP leader Xi Jinping in Singapore, the current Democratic Progress Party (DPP) government might be tempted to put the One China principle to the test (a principle adhered to both by the Chinese Communist Party and the Kuomintang). To the world's surprise, she got help from the US president-elect to do just that when he accepted a telephone call from her on 2 December 2016. However, when she subsequently made stopovers in the USA, no one from either the Obama administration or the incoming Trump administration met her. Hopefully, President Tsai Ing-wen's pragmatism will prevent her from utilizing an inexperienced US presidential administration to rock the boat in the Taiwan Strait. While economic integration has a demonstrated general potential to further the cause of peace, continued cross-strait integra-

---

4. At the 6th Congress in 1980, there were 177 delegations from fraternal parties in 118 different countries. Yet at the first five congresses there were also few foreign guests.

tion is likely to be the first casualty of any challenge to the One China principle.

Many countries, including several with a tradition for holding multi-party elections, have seen an increase in human rights violations. The Thai military seized power in a May 2014 coup and governed the country under emergency laws until it managed to get a new, illiberal constitution accepted in a referendum on 7 August 2016. The majority Malay Muslim provinces in the south voted heavily against, as did people in areas that remain loyal to the exiled former PM Thaksin Shinawatra, notably the northeastern and some of the northern provinces. Nonetheless, the constitution was adopted with a 61 per cent majority and a 59 per cent turnout. The polarized struggle in Thai politics since the early 2000s has made it difficult for any government to carry out a consistent economic policy, and the military has a tendency to give priority to its own budgetary needs. The Philippines' new president in August 2016, Rodrigo Duterte, made good immediately on his campaign promise to authorize extra-judicial killings by the police, and also encourage freewheeling vigilantes to engage in combating the country's endemic drugs trade. In the last few years, the Malaysian government of Najib Razak has also applied tough measures in order to stay in power, after alleged corruption on a large scale was disclosed at the highest level. Former PM Mahathir Mohamad and the long-standing opposition leader Anwar Ibrahim have found common cause in their quest to oust Najib from power. After Prime Minister Hun Sen's Cambodian People's Party nearly lost the parliamentary elections in 2013, the government has used lawsuits, arrests and new repressive laws with the likely aim to prevent Hun Sen's opponents from running in the 2018 elections.

As already mentioned, the region has not developed the cultural, normative, institutional or legal foundations for a viable peace, but has still been surprisingly peaceful for decades, due to conflict avoidance and a quest for economic growth. The peace is now being threatened by a number of troubling trends. What grounds could there be for expecting the peace to continue? In the last instance, it could be a combination of nuclear deterrence and economic interdependence, neither of which alone can be relied upon to secure the peace, but the combination of nuclear fear and economic hope, present at the same time, could perhaps have a sufficiently constraining effect on national leaders. All decision makers, especially in Beijing and Washington, know how difficult it is to keep a war limited if one of the parties sees escalation as the only alternative to a humiliating defeat.

Sources of Optimism

Amidst the troubling trends, there have also been some positive developments. The election of the charismatic Joko Widodo to the Indonesian presidency in 2014 may be mentioned, as well as Myanmar's establishment of a constitutional government in 2011 and the formation of a new government in March 2016, after Aung San Suu Kyi's National League for Democracy (NLD) had won parliamentary elections in a landslide. The country's 2008 constitution prevented Aung San Suu Kyi from being elected president by the National Assembly, but she instead took up a position as State Councillor and became the government's de facto leader. She is obliged, though, to negotiate constantly with the commander-in-chief, Min Aung Hlaing, who is constitutionally endowed with the right to designate three key ministers and appoint 25 per cent of all members of elected assemblies both on the Union level and the level of the country's seven states and seven regions. Unfortunately, the establishment of Aung San Suu Kyi's government has been followed by an upsurge instead of an end to Myanmar's internal armed conflicts, but she often declares peace to be her prime goal, and Myanmar's opening has created political space for various interests to organize themselves.

Among the positive developments should also be counted the ongoing peace processes in the Philippines and Myanmar, although they have moved into a difficult phase where many opposite interests must be accommodated within a transition from a centralized to a federal form of government.

Can the regional peace hold amidst all the international tension, the return to more authoritarian governance in several countries, and as political turmoil has arrived to countries that used to be stable? If my developmental peace theory holds, then peace depends on the capacity of national leaders to focus on economic and social development. As long as the leaders of the most influential powers see stable economic development as their main goal, we are unlikely to see an outbreak of major war. However, it may be difficult for politicians to maintain a focus on development if their economic initiatives do not yield further improvement of people's lives. An economic recession of the kind experienced by Russia in the 1990s and again in 2009, would make it hard to keep development within an open system of trade as a top priority. Calls are heard for protectionist measures, primarily in the United States, which could be precursors for war.

On the other hand, neither China nor the USA had done much until Trump entered the White House to reduce their economic dependence on each other. No sanctions or protectionist laws had been adopted, and the two countries tried to resolve their trade-related disputes within the WTO framework and abide by its rulings. Both the OBOR and the now defunct TPP built on a desire to shape the terms of international integration. If the great power leaders continue to understand how important the global system of trade and finance is for the well-being of their populations, and carry with them an existential fear of nuclear war, then they are likely to show the modicum of restraint that is necessary to eschew an outbreak of war. But this likelihood decreases if they give higher priority to honour, status or territorial claims than to the national economy, or try to fix economic problems with protectionist measures. The presidents of China and the USA and the Prime Minister of Japan are all aware of the economy's primacy and of their dependence on each other. If the regional economy stagnates, then it will be more difficult to maintain a system of open trade. Leaders might then look for shortcuts to popularity.

By contrast to the five troubling trends enumerated above, the uninterrupted integration of East Asian economies gives reason to assume that the peace will be prolonged. Demographic ageing may also enhance peace. As Henrik Urdal (2017) argues, medical services and pensions are expensive and the elderly people who demand their maintenance and improvement are politically influential. This budget pressure should make it less desirable to engage in any arms race. Low fertility rates also make it difficult to recruit young soldiers. Already in the next decade, China's commitment to its own ageing population may put brakes on its economic growth. This could allow the United States to remain the world's preponderant power without needing to do anything to halt China's rise, since its population has a more balanced age structure.

While all of this seems logical, we have no experience to build upon when assuming that demographic ageing promotes peace. The age structure we now see emerging in the world as a whole, which will put an end to global population growth towards the end of this century, is something entirely new, although some national populations have already been ageing for some time. Japan, again, is in the vanguard. As yet, however, Japan's and China's ageing have not generated more peaceful attitudes. Instead there has been a revival of nationalist animosities. A Pew survey (Stokes 2016) confirms that the Japanese and Chinese remain deeply suspicious of each other. Fifty-five per cent of the Japanese felt that Japan had apologized enough for what it did in the past. Only 10 per cent of the Chinese agreed. Eighty-six per cent of the Japanese and 81 per cent of the Chinese held an unfavourable view of the other, but this was actually a slight improvement from 2013.

Another trend conducive to peace is the strengthening of state capacity to deliver services and repress opposition. Improved provision of health and education services gives people a stake in the government's affairs. Citizens can see that they gain something of value from the taxes they pay. And, the police and military are more effectively keeping populations under control. While this improved capacity can be worrisome for those concerned with human rights, it has reduced the number of deaths by deterring would-be rebels from using violence to pursue their political goals.

New methods of surveillance and communication, and the building of internal transportation networks, have made it more difficult for armed rebellions to succeed. The jungle no longer gives much protection, so rebels find it difficult to create safe havens where they can regroup and train their combatants. Instead they must hide among people in the cities and worry constantly about possible informers or, alternatively, engage in peaceful political means to pursue their goals. East Asia has seen relatively little terrorism. Malaysia, Singapore and Indonesia are fairly strong states and have proved capable of uncovering and disarming their most dangerous internal enemies. New research by Isak Svensson (2017) supports the idea that these factors go some way towards explaining why, contrary to expectations, Southeast Asia has not so far developed into much of a second front in the global jihadist movement.

Yet another hopeful trend is the expansion of contact between the

USA and China on many levels, not least military. This enables decision makers to make each other aware of intentions, concerns and red lines. Obama and Xi Jinping both realized the importance of their relationship. There was a willingness on both sides to try to understand the other's way of thinking and to look for ways to prevent disputes from developing into conflicts, and conflicts from escalating into war. Hopefully, Xi Jinping and Trump will also reach some kind of minimal mutual understanding, building on the need to prevent a catastrophic war. The two countries' militaries may contribute to this by developing closer contact, and agreeing on shared mechanisms of crisis management.

Given these positive trends and the general awareness of economic interdependence and mutual nuclear deterrence, it seems likely – in spite of the several provocative statements by Trump and his advisors in the weeks before he was sworn in as president – that no American or Chinese leader, and also no other leader in the region (including Kim Jong Un), will make reckless military moves. Yet there is no way of denying the fragility of the East Asian Peace. We know from history that wars can break out between nations even when their leaders do not want it.

A big war might break out in three main ways. First, two great powers (China and the USA) could engage in a game of chicken, with each side expecting the other to back out and neither of them cracking. Second, a conflict between two local parties might pull China and the USA in on opposite sides, as could happen in Korea, the Taiwan Strait, or the East or South China Seas. Third, a government (e.g., Myanmar, the Philippines or North Korea) may lose control of its own population if rebellions take place in conjunction with factional struggles within the regime, whereafter the great powers intervene to restore order and then get into conflict with each other. This is the Syrian scenario, which did not, however, lead to any direct clashes between the intervening powers.

A regime collapse in North Korea could be dangerous given that country's location between China, Russia and Japan. All Chinese remember how the decline and fall of the Qing dynasty led to warlordism, foreign dominance, revolution, and a series of civil and external wars, including two with Japan: 1894–95 and 1931–45. Yet this state failure scenario is not as much discussed as the game-of-chicken and the activation-of–alliance-commitment scenarios.

Ten Peace Proposals

In light of all these dangers, what can be done to make the East Asian Peace more viable? Let me end by imagining a minor utopia. I say 'minor' because I do not intend to pronounce a regional nirvana or harmonious society. Yet the ten points below are utopian in the sense that none will be realized in full. Minor utopias are never realized in their totality, but, under favourable circumstances, they may inspire positive, essential change (Winter 2006).

If just some of what follows can be implemented, the East Asian Peace will become more viable. My proposals are inspired by Lyle Goldstein's 2015 book, *Meeting China Halfway*, which proposes a number of concrete steps to be taken by the USA and China to unleash what Goldstein calls 'cooperation spirals'. This is an excellent term, and many of Goldstein's proposals could easily be implemented with just a modicum of political will.

My ten proposals below are more comprehensive and demanding: they offer foundations for interstate and intrastate peace in all of East Asia, and they seek not only to overcome the structural weaknesses of the East Asian Peace and turn around the five troubling trends analysed above, but also to give regional peace the new momentum needed to render it viable. Let us imagine that South Korea or Mongolia decides to make an effort to create such momentum by following up an idea discussed among peace researchers in the region, namely to initiate an Asian 'Helsinki process'. The Helsinki agreement of 1975 led to the establishment of the Organization for Security and Cooperation in Europe (OSCE). The countries of East Asia could initiate a similar process, which might include some of the following steps:

1. Set green growth as top priority. Untrammelled economic growth can no longer be the paramount priority leading nations to seek peace. Environment-friendly growth must come in its place. Climate change could enhance global peace because it forces people, governments and nations to work together to save the planet.

Green growth, based on services and environment-friendly technologies, relies on renewable energy, or on gas instead of coal and oil. It uses 3D printing technologies, thus lessening the pressure on transportation. Green, sustainable growth should be the prime goal of nations, the measure they use for gauging their competitive edge. Such a focus does not suggest a reactionary return to autarkic models of self-sufficient local communities. It depends on open, transnational markets where environment-friendly solutions compete. Trade hindrances and economic sanctions would hamper green growth, but laws and regulations – both national and treaty-based – are needed to guide markets in a green direction.

The United States and Japan should join the Asian Infrastructure Investment Bank (AIIB), which was set up on China's initiative, and the AIIB should adopt a greener profile. China needs to stimulate its households to use their market power to buy the greenest and most user-friendly products and solutions from anywhere in the world. Radical economic reforms will be needed in the USA, EU, China and Japan to create more balance in their economic interactions. Japan should give China more access to its huge market.

Although the US has now abandoned the TPP, many of its constitutive elements may be included in a multilateral agreement among its remaining parties, or in bilateral trade and investment agreements, and form the basis for a trading system that may eventually include both China and the USA. China should further develop its own proposal for a Free Trade Area of the Asia-Pacific (FTAAP), and open it up to all interested countries. Japan and the USA should be invited to participate in China's One Belt One Road (OBOR) initiative. Full support must be given to the WTO's attempts to remove global hindrances against trade in services.

While it may seem strange to set green growth as the first point in a peace proposal, this follows from an insight that emerged from our research: key decisions leading to peace are often made by people who pursue other goals than peace, and need peace in order to achieve them. While peace activists make important contributions to peace by influencing public opinion, and while negotiators, peace facilitators and specialists of various kinds hammer out the solutions that make peace possible, it remains the case that top-level decision makers – those empowered to decide whether or not to use force – are most often motivated by goals other than peace as such. They see peace as a means to achieve other aims.

China is heavily polluted, with contaminated rivers, scarcity of clean water, a series of poisoning scandals and an appalling air quality in its cities. This makes people angry and has already caused much unrest. In order to save China from pollution and the planet from global warming, China must stick to its Peaceful Development doctrine. Green growth policies may foster hopes of a better future, as well as reduce the risk of both internal and international war.

2. Create new types of power relations. Under Xi Jinping, China has proposed the creation of a new type of major power relations, not based on formal alliances but rather on partnerships premised on respect for each other's political systems and core interests. The United States has so far turned a cold shoulder to the suggestion. Liberal Americans want China to become a pluralistic democracy and a responsible global shareholder, and overcome old and long-irrelevant ideas about spheres of influence. I believe there should be room for compromise between these two outlooks, and it does not seem inconceivable that Presidents Xi and Trump will be better able to reach a deal based on respect for each others's core interests than their predecessors.

It is easy for a superpower, sitting on its own continent with huge oceans on either side, to berate others for thinking in terms of spheres of influence. As China grows more confident in its global power, it is likely to gradually acquire an outlook similar to that of US liberals today, but not immediately. For quite some time, China will continue to feel vulnerable and therefore seek reductions in what it perceives as US military containment. The United States should make itself ready to satisfy this need, while making its step-by-step withdrawal contingent on Chinese good neighbour policies, so the security needs of Japan, South Korea, the Philippines, Vietnam, Malaysia and Indonesia can be met, and Taiwan can be reassured against any attack from the mainland.

To make a compromise possible, the USA, China and Japan must increase contacts between their military forces, hold joint exercises, engage together in UN peace keeping, conduct joint anti-piracy operations, cooperate in fighting transnational crime and weapons proliferation, and prepare for joint search and rescue operations.

As an immediate measure, joint study groups should be formed to go through possible conflict scenarios and find reliable ways of preventing them. All East Asian governments should be motivated to ensure full civilian control of their military forces so they do not use political power to unduly boost their budgets or enrich their senior officers. Multilateral arms control negotiations should be revived to set limits to the amount of weapons each nation may keep for its defence. This could build trust, increase shared knowledge and provide citizens of both countries with concrete examples of the benefits that could follow from the sort of political compromises that I propose.

3. *Use informal diplomacy.* Diplomacy is not and need not be limited to 'track one' government-to-government interaction. I call upon transnational networks of politicians, analysts and business leaders to generate 'track two' diplomatic processes aiming to create cooperation spirals in which pairs of states take a succession of concrete steps to reassure each other while at the same time creating common goods. This is a simple proposal. After transnational groups of civil society actors have developed shared ideas of how to manage or resolve a critical issue, governments may take up these ideas and transform them into track one state-to-state cooperation.

This has been the key idea behind the Council for Security Cooperation in the Asia Pacific (CSPAC), whose various regional and country committees have offered multiple ideas over the years to the regional governments. All good people should be called upon to launch additional proposals for what governments can do in order to build confidence and launch initiatives leading to long-term cooperation. In our research programme, Mikael Weissmann (2012) has shown how transnational networks of people who have access to decision makers can effectively promote peace.

4. *Strengthen national and international law.* Laws do not create peace, but they can make it more viable by providing clarity, both nationally and internationally, about what is acceptable or not as well as the cost of engaging in unacceptable behaviour. The practice of law is developing quickly in East Asia. Legislative assemblies are assuming a greater role, courts are becoming more independent, the quality of legal education is improving, and access to legal services is widening. These positive trends are likely to continue.

When people feel protected by the law, they have less need to rebel. Also, if the cost of failed rebellion, and the likelihood that it will fail, become part of the common knowledge, the use of armed struggle as a political tactic must be less appealing – particularly if the right to fight for a cause with non-violent means is protected under the law. On the international level, as shown by Scott (2017) and Goertz et al. (2016), China has benefited enormously from 20th-century legal developments, as national sovereignty, equality among states, non-aggression, non-interference and non-secession have become basic principles.

China enthusiastically supported the United Nations Convention on the Law of the SEA (UNCLOS) when it was negotiated from 1973–82, with its anti-hegemonic profile and emphasis on the rights of coastal states. UNCLOS provides a constitution for the oceans that defines how rights and duties in the sea, under the seabed, and in the air, shall be allocated peacefully among states on the basis of distance from coasts. The sea as such cannot be conquered or controlled. It is open, but coastal states can claim the sovereign right to all resources within 200 nautical miles of their coast – under certain conditions even further out as well.

In cooperation with the Republic of China in Taiwan (which originally developed the Chinese claims in the South China Sea), Beijing must find ways to conform its maritime zone claims to UNCLOS, which it signed in 1982 and ratified in 1996. Without doing this it cannot arrive at any maritime boundary agreement with its riparian neighbour states. Although China has dismissed the 12 July 2016 ruling by an Arbitral Tribunal established at the request of the Philippines, it will have to engage with the tribunal's arguments. It is not so that all of its conclusions are necessarily carved in stone.

China could boost its regional security by resolving its maritime disputes on the basis of international law. This would remove grounds for conflict and reduce the temptation felt by China's neighbours to seek US military protection. Much arduous work will be needed in order to arrive at boundary agreements between China and all of its neighbours, but then it must be all the more important for Beijing to launch a step-wise process that can yield these treaties. A first step might be to agree on which parts of the sea and seabed that *cannot be disputed under UNCLOS* because they can only be claimed by one state. It will be painful for China to adjust its position to what is possible under UNCLOS since it has for a long time upheld legally untenable claims. Yet, since the other states know their rights, there is no other way for China to reach a voluntary agreement than to limit and restate its claims on the basis of UNCLOS.

As a matter of even greater short term priority, China and ASEAN should move forward with agreeing on a Code of Conduct in the South China Sea in a way that builds on their 2002 Declaration on the Conduct of Parties. All construction of artificial islands or installations on small reefs or rocks must cease. Both bilateral and multilateral negotiations are needed in order to establish joint management of fisheries in disputed zones. It is more urgent to cooperate on fish than oil. Fish is a renewable resource if properly managed. Oil takes millions of years to produce but just a short time to consume. The economic stakes are high in the oil business, with huge investments required simply for exploration and even greater investments for extraction. If discoveries are made, then companies and states may reap huge revenues, although less when the oil price is low. Fishing is a much less costly business, but overfishing is a serious problem that needs to be solved through a regional initiative. While this is done, the sovereignty dispute regarding the many small islands may continue to be handled in the way recommended by Deng Xiaoping: leave it to future generations.

5. *Build regional institutions.* ASEAN's role in facilitating conflict management and resolution within and between its member states should be enhanced, with institutions housed for that purpose at its headquarters in Jakarta. Ways of enhancing and solidifying the regional peace should be on the agenda at every meeting of the ASEAN Regional Forum and the East Asian Summits.

Trilateral summits among China, Japan and South Korea should not just discuss their economic integration, but also look for ways to engage North Korea.

At a time when Western countries are likely to be less proactive than in the past when it comes to developing world trade, East Asia's regional organizations must take a greater responsibility for developing initiatives in the direction of facilitating environment-friendly growth internationally. China should initiate greater cooperation with Japan, and invite both Japan and the USA to take part in the One Belt One Road (OBOR) initiative.

China should continue its quest for greater influence in the World Bank, International Monetary Fund and Asian Development Bank, while at the same time using its own initiative, the Asian Infrastructure

Investment Bank (AIIB), as an instrument for enhancing green growth in the East Asian region

6. Reconcile historical identities. Reconciliation processes and truth commissions both within and between nations should be stimulated. This may sometimes be done through formal, state-led processes, but well-funded civil society initiatives, engaging museums, media, artists, writers and professional historians are more likely to have a lasting effect on mindsets. Rather than trying to build consensus around an overall narrative, one should seek to develop conciliatory attitudes, space for tolerance and, where possible, acknowledgement of historical facts that everyone needs to incorporate into their narrative.

It works better to heal historical wounds with open, critical reflection on the basis of meticulous empirical research than try to reach an agreed version of history through negotiations. Historical facts, once established beyond reasonable doubt, are not negotiable. However, both political and scholarly space must be open to evolution in the ways facts are interpreted and explained in historical narratives. Many different narratives may be composed on the basis of the same facts, and most of them will change with time. A requisite for reconciliation is to acknowledge essential facts, however disagreeable to oneself.

Reconciliation is best achieved when guilt is admitted voluntarily and a hand is reached out to the victims. If the Japanese Emperor would make a journey of reconciliation to Seoul, Pyongyang, Nanjing and Singapore, this could open new venues to regional peace. Those who believe it is difficult for the Japanese to understand why this should be important might recall the powerfully warm response US President Obama received in 2015, when he visited Hiroshima. Although he did not apologize, many Japanese citizens felt a sense of healing as a result of the respect he paid to the victims of America's perhaps most heinous crime.

7. Engage North Korea. The South Korean government should revive Kim Dae-jung's Sunshine Policy vis-à-vis North Korea. The policy of economic and cultural engagement should be de-linked from the nuclear issue, since the fearful North Korean regime will become ever more adamant in its quest for a nuclear deterrent if the outside world sets denuclearisation as a condition for engagement.

Talks with the aim of securing a moratorium on further testing and prevent proliferation to other countries should be conducted in a special forum, which could well again be the Six Party Talks, with China hosting Russia, Japan, the USA, North and South Korea. Americans need to give up their hope that China will turn the screws on North Korea. Like South Korea, China is well advised to de-link economic and nuclear issues in its dealings with Pyongyang. Although US diplomats might resist such a strategy, China risks generating tremendous Korean resentment if it attempts to force Kim Jong Un from power and establish itself as the power broker between factions in his entourage.

North Korea should declare a moratorium on nuclear and missile testing, and then, without any preconditions, the USA should enter into talks aiming at a peace treaty formally to end the Korean War and establish diplomatic relations among all parties. UN sanctions should be lifted step by step, each time North Korea fulfils certain verifiable conditions. South and North Korea should formalize a boundary on land and at sea, tracing the Demilitarized Zone (DMZ) and changing the maritime Northern Limit Line, as a step towards re-establishing cross-border infrastructure and economic cooperation, and in the longer term a confederal union.

It is essential to upend the current downward spiral in North Korea's foreign relations into a cooperation spiral. A key to doing that is foreign recognition of the North Korean people's potential for economic, educational and technological development, if allowed to compete on an even global playing field and integrate with the rest of the Northeast Asian powerhouse. North Korea sits right in the middle of one of the world's most dynamic zones.

8. *Deepen cross-strait integration.* Beijing and Taipei should keep up the economic integration that happened across the Taiwan Strait under the eight-year presidency of Ma Ying-jeou (2008–16). Initiate a permanent political dialogue between the mainland and Taiwan-based governments to develop new integrative proposals, and also give the government in Taiwan a diplomatic role together with the PRC in international forums, both regionally and globally.

The PRC should, under the One China principle, offer Taiwan a special entity status at the ASEAN+3 and East Asian Summit meetings. China should reduce the number of missiles targeting Taiwan, and the USA should cease its arms sales.

The governments in the Chinese mainland and on Taiwan should take joint initiatives to manage and eventually resolve those maritime disputes where they both maintain claims on behalf of One China. This concerns the dispute over the Senkakus/Diaoyu Islands with Japan, the Spratly Islands with Vietnam, Malaysia, Brunei and the Philippines, and huge water zones, where cooperation on fishery management is urgent. Joint fishery management and initiatives to preserve the marine environment in endangered coral reefs should be linked to a moratorium on the construction of artificial islands.

9. Create federal peace. China, Japan, the USA and the EU should coordinate their efforts to provide attention and support to the unfinished peace processes in the Philippines and Myanmar, and the one that has barely started in south Thailand. All three countries need flexible federal solutions to satisfy the needs of their various ethnic communities.

Women must take an active role in these peace processes (as they have to some extent in the Philippines), and gender issues must be taken systematically into consideration when agreements and new laws are drafted and agreed upon. If Thailand, the Philippines and Myanmar can achieve internal peace, and new internal conflicts do not break out in other countries, then there would not be one single internal armed conflict left in East Asia. It would be a region with zero armed conflicts.

Some of the peace processes have been long and arduous already, with ceasefires being repeatedly signed and broken. Robust monitoring of ceasefires is needed, with unbiased foreign participation, and lessons should be learned from successful peace processes elsewhere. In the Philippines and Myanmar, there is now a momentum for replacing a centralised system of government with a federal system, under which a substantial amount of autonomous power shall be retained at the local level. These transitions are highly demanding when multiple ethnic groups have different or even opposite interests.

There may be much to learn from other federal countries in terms of flexibility in how powers and resources are divided or shared between the federal union, its constituent states, autonomous areas within those states, and how the interests of minorities without specific homelands are protected. Participants in the national political dialogues in the Philippines and Myanmar must understand that a one-size-fits-all system is impossible. Flexibility is key. The Thai government should also realize, the sooner the better, that the solution to the armed conflict in the Malay Muslim south must also be based on a high level of local autonomy.

10. Promote peaceful values. Our research has shown that societies valuing gender equality and protection of ethnic, religious and sexual minority rights are unlikely to be violent. Such values should be promoted in the schools and media, not only for their own sake but also because they contribute to peace.

Attention must be given to the dark side of the East Asian Peace, the side that threatens its viability: violent repression, extra-judicial killings, domestic violence against children and women, capital punishment, torture, and disrespect for the cultural and other rights of ethnic and religious minorities.

Our research has also looked into the growing nationalist trend and East Asia's history struggles. Let me express a hope that *East Asian Peace* may become a household concept, and that schools, museums and the media will do their best to make young Asians aware of how much longer and better their lives are, compared with their parents and grandparents, due to peaceful development.

If only some of these proposals are followed up, then there could be a change in the way people see their future. They might even realise that if a vast region like East Asia can be free from war, then it is also possible to achieve world peace.

References

Baev, Pavel and Stein Tønnesson (2015) 'Can Russia keep its special ties with Vietnam while moving closer and Closer to China?' *International Area Studies Review* 18(3): 312–325.

——— (2017) 'The Troubled Russia-China Partnership as a Challenge to the East Asian Peace', *Fudan Journal of the Humanities and Social Sciences*, doi: 10.1007/s40647-017-0166-y.

Barron, Patrick, Sana Jaffrey and Ashutosh Varshney (2016) 'When large conflicts subside: The ebbs and flows of violence in post-Suharto Indonesia', *Journal of East Asian Studies* 16(2): 191–217.

Bernstein, Richard and Ross H. Munro (1997) *The Coming Conflict with China.* New York: Random House.

Bjarnegård, Elin (2015) 'Addressing Fear and Injustice to Create an East Asian Culture of Peace', *Global Asia* 10(4): 20–25.

——— (2017) 'The Unequal Peace', in Elin Bjarnegård and Joakim Kreutz (eds) *Debating the East Asian Peace.* Copenhagen: NIAS Press.

Bjarnegård, Elin, Karen Brounéus and Erik Melander (forthcoming) 'The Personal is the Political? Violent Childhood Experiences and the Risk of Political Violence as Adults in Thailand', Manuscript under review.

Bjarnegård, Elin and Joakim Kreutz, eds (2017) *Debating the East Asian Peace.* Copenhagen: NIAS Press.

Bjarnegård, Elin and Erik Melander (2011) 'Disentangling gender, peace and democratization: the negative effects of militarized masculinity', *Journal of Gender Studies* 20: 139–154.

——— (2013) 'Revisiting Representation: Communism, Women in Politics, and the Decline of Armed Conflict in East Asia', *International Interactions* 39(4): 558–574.

——— (2014) 'Thailand's Missing Democrats: Reds, Yellows, and the Silent Majority', *Foreign Affairs*, 22 May.

—— (2017) 'Pacific Men: How the Feminist Gap Explains Hostility' *The Pacific Review*, doi:10.1080/09512748.2016.1264456.

Bjarnegård, Elin, Erik Melander, Gabrielle Bardall, Karen Brouneus, Erika Forsberg, Karin Johansson, Angela Muvumba Sellström and Louise Olsson (2015) 'Gender, Peace and armed conflict', *SIPRI Yearbook*, Oxford: Oxford University Press.

Bremmer, Ian (2006) *The J Curve: A New Way to Understand Why Nations Rise and Fall*. New York: Simon & Schuster.

Brooks, Stephen G. and William C. Wohlforth (2016) 'The Rise and Fall of the Great Powers in the Twenty-first Century', *International Security* 40(3): 7–53.

Buzan, Barry and Ole Wæver (2003) *Regions and Powers: The Structure of International Security*. Cambridge: Cambridge University Press.

'Cabinet Decision on Development of Seamless Security Legislation to Ensure Japan's Survival and Protect its People', 1 July 2014: http://www.cas.go.jp/jp/gaiyou/jimu/pdf/anpohosei_eng.pdf, accessed 16 October 2016.

Cai Dingjian (2005) 'The development of constitutionalism in the transition of Chinese society', *Columbia Journal of Asian Law* 19: 1–29.

Callahan, William A. (2013) *China Dreams: 20 Visions of the Future*. Oxford: Oxford University Press.

Campbell, Kurt M. (2016) *The Pivot: The Future of American Statecraft in Asia*. New York: Twelve.

Chan, Steve (2013) *Enduring Rivalries in the Asia-Pacific*. Cambridge: Cambridge University Press.

Chang, Gordon G. (2002) *The Coming Collapse of China*. London: Arrow.

—— (2006) 'Halfway to China's Collapse', *Far Eastern Economic Review* 169(5) June: 25–28.

—— (2011) 'The Coming Collapse of China: The 2012 Edition', *Foreign Policy*, 29 December.

Chiang Kai-shek (1985 [1943]) *China's Destiny*. New York: Praeger.

Clinton, Hillary (2011) 'America's Pacific Century', *Foreign Affairs*, 11 October.

Coulomb, Cathérine (2007) *Chine, le nouveau centre du monde?* Paris: l'Aube.

Copeland, Dale C. (1996) 'Economic Interdependence and War: A Theory of Trade Expectations', *International Security* 20(4): 5–41.

—— (2003) 'Economic Interdependence and the Future of U.S.-Chinese Relations', In G. John Ikenberry and Michael Mastanduno, eds, *International*

Relations Theory and the Asia-Pacific. New York: Columbia University Press: 323–352.

———— (2015) *Economic Interdependence and War.* Princeton NJ: Princeton University Press.

Coronel-Ferrer, Miriam (2011) 'Political Violence and Political Survival: Philippine Presidentialism under Gloria Macapagal Arroyo', Paper presented to the 1st Annual Conference of the East Asian Peace programme, Uppsala 16–18 September.

———— (2015) 'Reflections on the peace process in the Philippines', Keynote address to the East Asian Peace programme's fifth annual conference in Singapore, 6–8 November: www.youtube.com/watch?v=Or2GIwuy52Q, accessed 16 October 2016.

Dafoe, Allan and Jessica Chen Weiss (2015) 'Authoritarian Audiences in International Crises: Evidence from China', Paper presented to the 5th Annual Conference of the East Asian Peace programme, Singapore 6–8 November.

Davenport, Christian, Erik Melander and Patrick Regan (forthcoming). *The Peace Continuum.* Oxford: Oxford University Press.

Deutsch, Karl W. et al. (1957) *Political Community and the North Atlantic Area.* New York: Greenwood.

Dickson, Bruce J. (2016) *The Dictator's Dilemma: The Chinese Communist Party's Strategy for Survival.* Oxford: Oxford University Press.

Domenach, Jean-Luc (2009) *La Chine m'inquiète.* Paris: Perrin.

Domenach, Jean-Luc and George Holoch (2012) *China's Uncertain Future.* New York: Columbia University Press (updated English language edition of Domenach 2009).

Dower, John W. (1999) *Embracing Defeat: Japan in the Wake of World War II.* New York: Norton.

———— (2014) 'The San Francisco System: Past, Present, Future in U.S.–Japan–China Relations', *The Asia-Pacific Journal* 12(8/2).

Eck, Kristine (2015a) 'Repression by Proxy: How Military Purges and Insurgency Impact the Delegation of Coercion', *Journal of Conflict Resolution* 59(5): 924–946.

———— (2015b) 'Cracking Down on Conflict: East Asia's Repressive Peace', *Global Asia* 10(4): 46–51.

———— (2017) 'The Repressive Peace', in Elin Bjarnegård and Joakim Kreutz (eds) *Debating the East Asian Peace.* Copenhagen: NIAS Press.

Eck, Kristine and Christopher Fariss (2015) 'Respect for Human Rights in East Asia and the World', Paper presented to the 5th Annual Conference of the East Asian Peace programme, Singapore 6–8 November.

The Economist (2010) 'The worldwide war on baby girls', 4 March.

—— (2017) 'The war on baby girls winds down', 21 January.

Engvall, Anders and Magnus Andersson (2014) 'The Dynamics of Conflict in Southern Thailand', *Asian Economic Papers* 30(3): 169–189.

Fenby, Jonathan (2014) *Will China Dominate the 21st Century?* Cambridge: Polity Press.

Friedberg, Aaron (2011) *A Contest for Supremacy: China, America, and the Struggle for Mastery in Asia.* New York: Norton.

Fravel, M. Taylor (2008) *Strong Borders, Secure Nation: Cooperation and Conflict in China's Territorial Disputes.* Princeton: Princeton University Press.

Fukuda Takeo, 'Speech to the House of Councillors, 22 March 1972', Cited in Hagström and Hanssen (2015).

Gibler, Douglas M. (2012) *The Territorial Peace: Borders, State Development, and International Conflict.* Cambridge: Cambridge University Press.

Gill, Bates (2016) 'The enduring paradox of US-China relations', The Tan Chin Tuan lecture at Yale-NUS College, Singapore, 29 January: www. yale-nus.edu.sg/newsroom/29-january-2016-the-enduring-paradox-of-us-china-relations/, accessed 16 October 2016.

Global Peace Index Report (2016) *Executive Summary*, Glossary: 4: http:// static.visionofhumanity.org/sites/default/files/GPI%202016%20 Report_2.pdf accessed 16 October 2016.

Goertz, Gary, Paul F. Diehl and Alexandru Balas (2016) *The Puzzle of Peace: The Evolution of Peace in the International System.* Oxford: Oxford University Press.

Glosny, Michael A. and Philip C. Saunders (2010) 'Debating China's Naval Nationalism', *International Security* 35(2): 161–175.

Goldsmith, Benjamin E. (2013) 'Different in Asia?: Developmental States, Trade, and International Conflict Onset and Escalation', *International Relations of the Asia-Pacific* 13(2): 175–205.

—— (2014a) 'The East Asian Peace as a Second-Order Diffusion Effect', *International Studies Review* 16(2): 275–289.

—— (2014b) 'Domestic Political Institutions and the Initiation of International Conflict in East Asia: Some Evidence for an Asian Democratic Peace', *International Relations of the Asia-Pacific* 14(1): 59–90.

—— (2017) 'Peace by Trade', in Elin Bjarnegård and Joakim Kreutz (eds) *Debating the East Asian Peace*. Copenhagen: NIAS Press.

Goldstein, Lyle J. (2015) *Meeting China Halfway: How to Defuse the Emerging US-China Rivalry*. Washington DC: Georgetown University Press.

Gombert, David C., Astrid Stuth Cevallos and Cristina L. Garrafola (2016) *War with China: Thinking through the Unthinkable*. Santa Monica, CA: RAND.

Gries, Peter Hays (2004) *China's New Nationalism*. Berkeley: University of California Press.

Guthrey, Holly L. (2015a) *Victim Healing and Truth Commissions: Transforming Pain through Voice in Solomon Islands and Timor-Leste*. Basel: Springer.

—— (2015b) 'Forgetting Undermines the East Asian Peace', *Global Asia* 10(4): 32–39.

—— (2016) 'Local Norms and Truth Telling: Examining Experienced Incompatibilities within Truth Commissions of Solomon Islands and Timor-Leste', *The Contemporary Pacific* 18(1): 1–29.

—— (2017) 'The Unforgiving Peace', in Elin Bjarnegård and Joakim Kreutz (eds) *Debating the East Asian Peace*. Copenhagen: NIAS Press.

Haas, Mark L. (2007) 'A Geriatric Peace? The Future of U.S. Power in a World of Aging Populations', *International Security* 32(1): 112–147.

Hagström, Linus and Ulv Hanssen (2015) 'War is Peace: The Rearticulation of "Peace" in Japan's China Discourse', *Review of International Studies* 42(2): 266–286.

Halper, Stefan (2010) *The Beijing Consensus: How China's Authoritarian Model Will Dominate the Twenty-First Century*. New York: Basic Books.

Hara, Kimie, ed. (2015) *The San Francisco System and Its Legacies: Continuation, Transformation and Historical Reconciliation in the Asia-Pacific*. Milton Park: Routledge.

Hegre, Håvard et al. (2013) 'Predicting Armed Conflict, 2010–2050', *International Studies Quarterly* 57: 250–270.

Heldmark, Thomas and Rolf Wrangnert (2015) *East Asian Peace Annual Conference 2015*. Video film: https://www.youtube.com/watch?v=Or2GIwuy52Q, accessed 16 November 2016.

Heldmark, Thomas and Rolf Wrangnert (2016) *East Asia's Surprising Peace*. Video film: https://www.youtube.com/watch?v=PZLQ0vmxi68 (YouTube also has Chinese- and Japanese-language versions), accessed 16 October 2016.

Hudson, Valerie M. & Andrea M. den Boer (2004) *Bare Branches: The Security*

Implications of Asia's Surplus Male Population. Cambridge MS: MIT Press.

Hughes, Christopher R. (2006) *Chinese Nationalism in the Global Era.* London: Routledge.

Hung Ho-fung (2016) *The China Boom: Why China Will Not Rule the World.* New York: Columbia University Press.

Hyer, Eric (2015) *The Pragmatic Dragon: China's Grand Strategy and Boundary Settlements.* Copenhagen: NIAS Press.

Ikenberry, G. John (2008) 'The Rise of China: Power, Institutions, and the Western Order', In Robert S. Ross and Zhu Feng (eds) *China's Ascent: Power, Security, and the Future of International Politics.* Ithaca NY: Cornell University Press: 89–114.

——— (2015) 'Introduction: The United States, China, and the Global Order', In G. John Ikenberry, Wang Jisi and Zhu Feng (eds) *America, China, and the Struggle for World Order: Ideas, Traditions, Historical Legacies, and Global Visions.* New York: Palgrave Macmillan.

Imazu Hiroshi, 'Speech to the House of Representatives, 26 July 2012', Cited in Linus Hagström and Ulv Hanssen (2015).

Isaacs, Harold R. (1947) *No Peace for Asia.* Boston: MIT Press.

Jacques, Martin (2009) *When China Rules the World: The Rise of the Middle Kingdom and the End of the Western World.* London: Allen Lane.

Jong Kun Choi (2016) 'Crisis Stability or General Stability? Assessing Northeast Asia's absence of War and Prospects for Liberal Transition' *Review of International Studies* 42(2): 287–309.

Kang, David (2007) *China Rising: Peace, Power, and Order in East Asia.* New York: Columbia University Press.

Kastner, Scott L. (2010) *Political Conflict and Economic Interdependence across the Taiwan Strait and Beyond.* Singapore: NUS Press.

——— (2015) 'Economic Interdependence and the Prospects for Peace in the Taiwan Strait', Paper presented to the 5th Annual Conference of the East Asian Peace programme, Singapore 6–8 November.

——— (2016) 'Is the Taiwan Strait Still a Flash Point? Rethinking the Prospects for Armed Conflict between China and Taiwan', *International Security* 40(3): 54–92.

Khong Yuen Foong (2014) 'Foreign Policy Analysis and the International Relations of Asia', in Saadia M. Pekkanen, John Ravenhill and Rosemary Foot (eds) *The Oxford Handbook of the International Relations of Asia.* Oxford: Oxford University Press.

Kissinger, Henry (2011) *On China*. New York: Penguin.

Kivimäki, Timo (2001) 'The Long Peace of ASEAN' *Journal of Peace Research* 38(1): 5–25.

—— (2010) 'East Asian Relative Peace – Does It Exist? What Is It?' *The Pacific Review* 23(4): 503–526.

—— (2014) *The Long Peace of East Asia*. London: Ashgate.

Koda, Yoji (2015) 'Significance of the Guidelines for Japan-US Defense Cooperation and Japan's Defense Legislation in 2015', *AJISS Commentary* No. 218, 9 September: http://www2.jiia.or.jp/en_commentary/201509/09-1.html, accessed 26 October 2016.

Kreutz, Joakim (2014) 'Why China Supported Democratization in Burma/Myanmar', Working paper.

—— (2015) 'Outsiders Matter: External Actors and the Decline of Armed Conflict in Southeast Asia', *Global Asia* 10(4): 17–19.

—— (2016) 'Authoritarian Politics and Communal Violence: Explaining Inter-Religious Clashes in Burma/Myanmar', Working paper.

—— (2017) 'Peace by External Withdrawal', in Elin Bjarnegård and Joakim Kreutz (eds) *Debating the East Asian Peace*. Copenhagen: NIAS Press.

Lampton David M. (2008) *The Three Faces of Chinese Power: Might, Money, and Minds*. Berkeley, CA: University of California Press.

—— (2014) *Following the Leader: Ruling China, from Deng Xiaoping to Xi Jinping*. Berkeley CA: University of California Press.

Legro, Jeffrey W. (2000) 'The Transformation of Political Ideas', *American Journal of Political Science* 44(3): 419–32.

—— (2008) 'Purpose Transitions. China's Rise and the American Response', In Robert S. Ross and Zhu Feng (eds) *China's Ascent: Power, Security and the Future of International Politics*. Ithaca, NY: Cornell University Press: 163–187.

Leifer, Michael (1999) 'The ASEAN peace process: A category mistake', *The Pacific Review* 12(1): 25–38.

Leonard, Mark (2008) *What Does China Think?* London: Fourth Estate, 2008.

Li, Cheng (2016) *Chinese Politics in the Xi Jinping Era: Reassessing Collective Leadership*. Washington, DC: Brookings.

Li, Rex, 'A Constructivist Analysis of the Relative Peace in the Taiwan Strait', unpublished paper, 2016.

Liu Mingfu (2010) *The China Dream: Great Power Thinking and Strategic Positioning of China in the Post-American Age*. New York: CN Times Books.

Luttwak, Edward N. (2012) *The Rise of China vs. the Logic of Strategy*. Cambridge MA: The Belknap Press of Harvard University Press.

Ljunggren, Börje (2015a) *Den kinesiska drömmen: Utmaningar för Kina och världen* [The Chinese dream: challenges for China and the world]. Stockholm: Hjalmarson & Högberg.

———— (2015b) 'The Chinese Dream: Does it Challenge East Asia's Peace?' *Global Asia* 10(4): 52–56.

———— (2017). *Den kinesiska drömmen – Xi, makten och utmaningarna* [The Chinese dream: Xi, power and challenge]. Stockholm: Hjalmarson & Högberg.

Mann, James (2007) *The China Fantasy; How Our Leaders Explain Away Chinese Repression*. New York: Viking Penguin.

Mearsheimer, John J. (2001) *The Tragedy of Great Power Politics*. New York: W. W. Norton.

Melander, Erik (2015) 'Gender and Masculine Honor Ideology: Why They Matter for Peace', *Global Asia* 10(4): 40–45.

———— (2017) 'The Masculine Peace', in Elin Bjarnegård and Joakim Kreutz (eds) *Debating the East Asian Peace*. Copenhagen: NIAS Press.

———— (forthcoming) 'A Procedural Approach to Quality Peace', in Christian Davenport, Erik Melander and Patrick Regan, *The Peace Continuum*. Oxford: Oxford University Press.

Ministry of Foreign Affairs of Japan (2015) 'The Guidelines for Japan–US Defense Cooperation', 27 April: http://www.mofa.go.jp/files/000078188. pdf, accessed 16 November 2016.

Moody, Andrew (2009) 'When China rules the world', *China Daily* 19 September: http://www.chinadaily.com.cn/cityguide/2009-09/09/content_8671223.htm, accessed 16 November 2016.

Nag, Rajat M. (2011) 'Realizing the Asian Century', Speech at the *Seminar on Asia 2050*, 18 October: https://www.adb.org/news/speeches/seminar-asia-2050, accessed 16 November 2016.

Nasution, Abdul Haris (1965) *Fundamentals of Guerrilla Warfare*. New York: Praeger.

Nathan, Andrew (2003) 'Authoritarian Resilience', *Journal of Democracy* 14(1): 6–17.

———— (2015) 'Andrew J. Nathan discusses China in China File', Asia Society blog, 22 December: http://www.chinafile.com/conversation/china-2016, accessed 16 November 2016.

Nathan, Andrew and Andrew Scobell (2012) *China's Search for Security*. New York: Columbia University Press.

Navarro, Peter (2008) *The Coming China Wars: How They Will be Fought. How They May be Won*. Upper Saddle River, NJ: FT Press.

——— (2015) *Crouching Tiger. What China's Militarism Means for the World*. Amherst, NY: Prometheus (with a foreword by Gordon G. Chang).

Navarro, Peter and Greg Autry (2011) *Death by China: Confronting the Dragon. A Global Call to Action*. Upper Saddle River, NJ: FT Press.

Obama, Barack (2011) 'Remarks by President Obama to the Australian Parliament', Office of the Press Secretary, the White House, 17 November: https://www.whitehouse.gov/the-press-office/2011/11/17/remarks-president-obama-australian-parliament, accessed 26 October 2016.

Odgaard, Liselotte, Thomas Mandrup & Cedric de Coning, eds (2014) *BRICS and Coexistence: An Alternative Vision of World Order*. London: Routledge.

Odgaard, Liselotte & Thomas G. Nielsen (2014) 'China's Counterinsurgency Strategy in Tibet and Xinjiang', *Journal of Contemporary China* 23(87): 1–21.

Overholt, William H. (2008) *Asia, America, and the Transformation of Geopolitics*. Cambridge: Cambridge University Press.

Page, Jeremy (2010) 'China Tests New Political Model in Shenzhen', *The Washington Post* 18 October: http://online.wsj.com/article/SB1000142 405270230425040457555810330325161616.html?mod=googlenews_wsj, accessed 16 November 2016.

Pei Minxin (2006) *China's Trapped Transition: The Limits of Developmental Autocracy*. Cambridge MA: Harvard University Press.

——— (2015) 'The Twilight of Communist Party Rule in China', *The National Interest* 12 November.

——— (2016) *China's Crony Capitalism: The Dynamics of Regime Decay*. Cambridge, MA: Harvard University Press.

Phillips, Tom and Christy Yao (2016) '"Brutal, amoral, ruthless, cheating": how Trump's new trade tsar sees China', *The Guardian*, 22 December: www.theguardian.com/world/2016/dec/22/brutal-amoral-ruthless-cheating-trumps-trade-industrial-peter-navarro-views-on-china, accessed 10 January 2017.

Rachman, Gideon (2016) *Easternisation: War and Peace in the Asian Century*. London: The Bodley Head.

Ren Xiao (2016) 'Idea Change Matters: China's Practices and the East Asian

Peace', *Asian Perspective* 40(2): 329–356.

Ringen, Stein (2016) *The Perfect Dictatorship: China in the 21st Century*. Hong Kong: Hong Kong University Press.

Roach, Steven (2014) *Unbalanced: The Codependency of America and China*. New Haven, CT: Yale University Press.

Ross, Robert S. (1999) 'The Geography of the Peace: East Asia in the Twenty-first Century', *International Security* 23(4): 81–118.

——— (2009a) *Chinese Security Policy: Structure, Power and Politics*. New York: Routledge.

——— (2009b) 'China's Naval Nationalism. Sources, Prospects, and the U.S. Response', *International Security* 34(2): 46–81.

——— (2014) 'The Rise of the Chinese Economy and the East Asian Security Order', Paper presented to the 4th Annual Conference of the East Asian Peace programme, Beijing, 29 October–1 November.

——— (2017) 'The Great Power Challenge to the East Asian Peace', in Elin Bjarnegård and Joakim Kreutz (eds) *Debating the East Asian Peace*. Copenhagen: NIAS Press.

Russett, Bruce and John Oneal (2001) *Triangulating Peace: Democracy, Interdependence and International Organizations*. New York: Norton.

Ryu Yongwook (2013) 'The 'History Problem': Aggressive Intentions, and China's Threat Perception of Japan', Paper presented to a programme workshop in Krusenberg, Uppsala, 6–8 June 2013.

——— (2015) 'To Revise or Not to Revise: Conservative Nationalism, the 'Peace Constitution' and National Identity in Japan', Paper presented to the 5th Annual Conference of the East Asian Peace programme, Singapore, 6–8 November.

——— (2017) 'The Nationalist Threat to the East Asian Peace', in Elin Bjarnegård and Joakim Kreutz (eds) *Debating the East Asian Peace*. Copenhagen: NIAS Press.

Sabillo, Jill (2016) 'Peace panel head renews call for BBL passage to counter extremism', *Philippines Inquirer* (18 January): http://newsinfo.inquirer.net/756322/peace-panel-head-renews-call-for-bbl-passage-to-counter-extremism, accessed 16 November 2016.

Sadan, Mandy (2013) *Being and Becoming Kachin: Histories Beyond the State in the Borderworlds of Burma*. Oxford: Oxford University Press.

———, ed. (2016) *War and Peace in the Borderlands of Myanmar: The Kachin Ceasefire, 1994–2011*. Copenhagen: NIAS Press.

Scott, Shirley V. (2017) 'Peace by International Law', in Elin Bjarnegård and Joakim Kreutz (eds) *Debating the East Asian Peace*. Copenhagen: NIAS Press.

Shambaugh, David (2005) 'Return to the Middle Kingdom?' in David Shambaugh (ed.) *Power Shift: China and Asia's New Dynamics*. Berkeley CA: University of California Press: 23–47.

———— (2008) *China's Communist Party: Atrophy and Adaptation*. Berkeley: University of California Press.

———— (2010) 'A New China Requires a New US Strategy', *Current History* 109(728), September: 219–227.

———— (2013) *China Goes Global: The Partial Power*. Oxford: Oxford University Press.

———— (2015) 'The Coming Chinese Crackup', *The Wall Street Journal*, 6 March.

———— (2016) *China's Future*. Cambridge: Polity Press.

Shirk, Susan L. (2007) *China, Fragile Superpower: How China's Internal Politics Could Derail Its Peaceful Rise*. Oxford: Oxford University Press.

Slater, Dan (2010) *Ordering Power: Contentious Politics and Authoritarian Leviathans in Southeast Asia*. Cambridge: Cambridge University Press.

Song Yann-huei and Stein Tønnesson (2013) 'The Impact of the Law of the Sea Convention on Conflict and Conflict Management in the South China Sea', *Ocean Development and International Law* 44(3): 235–269.

Song Yann-huei and Zou Keyuan, eds (2014) *Major Law and Policy Issues in the South China Sea: European and American Perspectives*. London: Ashgate.

South, Ashley and Christopher M. Joll (2016) 'From Rebels to Rulers: The Challenges of Transition for Non-state Armed Groups in Mindanao and Myanmar', *Critical Asian Studies* 48(2): 168–192.

Staniland, Paul (forthcoming) 'Armed Politics and the Study of Intrastate Conflict', *Journal of Peace Research*.

Stashwick, Steven (2016) 'That Chinese Frigate in the Senkakus was a Bad Move for China', *The Diplomat* 13 June.

Steinfeld, Edward S. (2010) *Playing Our Game: Why China's Rise Doesn't Threaten the West*. Oxford: Oxford University Press.

Stokes, Bruce (2016) 'Hostile Neighbors: China vs. Japan', Washington, D.C.: Pew Research Center, 13 September: http://www.pewglobal.org/2016/09/13/hostile-neighbors-china-vs-japan/, accessed 26 October 2016.

Svensson, Isak (2011) 'East Asian Peacemaking: Exploring the Patterns of Conflict Management and Conflict Settlement in East Asia', *Asian Perspective* 35(2): 163–185.

—— (2015) 'A Surprising Calm: The Religious Peace in East Asia', *Global Asia* 10(4): 26–30.

—— (2017) 'Peace by Avoidance of Religious Civil Wars', in Elin Bjarnegård and Joakim Kreutz (eds) *Debating the East Asian Peace*. Copenhagen: NIAS Press.

Svensson, Isak and Mathilda Lindgren (2011) 'From Bombs to Banners? The Decline of Wars and the Rise of Unarmed Uprisings in East Asia', *Security Dialogue* 42(3): 219–237.

Taylor, Jay (2009) *The Generalissimo: Chiang Kai-shek and the Struggle for Modern China*. Cambridge MA: Harvard University Press.

Togo Kazuhiko (2014) 'PacNet #70 - Revision of Article 9 and its implications', *Newsletter*, Center for Strategic and International Studies, 2 September: http://bit.ly/pacnet70, accessed 16 November 2016.

Tønnesson, Stein (2014) 'China's National Interests and the Law of the Sea: Are They Reconcilable?' in Wu Shicun and Nong Hong (eds) *Recent Developments in the South China Sea*. London: Routledge: 199–227.

—— (2015a) 'The South China Sea: Law Trumps Power', *Asian Survey* 55(3): 455–477.

—— (2015b) 'Deterrence, Interdependence, and Sino–US Peace', *International Area Studies Review* 18(3): 297–311.

—— (2015c) 'Explaining East Asia's Developmental Peace: The Dividends of Economic Growth', *Global Asia* 10(4): 10–15.

—— (2016a) 'Will Nationalism Drive Conflict in Asia?' *Nations and Nationalism* 22(2): 232–242.

—— (2016b) 'The Tonkin Gulf Model of Conflict Resolution', in C.J. Jenner and Tran Trong Thuy (eds) *The South China Sea*. Cambridge: Cambridge University Press: 151–170.

—— (2016c) 'UN compulsory arbitration: a tough test for China', Brussels: European Union Institute for Security Studies (EUISS) Report.

—— (2016d) 'The Case for Negative Peace Research', Paper presented to the International Studies Association conference in Atlanta, Georgia, 17 March.

—— (2017) 'Peace by Development', in Elin Bjarnegård and Joakim Kreutz (eds) *Debating the East Asian Peace*. Copenhagen: NIAS Press.

—— (forthcoming) 'Article 9 in the East Asia Peace', in Kevin Clements (ed.) *Identity, Trust and Reconciliation in East Asia: Dealing with Painful History to Create a Peaceful Present*. London: Palgrave.

Tønnesson, Stein and Pavel Baev (2017) 'Stress-test for Chinese restraint: China evaluates Russia's use of force', *Strategic Analysis*: http://dx.doi.org/10.10 80/09700161.2017.1278878.

Tønnesson, Stein and Elin Bjarnegård (2015) 'Why So Much Conflict in Thailand?' *Thammasat Review* 18(1): 132–161.

Urdal, Henrik (2017) 'Peace by Demographic Changes', in Elin Bjarnegård and Joakim Kreutz (eds) *Debating the East Asian Peace*. Copenhagen: NIAS Press.

Wade, Robert (1990) *Governing the Market: Theory and the Role of Government in East Asian Industrialization*. Princeton NJ: Princeton University Press.

Wallensteen, Peter (2015a) *Quality Peace: Peacebuilding, Victory and World Order*. Oxford: Oxford University Press.

—— (2015b) 'Comparing Conditions for Quality Peace', in *International Security Studies*, Beijing: Social Sciences Academic Press 1(1): 59–76.

Wang Dong and Yin Chengzhi, 'Efficient Deterrence and Cross-Strait Relations', unpublished paper, 2016.

Weiss, Jessica Chen (2014) *Powerful Patriots: Nationalist Protest in China's Foreign Relations*. Oxford: Oxford University Press.

Weissmann, Mikael (2012) *The East Asian Peace: Conflict Prevention and Informal Peacebuilding*. Houndmills, Basingstoke: Palgrave Macmillan.

White, Hugh (2012) *The China Choice: Why We Should Share Power*. Oxford: Oxford University Press.

Winter, Jay (2006) *Dreams of Peace and Freedom: Utopian Moments in the Twentieth Century*. New Haven CT: Yale University Press.

Xi Jinping (2014) *The Governance of China*. English edition. Beijing: Foreign Languages Press.

Yan Xuetong (2017) 'China Can Thrive in the Trump Era,' *New York Times*, 25 January.

Zhao Suisheng (2004) *A Nation-State by Construction*. Stanford: Stanford University Press.

Zheng Yongnian (2010) *The Chinese Communist Party as Organizational Emperor*. London: Routledge.

Zou Keyuan (2012) 'Building a 'Harmonious World': A Mission Impossible?' *Copenhagen Journal of Asian Studies* 30(2): 74–99.

————(2014) 'Maintaining Maritime Peace in East Asia: A Legal Perspective', *Journal of Territorial and Maritime Studies* 1(2): 27–49.

Zou Keyuan and Stein Tønnesson (2015) 'Legal Foundations of the East Asian Peace', Paper presented to the 5th Annual Conference of the East Asian Peace programme, Singapore 6–8 November.

Appendix

Participants in the East Asian Peace Programme

Advisory Board
Kevin Clements, University of Otago; Bates Gill, Australian National University; Börje Ljunggren, Lund University; Moon Chung-in, Yonsei University; Robert S. Ross, Boston College; Thommy Svensson, Nordic Institute of Asian Studies; Peter Wallensteen (chair), Uppsala University; Wang Yizhou, Peking University.

Core Group
Stein Tønnesson (programme leader), Uppsala University/Peace Research Institute Oslo; Erik Melander (deputy programme leader), Uppsala University; Susanne Schaftenaar (programme coordinator, 2011–13), Uppsala University; Holly Guthrey (programme coordinator, 2014–17), Uppsala University; Elin Bjarnegård, Uppsala University; Kristine Eck (2013–17), Uppsala University; Timo Kivimäki (2011–12), University of Bath; Joakim Kreutz (2013–17), Uppsala University; Isak Svensson, Uppsala University.

Research Associates
Pavel Baev, Peace Research Institute Oslo; Karen Brounéus, Uppsala University; Miriam Coronel Ferrer, University of the Philippines; Allan Dafoe, Yale University; Anders Engvall, Stockholm School of Economics; Benjamin E. Goldsmith, University of Sydney; Linus Hagström, Swedish Defence University; Hoang Anh Tuan, Diplomatic Academy of Vietnam; Jong Kun Choi, Yonsei University; Rex Li, Liverpool John Moore's University; Liselotte Odgaard, Royal Danish

Defence College; Thitinan Pongsudhirak, Chulalongkorn University; Robert S. Ross, Boston College; Ryu Yongwook, Australian National University; Yann-huei Song, Academia Sinica; Ashley South, Chiang Mai University; Paul Staniland, University of Chicago; Nina von Uexküll, Uppsala University; Henrik Urdal, Peace Research Institute Oslo; Wang Dong, Peking University; Jessica Weiss, Cornell University; Mikael Weissmann, Swedish Institute of International Affairs; Ren Xiao, Fudan University; Zou Keyuan, University of Central Lancashire.

Guest researchers, research assistants and participants in workshops and conferences
Karin Bäckstrand, Lund University; Patrick Barron, Asia Foundation; Rikard Bengtsson, Lund University; Tomas Bergström, Lund University; Magdalena Bexell, Lund University; Annika Björkdahl, Lund University; Dennis J. Blasko, Wilson Center; Anne Brown, University of Queensland; Seyom Brown, Massachusetts Institute of Technology; Tobias Carlsson, Lund University; Steve Chan, University of Colorado-Boulder; Wisit Chatchawantipakorn, Thailand; Maj. Gen. Chen Zhou, Chinese Academy of Military Science; Chih-mao Tang, Soochow University; Sasiwan Chingchit, Asia Foundation; Ajin Choi, Yonsei University; Chong Ja Ian, National University of Singapore; Kavi Chongkittavorn, Chulalongkorn University; Thao Minh Chu, Diplomatic Academy Vietnam; Mihai Crouicu, Uppsala University; Johan Davidsson, Lund University; John Delury, Yonsei University; Prasenjit Duara, Asia Research Institute; Vanda Felbab-Brown, Brookings Institute; Chris Fariss, Pennsylvania State University; Annika Fredén, Lund University; Lars Peter Fredén, Ambassador of Sweden, China; Evelyn Goh, Australian National University; Stephen Gray, Adapt Research and Consulting, Yangon; Natasha Hamilton-Hart, University of Auckland; Sophia Hatz, Uppsala University; Bill Hayton, Chatham House; Maria Hedlund, Lund University; Thomas Heldmark, Journalist; Christopher Hill, University of Denver; Victoria Hui, University of Notre Dame; Anna Jarstad, Umeå university; Renee Jeffery, Griffith University; Nicole Jenne, European University Institute; Magnus Jerneck, Lund University; Jia Qingguo, Peking University; Srisompob Jitpiromsri, Prince of Songkhla University, Pattani; Christopher M. Joll, Chiang Mai University; Kristina Jönsson, Lund University; Hae-Won Jun, Korea National Diplomatic Academy;

Scott Kastner, University of Maryland; Lia Kent, Australian National University; Nicholas Khoo, University of Otago; Mikyoung Kim, Hiroshima City University; David Lake, University of California, San Diego; Terence Lee, National University of Singapore; Melissa Loja, University of Hong Kong; Chunrong Liu, Fudan University, Shanghai; Emma Lund, Lund University; Shanshan Mei, American University; Eugenie Merieau, Science Po Paris/Thammasat University; Marte Nilsen, Peace Research Institute Oslo; Nicola Nymalm, Swedish Institute of International Affairs, Stockholm; Malin Oud, independent consultant, Stockholm; Wooyeal Paik, Sungkyunkwan University; T. J. Pempel, University of California at Berkeley; Anders Persson, Lund University; Henrik Persson, Swedish Embassy to Korea; Cao Qun, China Institute of International Studies; Ratchawadee Saengmahamat, (Thailand); Shirley Scott, University of New South Wales; Jung Min Seo, Yonsei University; Ria Shibata, University of Otago; Paulynn Sicam, peace negotiator, Manila; Tang Siew Mun, ASEAN Studies Centre/Yusof Ishak Institute; Dan Slater, University of Chicago; Ashley South, Chiang Mai University; Eric Skog, Uppsala University; Marie Söderberg, Stockholm School of Economics; Chandra Lekha Sriram, University of East London; Stithorn Thananithichot, King Prajadhipok Institute; Tetsuya Toyoda, Wilson Center; Jessica Trisko Darden, American University; Vu Truong, Vietnam; Pauline Tweedie, Asia Foundation; Vu Hong Trang, Vietnam; Wang Zheng, Seton Hall University; Josepha Ivanka Wessels, Lund University; Rolf Wrangnert, film producer, Stockholm; Wen-Chin Wu, National Taiwan University/Academy Sinica; Fiona Yap, Australian National University; Young Ho Kim, National Defence University, Seoul; Fariborz Zelli, Lund University; Zhang Rongmei, Yunnan University, Kunming.

Index

f=figure; n=footnote; t=table;
bold=extended discussion or a term emphasised in the text

—